British films of the 1970s

Manchester University Press

British films of the 1970s

Paul Newland

Manchester University Press

Published by Manchester University Press
Altrincham Street, Manchester M1 7JA, UK
www.manchesteruniversitypress.co.uk

British Library Cataloguing-in-Publication Data
A catalogue record for this book is available from the British Library

ISBN   978 1 5261 1683 3 paperback

First published by Manchester University Press in hardback 2013

This edition first published 2017

The publisher has no responsibility for the persistence or accuracy of URLs for any external or third-party internet websites referred to in this book, and does not guarantee that any content on such websites is, or will remain, accurate or appropriate.

Typeset by 4word Ltd, Bristol
Printed in Great Britain
by TJ International Ltd, Padstow

Contents

Acknowledgements

First, I would like to thank the Arts and Humanities Research Council for funding research into the archive of the film producer Gavrik Losey, held in the Bill Douglas Centre at the University of Exeter. I was lucky enough to be employed as the postdoctoral research associate on this project in the School of Arts, Languages and Literatures at the University of Exeter between 2006 and 2008. This book represents the culmination of that work. Second, I would like to thank the Department of Theatre, Film and Television Studies at Aberystwyth University for granting me research leave for a semester in 2011 in order to finish this book, and for funding some short research trips. Third, I would like to thank the British Academy for awarding me a grant to research *Babylon* (Franco Rosso, 1980).

During the researching and writing of this book I have benefited greatly from the experience and generosity of a number of individuals – industry professionals, academic colleagues and very good friends. Many, many thanks to Kate Woodward, Sue Harper, Duncan Petrie, and Andrew Spicer for generously reading drafts of sections of this book, and offering sound suggestions concerning how I might improve it. Thanks to Gavrik Losey for engaging warmly with my research, and educating me enthusiastically about the finer points of British cinema in the 1970s and beyond. Thanks to Waris Hussein, Lord Puttnam and Franco Rosso for making themselves available for interviews. I would like to thank Duncan Petrie for his support and encouragement during my days at the University of Exeter and subsequently. I also want to thank Steve Neale for his careful guidance of my work during the Gavrik Losey research project. For their support and encouragement (in a number of different ways), I want to further thank (in no particular order) Sarah Street, Justin Smith, Charlotte Brunsdon, Claire Monk, Dan North, Paul Williams, Kate Egan, Helen Hanson, Phil Wickham, Will Stone, Sid Stronach and Tim Noble. I also owe a debt of gratitude to my students.

Thanks to the staff at the British Film Institute Reading Room, the Bill Douglas Centre at the University of Exeter, and the Hugh Owen library at Aberystwyth University. And to the contributors to the 'Don't Look Now?' conference I organised at the University of Exeter in July 2007.

Many thanks to Adrian Kear and Jamie Medhurst, my Heads of Department at Aberystwyth University, for their belief in me and my work, and their commitment to research in the Department of Theatre, Film and Television Studies. I also want to record my gratitude to the management team and administrative staff in the Department – especially Kath Williams, Ceris Medhurst-Jones, Glenys Hartnell, and Catrin Davies. And many thanks go to the staff at Manchester University Press, who were supportive of this book from the beginning.

Thanks to my parents, Roy and Mary, for their continuing love and support. And to Peter and Liz Nellist for everything they continue to do to help Kate, myself, and our family. Thanks to Annabel and Edward, whose many appearances in my office at home when I was writing this book were always very welcome interruptions, even if I didn't always make this clear at the time. Finally, thanks, most of all, to Kate, without whom this book would simply not have been possible.

PAUL NEWLAND
Aberystwyth, February 2012

Introduction

Film-making fragments: *Nobody Ordered Love* and *Long Shot*

A long-forgotten film, *Nobody Ordered Love* (Robert Hartford-Davis, 1971), tells the story of the trials and tribulations of individuals attempting to put together a British film during the early 1970s. The narrative follows a hustling opportunist, Peter Triman (Tony Selby), and a director, Peter Medbury (John Ronane), through their struggles to make an epic First World War film entitled *The Somme*. The production process is fraught with problems. Initially, the shoot is disrupted by the behaviour of the star, the former sex symbol Alice Allison (Ingrid Pitt).[1] Medbury decides that he wants the part to be recast, but his financial backer, Leo Richardstone (Peter Arne), insists on a star name for the film. While Alice continues to cause grief on set, Medbury auditions an up-and-coming starlet, Caroline Johnson (Judy Huxtable). Meanwhile, Triman exploits Alice's alcoholism, getting her drunk on whisky and trying to seduce her. But she is found dead the next morning, from a self-inflicted stab wound. After a disagreement regarding the ways in which Alice was treated, Medbury tells Triman his behaviour has infringed a morality clause in his contract, and that he will not countenance working with Triman on his next production. In revenge, Triman arranges for the negative of *The Somme* to be destroyed in an 'accident'.[2]

Nobody Ordered Love thus finds dramatic potential in the myriad difficulties faced by film-makers during the early 1970s, and operates within (and, indeed, reflects upon) a British film industry

1

evidently in the doldrums. In his important book on British cinema in the 1970s and early 1980s, *National Heroes* (1985), the film critic Alexander Walker begins his first chapter, 'State of Change', by arguing that 'The first few years of the 1970s brought home to British cinema and society what bad times lay ahead. Nothing seemed to be moving.'[3] Walker further points out that British cinema in the early 1970s 'looked like the country itself: it had a residual energy, but in the main was feeling dull, drained, debilitated, infected by a run-down feeling characteristic of British life'.[4] This view was shared by other writers and critics. In another book published in 1985, *The Once & Future Film*, John Walker suggested that in the 1970s there was 'no money to make films, no cinemas to show them in, no audiences to pay to see them'.[5]

Things had not always been this way. During the 1960s – after the successes of the so-called 'British New Wave' films, the Beatles films, and 'swinging London' films – American production companies set up offices in London, hoping to back the next big British film. The key studios operating production programmes in Britain were United Artists, Paramount, Warner Bros, Metro-Goldwyn-Mayer, Twentieth Century-Fox, Columbia, Universal, and Disney. In addition to the fashionable status of aspects of 1960s Britishness and the concomitant bankability of British stars, the increased levels of American finance that flooded into film-making in Britain during the 1960s can be explained at least in part by the quality and availability of British studios, and the relatively cheap labour during this period. American money imported into Britain to finance film-making through subsidiaries reached a peak of £31.3 million in 1968.[6] However, the British film industry suffered immensely from the withdrawal of much of this finance in the early 1970s. Indeed, by 1974, the sum imported by US companies had fallen to £2.9 million.[7] Meanwhile, funds available from the British-government-backed National Film Finance Corporation (NFFC) also dropped – between 1973 and 1981 it contributed only £4 million towards 31 feature films and six shorts.[8] Overall, as Linda Wood has pointed out, the total number of British films registered fell from 98 in 1971 to 36 in 1981.[9] So the 1970s was undeniably a difficult period for the British film industry. After the box office successes of the 1960s, then, this was a period of relative struggle for film-makers and producers. But by the 1980s a revival of sorts had occurred, exemplified by the Oscar triumph of *Chariots of Fire* (Hugh Hudson, 1981),[10] and further facilitated by the broadening of the American market as a consequence of the development of cable television, as well as the setting up of Channel 4 in 1982 – a television channel which developed an interest in financing low-budget British films.[11]

During the 1970s, the profound social and cultural changes that had occurred in the 1960s created a situation in which British film-makers had other hurdles to clear. For one, they could no longer rely on what they had once conceived of as a 'mass' audience when marketing their films.[12] As the post-war consensus began to fragment, so too did the family audience. As Sue Harper puts it, 'The mass audience, which had hitherto provided reliable profits, was no longer monolithic in its structure. It was replaced by a range of niche audiences, who had more specialist requirements and whose responses were less predictable.'[13] At the same time, it appeared that British culture was becoming more permissive. The British Board of Film Censors (BBFC) moved towards a more liberal position under the leadership of John Trevelyan and (from 1971) Stephen Murphy.[14] In July 1970, a new classification system brought in the AA category for those aged fourteen and over, and developed the X category for films suitable for those over eighteen as opposed to sixteen (which it had been previously).[15] With this, British cinemas suddenly found themselves entertaining smaller audiences, including those eager to see adult X-certificate productions (this begins to account for the boom in production of horror films and sexploitation films during the early 1970s). Old-style cinemas were converted into three-screen complexes, which further encouraged what Andrew Higson has termed diversification 'at the point of exhibition'.[16] Audiences for British films fragmented in other ways, too. Film gradually shifted from the cinema to the home, as the impact of the wider availability of colour television (and later video) was increasingly felt. So, in the 1970s, as Higson points out, 'Cinema itself was not in decline, but was going through a complex process of diversification and renewal.'[17] Indeed, this might now be regarded as a transitional period for British cinema; as a kind of 'interregnum'.

There is evidence to be found in a film released later in the decade that film-making in Britain was still by no means a straightforward process. *Long Shot* (Maurice Hatton, 1978) features two individuals, Charlie and Neville (Charles Gormley and Neville Smith), trying to put together a film about Aberdeen oilmen, to be called *Gulf and Western*. Searching for a director, they head to the 1977 Edinburgh Film Festival, where they seek out the seasoned American film-maker, Sam Fuller. Failing to find him, they finally secure the services of the German director, Wim Wenders. Wenders – who was at that time making a name for himself in the New German Cinema as the director of films such as *Alice in the Cities* (1974), *Kings of the Road* (1976), and *The American Friend* (1977) – is one of a number of individuals from the film industry who make appearances in the film, playing themselves. Searching for a star for the production, Charlie tracks down Susannah York at a theatre where she is engaged in rehearsals for *Peter Pan*, though he clearly is not aware of who she is, because he tells her how much he admired her performances in *The Go-Between* (Joseph Losey, 1970) and *Georgy Girl* (Silvio Narizzano, 1966), thus confusing her with two British stars who came to prominence in the 1960s: Julie Christie and Lynn Redgrave. But York happily co-operates, as do a number of other industry professionals, including director John Boorman and theatrical agent Dennis Selinger. *Long Shot* works, then, as a kind of farcical, self-reflexive, fictional documentary that highlights the problems independent producers faced when trying to get films made in Britain during the late 1970s.

Nobody Ordered Love and *Long Shot* provide an intriguing place to start when considering British film-making in the 1970s because, while they have not been remembered or fêted as examples of British cinema at its best (or, indeed, remembered at all), they do speak of the complexities of the industry; of its essentially fissured and fragmented nature. They also both clearly demonstrate that British film-makers had an awareness of the difficulties of the period; specifically, funding issues and declining audiences. This is further borne out by the fact that both films do not sit easily within acknowledged British film genres. As Sue Harper points out about a range of 1970s British productions, 'Instead of having clear-cut boundaries, films seem to have permeable membranes, and to segue between horror/sex films/history or comedy/realism/sex, for example. This tentativeness about genre, and the range of cross-generic type, suggests that film-makers were uncertain about public taste.'[18] Indeed, by creating generic hybrids, many film-makers appeared to be hedging their bets by appealing to as wide an audience as possible. In this book, I explore a number of films which do not sit easily within genres. These films offer evidence that ways of classifying, categorising, and making distinctions between films began to rupture in Britain in the 1970s. But as well as being a period in which boundaries between different types of films fell apart, the 1970s also saw large number of directors and performers working across genres, in cinema, television and theatre, and often transnationally. This fragmentary film-making climate is evidenced not only in the shifting generic qualities of *Nobody Ordered Love* and *Long Shot*, but also by the careers of some of the figures who appear in these films.

Nobody Ordered Love (a hybrid tragi-comedy-horror) stars the actress Ingrid Pitt as Alice Allison. Pitt remains much better known for her exotic roles (which often feature nudity) in films such as the Hammer horrors, *The Vampire Killers* (Roy Ward Baker, 1970) and *Countess Dracula* (Peter Sasdy, 1971), and the Amicus Productions horror, *The House That Dripped Blood* (Peter Duffell, 1971).[19] She went on to appear in the horror film *The Wicker Man* (Robin Hardy, 1973). But Pitt's career did not develop purely within the horror genre. She also features in *Where Eagles Dare* (Brian G. Hutton, 1968) (much of which was filmed at Borehamwood Studios in Hertfordshire, UK), and later in *Who Dares Wins* (Ian Sharp, 1982), and the James Bond film *Octopussy* (John Glen, 1983).[20] The production of *Nobody Ordered Love* also featured other professionals who had complex, chequered careers during the 1970s. Robert Hartford-Davis, the director, for example, was a seasoned exploitation film-maker who had worked across genres. He directed the British horror films *Incense for the Damned* (aka *Bloodsuckers*) (1970), starring Patrick Macnee, Peter Cushing, and Patrick Mower, and *The Fiend* (1971), starring Patrick Magee. But he also worked in the USA, directing the blaxploitation film *Black Gunn* (1972). During the previous decade he had directed *Saturday Night Out* (1964) for producer Tony Tenser, who remains best known (alongside

Michael Klinger) as the man behind the production of Roman Polanski's British-shot art house films *Repulsion* (1965) and *Cul-de-sac* (1966), the development of the production company Tigon, the production of Michael Reeves' notorious *Witchfinder General* (1968), and the sex comedy *Eskimo Nell* (Martin Campbell, 1974) – discussed in detail in the first chapter of this book.[21]

The Scottish film director, Charles Gormley, who also appears in *Long Shot*, co-founded the company Tree Films in 1972 with Nick Lewis and another budding Scottish film-maker, Bill Forsyth, who would later direct the British films *That Sinking Feeling* (1979), *Gregory's Girl* (1981), and *Local Hero* (1983). Tree Films was essentially set up to make Scottish feature films, but eventually produced a number of documentaries, including *A Place in the Country* (1972), *Polar Power* (1974), and *Keep Your Eye on Paisley* (1975). During the 1970s, Gormley (like a number of film-making professionals at that time) worked across national boundaries, commuting from Glasgow to Amsterdam to get work as a scriptwriter for Dutch film-makers. In this capacity he co-wrote the erotic Dutch film *Blue Movie* (Wim Verstappen, 1971), but also acted alongside Anthony Perkins and Bibi Andersson in *Twee vrouwen* (aka *Twice a Woman*) (George Sluizer, 1979). Moreover, Gormley took advantage of industrial developments in Britain during the early 1980s (such the creation of funding streams via Channel 4 and the Scottish Film Fund) to direct the Glasgow-set *Living Apart Together* (1982), featuring pop star B. A. Robertson, and produced by Gavrik Losey, who was busy during the 1970s working as an independent producer but also as a production manager on films made by Goodtimes, EMI, and Apple Films.[22] After securing a role in *Nobody Ordered Love*, Judy Huxtable's subsequent film appearance was to be in *Derek and Clive Get the Horn* (Russell Mulcahy, 1979), which features her second husband, Peter Cook, recording an album of foul-mouthed comedy improvisations with Dudley Moore at Richard Branson's Virgin Studios in London.

Susannah York, who features in *Long Shot*, also worked throughout the 1970s. She was cast in *The Same Skin* (aka *Country Dance* and *Brotherly Love*) (J. Lee Thompson, 1970), a British film (also starring Peter O'Toole) about an incestuous relationship that develops within an aristocratic Scottish family. York appears in the

American film *Happy Birthday, Wanda June* (Mark Robson, 1971), and in the Columbia-backed British film *Zee & Co* (aka *X, Y and Zee*) (Brian G. Hutton, 1972), which stars Michael Caine and Elizabeth Taylor as a bickering middle-aged couple. She stars in Robert Altman's US psychological thriller *Images* (1972), and in the British thriller *Gold* (Peter R. Hunt, 1974), alongside Roger Moore. She appears in a film adaption of the French dramatist Jean Genet's play, *The Maids* (Christopher Miles, 1974) alongside Glenda Jackson and Vivien Merchant (the play was filmed for the American Film Theatre). York also features prominently in the Polish director Jerzy Skolimowski's British psychological horror film *The Shout* (1978), discussed in detail in Chapter 7 of this book. She features in *Conduct Unbecoming* (Michael Anderson, 1975), a drama about army officers in India, starring Michael York, Richard Attenborough, and Trevor Howard. And she features in *That Lucky Touch* (Christopher Miles, 1975), a British/German film, also starring Roger Moore and Shelley Winters, about an international arms dealer. Moreover, Susannah York obtained work outside Britain and the USA during the decade, playing the title role in the Australian film, *Eliza Fraser* (Tim Burstall, 1976). And she appears in Richard Donner's British-made, American-financed *Superman* (1978) as Lara, Superman's biological mother on Krypton. So it is clear that York worked throughout the 1970s across a range of genres and across a range of national cinemas as well as in Hollywood. Her career alone demonstrates that a very wide range of films were made during this period; films which do not always sit within acknowledged genres or, for that matter, widely-understood concepts of national cinema.

The British film director Stephen Frears also appears in *Long Shot*. He is admired for his 1980s work on films such as *My Beautiful Laundrette* (1985), *Prick Up Your Ears* (1987), and *Sammy and Rosie Get Laid* (1987), and he has, of course, worked on critically acclaimed films in subsequent decades. But he came to prominence in the industry during the 1970s. Frears directed *Gumshoe* (1971), starring Albert Finney as a Liverpool bingo caller who dreams of being a private eye, and *Bloody Kids* (1979), a television film, written by Stephen Poliakoff, about alienated youths living in an Essex seaside town. Frears also made a number of television plays during the 1970s for the BBC's *Play for Today* and *Play of the Week*, working with

7

Alan Bennett on *A Day Out* (1972), *Me! I'm Afraid of Virginia Woolf* (1978), and *Doris and Doreen* (1978). As such, Frears' 1970s career echoes those of the stalwart British directors Ken Loach and Mike Leigh, who also made critically-acclaimed films for television as well as the cinema during this period. These, then, were complex careers in complex times for the industry.

The British 1970s

> Two years ago I awoke from the troubled sleep of apathy. There was born in me the dreadful feeling that something was wrong with the state of the nation. Everywhere I looked I saw decadence, apathy, cynicism and decay. Try as I might, I could not rid myself of the spectre that haunted me: the spectre of a dying culture.
>
> Malcolm Scrawdyke, *Little Malcolm and His Struggle Against the Eunuchs*
> (Stuart Cooper, 1974)

Writing about the 1970s, Leon Hunt recognises that 'In popular accounts of the period, it's the "decade that style/taste forgot", an object of pleasurable, kitsch embarrassment.'[23] Many of us have our own view of what characterises the British 1970s, often drawn from personal memories, our knowledge of the idiosyncrasies of fashions or styles, familiar historical narratives, or, indeed, the visual iconography of films and television programmes. But Sue Harper astutely reminds us that 'We know that history does not naturally organize itself in neat decades. To a certain extent, the 1970s "is a sort of fiction".'[24] If the British 1970s is a sort of 'fiction', it is a fiction ostensibly concerned with crisis, but also with transformation and opportunity. This much is evident in a number of British films of the period. For example, the 1971 film, *Sunday Bloody Sunday*, was made on the back of the British director John Schlesinger's considerable success in America for United Artists with the US-shot *Midnight Cowboy* (1969). Alexander Walker saw *Sunday Bloody Sunday* as a 'transitional film embodying a terminal feeling'.[25] What he appeared to mean by this was that the film manages to dwell upon principle characters drawn from 'the newly beleaguered middle class';[26] figures whose confidence in the kind of decent life that Britain once promised them has now seemingly dissipated. *Sunday Bloody Sunday* is set (and was shot) in London, and, as Walker notes, the film's characters 'resemble the capital city they inhabit: apprehensive people undergoing a state of change, uncertain of the next move'.[27] The film (starring Glenda Jackson, Peter Finch, and Murray Head) certainly captures a profound sense of unease and insecurity at the heart of bourgeois London life.

Sunday Bloody Sunday begins with the middle-aged, Jewish physician, Alex (Peter Finch), looking into the camera, and asking a patient (Britain?) 'Now tell me if you feel anything at all?' The theme of a loss of feeling and a discernible spiritual numbness permeates the narrative. Walker notes that one of the central motifs of the film is the telephone answering service, 'which sustains the illusion that people are in contact with each other'.[28] Schlesinger's film certainly constructs relationships between characters in which communication becomes increasingly difficult. It is apparently harder and harder in this world for individuals to know what they want and how to get it. Naked self-interest is effectively seen to get them nowhere. Indeed, the film appears to suggest that an existence in a society in which attitudes to sex and relationships are rapidly changing (allowing individuals the freedom to do what they choose, when they choose) might in fact be characterised by loneliness and anxiety at best, and alienation and despair at worst. In other words, freedoms fought for and won during the 1960s might now, in the early 1970s, be coming at a profound cost. This film suggests that figures who display heightened levels of self-importance, selfishness, conceit, and vanity are now in danger of becoming narcissistic. Murray Head's character, Bob, for example, is a kinetic sculptor whose neon-lit pieces appear curiously shallow, self-indulgent, and pointless. Like the character himself, these objects are all bright surfaces and no depth. Other figures visibly move towards self-destruction. Indeed, the film offers a representation of the London drug scene which sees it as a grim problem rather than as hip and cool, exemplified by a sequence shot in an all-night pharmacy, depicting individuals waiting for their prescription fixes.

But while life in London is shown to be dark and dreary, there remains an element of human warmth in this film, as it draws out its 'theme of dawning middle-age and quiet desperation', as the critic Jan Dawson put it.[29] Tom Milne pointed out that, in *Sunday Bloody Sunday*, 'love, though it may not spring phoenix-like to life again, at least glows as a faint, treasured ember beneath the ashes piled up by life'.[30] Having said this, the economic frailty of the nation provides a fragmentary backdrop to the quotidian events in the film, even in their warmest moments. Penelope Gilliat wrote the screenplay, and chose to emphasise the fact that unemployment was increasingly becoming an issue in Britain in the early 1970s. Walker argues that this is realistic, 'as unemployment became *the* endemic social disease of the Seventies, even the professional classes were ravaged beyond moral repair'.[31] Not long after the beginning of the film, Alex Greville (Glenda Jackson) is seen driving through the streets of London in her Triumph Herald. We hear a news bulletin unfolding on her car radio in which the announcer clearly sets up the nature of the economic and socio-cultural climate: 'With Britain in the throes of its most serious economic crisis since the War, the Cabinet will be in almost continuous session over the weekend. So will trade union leaders faced with the threat of mass unemployment and militant unofficial strike action.' But the socio-cultural and economic crisis facing Britain during the early 1970s was not confined to cerebral films such as *Sunday Bloody Sunday*. The 'Carry On' film, *Carry On at Your Convenience* (Gerald Thomas, 1971), for example, manages to reflect on and mediate aspects of this period of economic instability. This film is a farce, ostensibly focused on the troubles enveloping a lavatory factory owned and run by W. C. Boggs (Kenneth Williams), where a shop steward with a Zapata moustache, Vic Spanner (Kenneth Cope), constantly clashes with Lewis Boggs (Richard O'Callaghan), and calls the workers out on strike. Of course, the lavatory factory might represent a microcosm of modern Britain here – struggling to get by in difficult times; troubled by internal conflict; and in all probability going down the tubes. This film is now regarded as one of the key texts of the 'Carry On' cycle,[32] even if its middle-class attack on the unions feels inappropriate in a film that was designed primarily for a working-class audience.[33]

Tom Nairn, writing in an influential book, *The Break-Up of Britain* (1977), saw a nation exemplified by 'rapidly accelerating backwardness, economic stagnation, social decay and cultural despair'.[34] At the level of the economy, key facts offer indisputable evidence of the myriad problems faced by the troubled nation. For example, throughout the 1970s, Britain struggled with high levels of inflation (especially after the 1973 OPEC oil crisis). Prices trebled between 1970 and 1980. British government debt reached a level of £9 billion by 1976, having been zero in 1970. In the league table of gross domestic product (GDP) growth for nations, Britain fell from a position of ninth in 1961 to thirteenth in 1966, to fifteenth in 1971, and down to eighteenth in 1976.[35] So, the nation was slipping behind its economic rivals. As Dominic Sandbrook puts it, 'By almost every measure, from investment and productivity to the rate of GDP growth per head and the growth of average real earnings, the Common Market countries were ahead.'[36] Unemployment grew from 3 per cent in 1971 to 5 per cent in 1979. The young were particularly hard hit.

Industrial conflict was also rife, and strikes loomed large in the public consciousness throughout the decade.[37] Indeed, the number of working days lost to strikes in 1970 was 11 million – the highest since the General Strike of 1926. But by 1972 the figure stood at 24 million.[38] Prime Minister Edward Heath spent much of 1971 trying to deal with the unions, and the Industrial Relations Act 1971 was passed in an attempt to bring them under control. But major miners' strikes followed in 1972 and 1973–74. During the 1972 strike, Heath declared a state of emergency, and floodlights on national monuments were turned off.[39] Power cuts were declared across the nation. During the 1973–74 miners' strike, the Conservative government put industry on a three-day working week to try to avoid further power cuts. Historian Alwyn Turner notes that the events of the winter of 1973–74 were so traumatic 'that they had shaken the confidence in the future of Britain, and there was a fear that disaster still lurked around the corner, a suspicion of crisis postponed'.[40] These events were satirised in the *Till Death Us Do Part* (BBC, 1965–75) television series episodes 'Strikes and Blackouts' and 'Three Day Week', written by Johnny Speight and broadcast in January 1974. When the Labour Government was returned to power in 1974 with Harold Wilson as Prime Minister, the new Chancellor of the Exchequer, Dennis Healey, set about attempting to redistribute wealth across the nation by raising the top rate of income tax to 83 per cent.[41] The new government also increased public spending. But, despite a large increase in the number of public sector workers, perceived standards in public services did not improve.[42] Industry continued to struggle throughout the period. Major industrial failures included Leyland and the prestigious car and engine maker, Rolls-Royce.[43] Furthermore, as the decade neared its close, 1978–79 saw the so-called 'winter of discontent' – widespread industrial action which helped to bring about the demise of Labour Prime Minister James Callaghan's government and subsequently see Margaret Thatcher's Conservative Party come to power in 1979.

If Britain faced economic crisis after economic crisis during the decade, many British people suffered anxieties concerning fundamental changes that were occurring to the composition of the nation.[44] In November 1973, Auberon Waugh told *Time* magazine that Britain was suffering from a 'mild attack of schizophrenia'.[45] From about 1968, the nation started to feel a lot less like a world power. The gradual fragmentation of the empire was impacting upon Britain's long-held status as a global force. Immigration from the former colonial territories was leading to the emergence of increased racial tensions, especially in inner-city areas. But the nation was also seemingly opening up to Europe. Prime Minister Edward Heath signed the Treaty of Accession in Brussels in January 1972, and Britain formally joined the European Economic Community on New Year's Day, 1973.[46] The British press was generally supportive of these developments, but, while the British were increasingly enjoying things European – Italian food, French wine, German cars – anxieties also developed concerning how far a closer union with the continent might affect traditional notions of Britishness. As Alwyn Turner puts it, 'Membership of the EEC was linked in the popular consciousness with what seemed like an assault on traditional images of Britain.'[47] The economic miracle that membership of the EEC promised never materialised.[48]

At the same time, the political crisis in Ulster was making itself increasingly visible on mainland Britain (details of how the conflict features in films of the period are explored in Chapter 8). Rising nationalism in Wales and Scotland was also evident. In 1974, the

Scottish National Party drew 30 per cent of the vote north of the border, and the issue of devolution dominated the last months of Callaghan's Labour administration.[49] The Scotland and Wales Act 1978 was passed, allowing for the creation of assemblies in Edinburgh and Cardiff. This movement towards separatism facilitated feelings of polarisation and fragmentation in 1970s Britain. But the British also had to deal with anxieties concerning criminal activity. Civil order was a real concern.[50] By the middle of the decade, all categories of crime were showing a significant annual increase.[51] All these developments fuelled the sense of a fragmenting socio-cultural landscape.[52] But on a more quotidian level, Britain was a nation going through a wide range of rapid, smaller shifts, seeing the development of new town centres, supermarkets, and tower blocks, but also new road signs, telephone numbers, county names, and postcodes. British people also had to deal with a new decimalised currency.[53] Britain was changing, irrevocably.

Out of this atmosphere came a culture (or a series of subcultures) that demonstrated a 'depth of both protest and exuberance'.[54] One need only think of the impact of black, feminist, gay and lesbian politics on the British cultural scene, the rise of the punk movement in the mid-1970s, and new outlets for underground cultural activities, including, of course, film-making (discussed at the end of Chapter 2).[55] The 1970s saw tangible shifts in gender politics, exemplified by the rise of the Women's Movement (discussed in Chapter 1). Britain in the 1970s was also characterised by increasingly visible sexual permissiveness (also discussed in Chapter 1). Indeed, according to Sandbrook, 'permissiveness had become a "political metaphor", and from this point on, protecting the embattled family was at the heart of conservative rhetoric'.[56] Marriage problems were coming more obviously out into the open – a key theme of a number of British films of the period (also discussed in Chapter 1). At the same time, countering this permissiveness was an enduring sexual conservatism. And Britain was further marked by intergenerational strife. These tensions can be witnessed being worked through in a number of British films of the decade. Meanwhile, the cultural life of the nation also displayed an increased level of nostalgia for earlier, simpler times. This is also a recurring theme of 1970s British films (discussed in Chapter 3).

So, as in the USA (but also across a range of Western nations), the 1970s in Britain was an era characterised by highly complex, conflicting ideological and aesthetic currents.[57] Indeed, in some ways, the profound socio-cultural shifts that encapsulate the ways in which a number of historians have framed socio-cultural and political life in 1970s Britain also pertain to other Western countries. Christopher Booker came up with the title 'The Death of Progress' for the first chapter of his book *The Seventies* (1980), within which he argues that 'the Seventies were in fact the most important decade of the twentieth century.'[58] He outlines his reasons for this position: 'The truth is that, in the past ten years, the old sources of optimism which have sustained the human race throughout the twentieth century (and which began to emerge a very long time before that) have begun to collapse on an unprecedented scale', and that the human race could no longer presume that an 'unimaginable future of light, knowledge and material abundance' lay around the corner.[59] Instead, it seems that a fundamental shift was seen to be occurring during the 1970s concerning the ways in which Western humanity saw itself and its future in the world. While the decade, for Booker, was a kind of prolonged 'morning after' to the 'euphoria and excesses of the Sixties', there was also something more profound going on.[60] A loss of confidence in the project of modernity could be detected.

The post-Enlightenment idea that humanity could create (through technological and scientific progress and innovation) a better future for itself had clearly come unstuck. Booker sees three aspects to what he terms the 'twentieth-century dream' which were challenged during the 1970s: the belief that science and technology could unlock the 'secrets of the universe' and thus create 'a materially secure and comfortable life for the majority of mankind'; the utopian belief that society could be improved through social and political reorganisation and greater state planning; and the belief that through dismantling the old repressive 'taboos' of the past, individuals could enjoy a 'much greater degree of freedom and self-realization'.[61] Others have seen this historical cultural shift as a move away from the certainties of old metanarratives and towards postmodernity.[62] This drift away from the 'twentieth-century dream' manifested itself in a number of areas; not least in architecture, which had seen the vast modernising urban projects of the 1960s start to fail on a spectacular scale (with the partial collapse of the Ronan Point tower block in east London in 1968 being one British example). Booker points out that 'nowhere did this loss of confidence in the Modern Movement go further than in the country which, in some ways, had embraced its ideas for comprehensive redevelopment more wholeheartedly than any, Britain'.[63] Perhaps representations of the failure of modernity (and of modern architecture in particular) are most strikingly evident in one of the most infamous films of the decade, *A Clockwork Orange* (Stanley Kubrick, 1971), in which key, brutal sequences were shot in the Thamesmead development in south east London – a vast, futuristic residential council estate.[64]

But other commentators have been keen to develop a more balanced, less dystopian narrative of the political and socio-cultural climate of Britain in the 1970s. After all, despite images of social breakdown, power cuts, the three-day week, and rampant bureaucracy and corruption, an analysis of national performance by the New Economics Foundation in 2004 found that Britain was a happier country in 1976 than at any time since.[65] By the early 1970s, more than half the British population owned their own homes. These properties were often 'markers of affluence, status, identity and independence, decorated in styles – garish patterned wallpaper, thick carpets, Formica surfaces, synthetic tiles – that were supposed to denote luxury and elegance'.[66] Many of these homes enjoyed the benefits of central heating, indoor lavatories, shiny new kitchens and bathrooms, telephones, and electronic appliances such as washing machines, fridges, and freezers.[67] The 1970s saw a continuation of the growth in the cultural and leisure market.[68] This was arguably the 'golden age' of British television. Indeed, by 1973, almost every family in Britain had a television set. Even working-class families were able to enjoy this revolution.[69]Alwyn Turner points out that Christmas 1973 in particular was, for many, 'actually a very happy time'; children excited by candlelit evenings waiting for Father Christmas, and the pop charts filled with cheery glitter pop. Slade's perennial 'Merry Xmas Everybody', perhaps the best-loved song of the era, was an 'antidote to the gathering doom'.[70] There were even successes for British football clubs on the European stage. And an increasing number of British people were enjoying the freedom to travel beyond the nation's shores. By 1973, 9 million Britons regularly holidayed outside the UK.[71] This trend (discussed in Chapter 2) was mocked by the comedy films *Carry On Abroad* (Gerald Thomas, 1972) and *Are You Being Served?* (Bob Kellett, 1977), and in the television series *Don't Drink the Water* (LWT, 1974–75), in which Blakey (Stephen Lewis) from *On the Buses* (LWT, 1969–73) retires to Spain. So, this was a period of profound change; change which was mediated across a wide variety of British films.

The aims of this book

The historical and biographical fragments pertaining to *Nobody Ordered Love* and *Long Shot* demonstrate that the 1970s careers of professionals involved in two minor films about the trials and tribulations of the British film industry are illustrative of a profoundly fragmented film-making culture. We can see that British actors did not only work within what we might think of as British national cinema. Many of these individuals were cast in films made in the USA, mainland Europe and Australia. We can also see that a number of film-makers, writers, actors, and producers were working increasingly across national boundaries during the 1970s, but also across cinema, television, and other forms of media such as advertising.[72] Dramatists, directors and actors more obviously associated with the highly-regarded world of British theatre also worked in cinema. Famous British pop and rock stars were cast in a number of films (not just musicals). So, British cinema of the 1970s was a variegated affair. It was certainly a period of struggle and difficulty; perhaps even of misery. But it was also an era of transition and change; and, in some areas, of revolution. The 1970s, then, felt for many like a period of opportunity. Within the cracks that appeared in a fragmenting industry, new spaces opened up for ground-breaking and original work; work that often gave expression to previously marginalised voices.[73] The primary purpose of this book is to examine a range of films that were made (often against great odds), and to explore the ways in which these films offer evidence that it was not only the British film industry that was going through a profound set of changes during the 1970s, but also the nation itself. British cinema of the 1970s is characterised by vicissitudes.

In his influential 1986 article, 'The Lost Continent', Julian Petley argued that large areas of British film history remained unexplored.[74] Thankfully, since the mid-1980s, a plethora of published material has allowed us to venture into the hinterlands of British film history, and historians are to be saluted for breaking this fertile new ground. Continued exploration has recently seen forays into the 1970s, which remained a relative wilderness until the publication of Robert Shail's edited collection *Seventies British Cinema* in 2008, my own edited collection *Don't Look Now* in 2010, and Sue Harper and Justin Smith's *British Film Culture in the 1970s: The Boundaries of Pleasure* (2012). I hope this current book will shed new light on this territory.

In this book I aim to retain an awareness of the tensions inherent in thinking about British national cinema in the 1970s. For Andrew Higson, national cinema is a fluid concept, 'subject to ceaseless negotiations'.[75] Higson points out that national cinema can be defined in economic terms, by focusing on the nature of the industry (infrastructures of production, distribution, and exhibition) rather than the texts themselves. And national cinema can be defined in terms of exhibition and consumption, and the ways in which producers market films internationally.[76] But, in addition to this, as Higson also notes, national cinema can be defined in terms of representation, and, specifically, the ways in which films construct images of nationhood (and the specificities of the iconography they employ to do this). It is the representational aspect of British national cinema that this book primarily explores, while, at the same time, retaining an interest in the industrial and economic contexts of the films under discussion, and their production, distribution, and exhibition histories.

The book examines a range of British films of the 1970s in eight chapters. But it does not offer a straightforward, chronological history of British film production during the period. While it does try to offer information about a substantial number of films, it does not offer an absolutely exhaustive account of 1970s British film texts and/or their historical contexts. I have chosen particular films for critical appraisal (or, indeed, for passing comment) primarily because it seems to me that they can be considered as rich texts that facilitate the construction of a series of intertwining narratives which might speak not only of the fragmenting nature of British film production and film culture but also of the flux and mutability of Britain (and Britishness) as witnessed in British film representations of the period. So, I am interested mainly in how far British films (of varying degrees of ambition and levels of artistic achievement) serve to evidence the vicissitudes of 1970s British socio-cultural life – how the films of British national cinema show 1970s Britain to itself and to the world. Because of this, I have taken the decision to limit my research to British films that represent Britain, either in the past or in the present, in all its ideological tensions and complexities.

My approach to choosing texts for discussion has been of necessity selective. It is perhaps the prerogative of cultural historians to move towards material that interests them personally, or even material they are passionate about. And, in my view, some of the films I discuss – *O Lucky Man!* (Lindsay Anderson, 1973), *Akenfield* (Peter Hall, 1974), *Requiem for a Village* (David Gladwell, 1975), *Pressure* (Horace Ové, 1975), *The Shout* (Jerzy Skolimowski, 1978), and *Radio On* (Chris Petit, 1979) – stand as some of the richest and most powerful seen in British national cinema, not only in the 1970s, but at any time. But others – while clearly not artistically impressive or always successful at the box office – also operate as intriguing texts which offer themselves up for close analysis, both at the level of their own textual specificity and semiotic richness, but also at the level of the ways in which they operate as fecund historical documents that might facilitate the exploration of broader contextual concerns regarding the vicissitudes of 1970s British cinema and social and cultural history. Taken together, the corpus of films explored in this book represents a vivid cross-section of the types of productions that managed to secure backing from a range of sources in difficult economic conditions. Some of these films are very well known; others less so. Some have been hailed as near-masterpieces; others dismissed (or indeed celebrated) as low-budget trash. Some have become cult films; others, in my view, could and should be of great interest but have been neglected critically until now. Some of these films were successful at the box office and launched the careers of admired individuals who would go on to become major figures in the business. Others barely made any money at all. But all of these films, when considered together, allow us to ask questions about the operation of a complex British film industry during the 1970s, and at the same time, the shifting nature of Britain and Britishness of the period.

In the writing of this book I wanted to evoke the essentially fragmented and fissured nature of not only British film production but also shifting notions of Britain as an idea, and a falling apart of concepts of Britishness that occurred during the 1970s. So, while I offer case studies of individual films, these studies often shift – or, indeed, fragment – to incorporate an appreciation of other film texts or contexts which one might not consider to have an obvious link to the initial film in question. Indeed, one of my central aims for this book is that it might uncover rich subterranean connections between films, film practitioners, and other extra-textual concerns. I do not want to set up an over-arching historical narrative in order to define 1970s British film culture and representations of Britishness, because the object of scrutiny so clearly resists this. To respect the sheer variety and diversity of film production, I want instead to remain alive to textual and contextual micro-histories, which, when considered together, might serve to evoke the vicissitudes so characteristic of the decade. As such, my discussions cover the unstable ebb and flow of genres; actors' performances and careers; the critical reception of films; the employment of studios and location shooting; innovations in production design; the employment of sound and concomitant developments in technology; diegetic and extra-diegetic music; and key aspects of camerawork, editing, and *mise-en-scène*. But these discussions often switch between films we might not usually place together within recognised, orthodox, and traditional critical frameworks. I take this approach because this is a cinema which cannot be understood in any useful way though traditional scholarly studies of topics such as genre, stardom, or studio production. This is a variegated period of film-making that lacks cohesion, and to lend it cohesion retrospectively would not be a useful exercise.

Moreover, British films of the 1970s cannot usefully be approached in terms of making distinctions (value judgements) between films of high and low artistic achievement, the 'popular' and the 'serious', or separating the semiotic specificities of highly regarded film texts from their socio-cultural contexts of production. Sue Harper and Justin Smith rightly argue that during this period 'the fragmented nature of the economic base gives rise to an inchoate body of films'.[77] In this book I want to show how far the most challenging and artistic of films and conversely, the most throwaway and, to some, seemingly worthless of films, might speak of Britain and Britishness in uncannily similar – and often curiously enlightening – ways.

While I have engaged in some necessary empirical research, I want to make it clear that my primary critical methodology remains close textual analysis. Above all, I am interested in what texts say about 1970s Britain; how they mediate socio-cultural change. My analysis is always keen to incorporate (or at least remain aware of) contextual material and concerns. This is of great importance to my methodology, because the industrial conditions of production and reception are, of course, key factors in the development of films as texts. Indeed, the economic conditions in which films are developed and released inform the formal qualities of these films, their aesthetics, and their systems of representation. In other words, film studios, production companies, and producers shape film budgets, which in turn shape the decisions directors, art directors, and production designers make concerning the look, tone, feel, and, ultimately, the quality of films. So, while British films of the 1970s offer us a deep repository of memories – and, as such, evidence of representational patterns that inform fragmentary notions of Britain and Britishness – they also often offer rich evidence of creative and industrial ingenuity. It also goes without saying that these films do not exist in a cultural vacuum. As such, while I am interested in the contexts of cinema history when examining individual films, I also try – where appropriate – to suggest useful thematic links to literature, poetry, and, of course, television programmes of the decade.

This book does not offer a comprehensive appraisal of every important (or, for that matter, impressive, or even interesting) film made in Britain during the 1970s or released during that period. From a personal perspective, ideally I would have liked to have covered in more detail the work of a wider range of extraordinary British film-makers who were working throughout the decade – with Nicolas Roeg and Ken Russell springing to mind here. But I am mindful of the fact that their legacies continue to be well documented elsewhere.[78]

While my focus is generally on films made for cinema distribution, I am aware that the 1970s was a rich period of film-making for television. As I am interested in representations of Britain on film during the 1970s, it is with some regret that, while I do refer to a range of films made for television, I have not been able to discuss as many films in detail as I would have liked, such as those made for *BBC Television Shakespeare* (BBC, 1978–85), *Play of the Month* (BBC, 1965–83), and one-off dramas such as the BBC's *Abigail's Party* (Mike Leigh, BBC, 1977), *The Stone Tape* (Peter Sasdy, BBC, 1972), and *Penda's Fen* (Alan Clarke, BBC, 1974). I certainly recognise that, as Dave Rolinson argues persuasively, 'During British cinema's difficulties in the 1970s, television drama became almost an alternative national cinema.'[79] It should not be forgotten that one of the most successful areas of British film production during the 1970s was television spin-offs, such as film versions of situation comedies, but also the *Monty Python* films: *Monty Python and the Holy Grail* (Terry Jones and Terry Gilliam, 1974) and *Life of Brian* (Terry Jones, 1979), as well as *And Now for Something Completely Different* (Ian MacNaughton, 1971).[80]

While this book offers an examination of a range of British films of the 1970s which places them within their historical contexts, I remain mindful of the fact that almost all of these films are dealing with representations of England and, as such, with aspects of (or ideas of) Englishness. I have certainly not made a conscious attempt to marginalise films that deal specifically with representations of Wales and Scotland. But it remains an inescapable fact that, in terms of the sheer numbers of films produced during the 1970s, Welsh and Scottish films are very thin on the ground compared to films made in (and about) England. English language films set in Wales during the period tend to focus on national artistic figures, aspects of widely-recognised Welsh culture, or the 'real lives' of

Welsh communities. These films include *Under Milk Wood* (Andrew Sinclair, 1972) – an adaptation of the play for voices by Dylan Thomas, starring Elizabeth Taylor, Richard Burton and Peter O'Toole. *Dylan* (Richard Lewis, 1978) tells the story of the infamous Welsh poet's final visit to the USA, and his death in New York. *Above Us the Earth* (Karl Francis, 1976) is a docu-drama about Welsh miners, charting the impact of a Rhymney Valley pit closure. And *Grand Slam* (John Hefin, 1978) is a BBC Wales comedy film about the successes of the Welsh rugby union team.[81] In 1970s Scotland, the work of Bill Douglas in his trilogy *My Childhood* (1971), *My Ain Folk* (1973), and *My Way Home* (1978) stands alongside the most poetic and moving films made in Britain (and indeed Europe) during the decade. Other films deal with the day-to-day realities of living in Scotland. For example, *Just Another Sunday* (John Mackenzie, 1975) – a BBC TV *Play for Today* – details sectarian violence that develops during a Protestant Orange Day Parade in the tough streets of Glasgow. *That Sinking Feeling* (Bill Forsyth, 1980) is a Glasgow-set comedy concerning four teenagers.[82] And the Scottish countryside features in films of the period such as *The Ballad of Tam Lin* (aka *The Devil's Widow*) (Roddy McDowell, 1970), which was based on a Scottish folk song and shot in the Scottish Borders, and *The Wicker Man* (Robin Hardy, 1973), which constructs a vision of a remote pagan community on a Scottish island.

We should remember that any history of British cinema is bound up with transnational developments, and we must necessarily be responsive to the shifts in the organisation of the US film industry, especially when one considers that so many British films of the period (particularly during the earlier part of the decade) were funded by US production companies. Indeed, many of the industrial issues confronting British film-makers during the 1970s also pertain to Hollywood. After all, writing about the American film industry in the 1970s, Peter Lev argues that 'in the 1960s and 1970s, the film audience shrank and fragmented, and the verities of the old studio system fell apart. Stars and genres were no longer enough to sell a picture'.[83] The major US studios lost $500 million between 1969 and 1972.[84] By the beginning of the 1970s, Hollywood had moved from investing in traditional, big-budget productions to developing an enthusiasm for new talents and low-budget films, which often demonstrated the influence of European art cinema.[85] If this was an era of 'nobody knows anything' – a period of uncertainty and disarray in Hollywood – it also provided moments of opportunity. As Lev puts it, 'If nobody knows anything, then everything is permitted.'[86] If it is true that creative moments in film history often take place in periods of social and political conflict – and there is evidence of this in the achievements of New American cinema as well as Italian neo-realism, the French *nouvelle vague* ('new wave'), and the German silent films – then British cinema of the 1970s also offers evidence of this, perhaps in the most unusual and unpredictable of places. Film production in Britain in the 1970s was so fragmented and disparate that it would be difficult (or indeed unhelpful) for us to assign a catch-all term to provide this period with a distinctive identity. But one thing this book does argue is that much British film-making of the 1970s was marked by a distinct hybridity. I want to begin by exploring how shifts in gender politics were represented in a range of British films of the 1970s.

Notes

1   At the time of writing, the prints of *Nobody Ordered Love* have seemingly disappeared. In 2012 the film remains one of the British Film Institute's most sought-after lost films, appearing in their '75 Most Wanted' list. As I have not been able to see the film, I have had to rely on the British Film Institute for information regarding the narrative – specifically, Kevin Lyons' piece, 'Nobody Ordered Love', available online at: www.bfi.org. uk/nationalarchive/news/mostwanted/nobody-ordered-love.html.

    Before her death in 2010, Ingrid Pitt suggested that a print of *Nobody Ordered Love* might still exist, as it has been screened (dubbed) on French television (see Maxford, 'Revelations and Revolutions: Ingrid Pitt', p. 45). Pitt also believed a print might be with Canal Plus, and that another print might be in Canada (see Bradley, 'The Bloody Countess: An Interview with Ingrid Pitt', p. 89).

2   For contemporary reviews of the film, see McGillivray, 'Nobody Ordered Love', and Fox, 'Nobody Ordered Love'.

3   A. Walker, *National Heroes*, p. 15.

4   A. Walker, *National Heroes*, p. 15.

5   J. Walker, *The Once & Future Film*, p. 23.

6   Dickinson and Street, *Cinema and State*, p. 240.

7   Dickinson and Street, *Cinema and State*, p. 240.

8   Dickinson and Street, *Cinema and State*, p. 241; Street, *British National Cinema*, p. 20.

9   Wood, *British Films 1971–1981*, p. 143.

10 Higson, 'A Diversity of Film Practices', p. 217.

11 Park, *Learning to Dream*, p. 61.

12 Higson, 'A Diversity of Film Practices', p. 217.

13 Harper, 'History and Representation: The Case of 1970s British Cinema', p. 29.

14 For more on the work of the BBFC, see Barber, 'British Film Censorship and the BBFC in the 1970s'.

15 See Sandbrook, *State of Emergency*, pp. 445–51.

16 Higson, 'A Diversity of Film Practices: Renewing British Cinema in the 1970s', p. 220.

17 Higson, 'A Diversity of Film Practices: Renewing British Cinema in the 1970s', p. 237.

18 Harper, 'Keynote Lecture: Don't Look Now? British Cinema in the 1970s Conference, University of Exeter, July 2007', p. 26.

19 Amicus was a British production company founded and managed by two Americans, Milton Subotsky and Max Rosenberg, at Shepperton Studios. Amicus made fourteen horror films between 1964 and 1974, featuring predominantly British casts (often including Peter Cushing and Christopher Lee) and settings. Amicus produced a number of British films in the 1970s that were not of the horror genre, including *At the Earth's Core* (Kevin Connor, 1974), *Creatures the World Forgot* (Don Chaffey, 1970), *The Land That Time Forgot* (Kevin Connor, 1974), *The People that Time Forgot* (Kevin Connor, 1977) and *Warlords of Atlantis* (Kevin Connor, 1978). See Bryce, *Amicus: The Studio that Dripped Blood*, and Hutchings, 'The Amicus House of Horror'.

20 Egan, 'Exploring the Critical Reception of Ingrid Pitt: Nudity, Feminism, Nostalgia and the 1970s', Culture, Change and Continuity symposium, Aberystwyth University, 15 September 2011.

21 For more on Tony Tenser, see Hamilton, *Beasts in the Cellar*; and for more on Michael Klinger, see Spicer, 'The Precariousness of Production: Michael Klinger and the Role of the Film Producer in the British Film Industry during the 1970s'.

22 For more on Gavrik Losey, see Newland, 'On Location in 1970s London: Gavrik Losey'; and Shaw, 'Picking up the Tab'.

23 Hunt, *British Low Culture: From Safari Suits to Sexploitation*, p. 1.

24 Harper, 'Keynote Lecture: Don't Look Now: British Cinema in the 1970s Conference, University of Exeter, July 2007', p. 23.

25 A. Walker, *National Heroes*, p. 16.

26 A. Walker, *National Heroes*, p. 16.
27 A. Walker, *National Heroes*, p. 17.
28 A. Walker, *National Heroes*, p. 17.
29 Dawson, 'Sunday Bloody Sunday', p. 164.
30 Milne, 'Sunday Bloody Sunday', p. 147.
31 A. Walker, *National Heroes*, p. 19.
32 Gerrard, 'What a Carry On! The Decline and Fall of a Great British Institution', p. 39.
33 Turner, *Crisis? What Crisis? Britain in the 1970s*, p. 79.
34 Nairn, *The Break-Up of Britain: Crisis and Neo-Nationalism*, p. 51.
35 Sandbrook, *State of Emergency*, p. 60.
36 Sandbrook, *State of Emergency*, p. 60.
37 Sandbrook, *State of Emergency*, p. 97.
38 Turner, *Crisis? What Crisis? Britain in the 1970s*, pp. 10–11.
39 Turner, *Crisis? What Crisis? Britain in the 1970s*, p. 12.
40 Turner, *Crisis? What Crisis? Britain in the 1970s*, pp. 103–4.
41 Turner, *Crisis? What Crisis? Britain in the 1970s*, p. 100.
42 Moore-Gilbert, 'Introduction: Cultural Closure or Post-avantgardism?', p. 3.
43 Moore-Gilbert, 'Introduction: Cultural Closure or Post-avantgardism?', pp. 2–3.
44 Laing, 'The Politics of Culture: Institutional Change in the 1970s', p. 30.
45 *Time*, 26 November 1973. Quoted in Sandbrook, *State of Emergency*, p. 7.
46 Sandbrook, *State of Emergency*, p. 168.
47 Turner, *Crisis? What Crisis? Britain in the 1970s*, p. 16.
48 Sandbrook, *State of Emergency*, p. 172.
49 Turner, *Crisis? What Crisis? Britain in the 1970s*, p. 228.
50 Moore-Gilbert, 'Introduction: Cultural Closure or Post-avantgardism?', p. 5.
51 Sandbrook, *State of Emergency*, p. 286.
52 Moore-Gilbert, 'Introduction: Cultural Closure or Post-avantgardism?', pp. 2–6.
53 Sandbrook, *State of Emergency*, p. 24.
54 Forster and Harper, 'Introduction', in Laurel Forster and Sue Harper (eds), *British Culture and Society in the 1970s*, p. 3.
55 Hunt, *British Low Culture: From Safari Suits to Sexploitation*, p. 1.
56 Sandbrook, *State of Emergency*, p. 454.
57 Lev, *American Films of the 70s: Conflicting Visions*, p. 182.
58 Booker, *The Seventies: Portrait of a Decade*, p. 5.
59 Booker, *The Seventies: Portrait of a Decade*, p. 5.
60 Booker, *The Seventies: Portrait of a Decade*, p. 7.

61   Booker, *The Seventies: Portrait of a Decade*, pp. 22–3.

62   For a detailed account of postmodernity, see Harvey, *The Condition of Postmodernity*; and Jameson, *Postmodernism, or, The Cultural Logic of Late Capitalism.*

63   Booker, *The Seventies: Portrait of a Decade*, p. 18.

64   Sounes, *Seventies: The Sights, Sounds and Ideas of a Brilliant Decade*, p. 126.

65   Turner, *Crisis? What Crisis? Britain in the 1970s*, p. ix.

66   Sandbrook, *State of Emergency*, p. 19.

67   Sandbrook, *State of Emergency*, p. 6.

68   Laing, 'The Politics of Culture: Institutional Change in the 1970s', p. 29.

69   Sandbrook, *State of Emergency*, p. 5.

70   Turner, *Crisis? What Crisis? Britain in the 1970s*, p. 22.

71   Turner, *Crisis? What Crisis? Britain in the 1970s*, p. 165.

72   For more on film-makers who worked in advertising, see Sargeant, 'Hovis, Ovaltine, Mackeson's and the *Days of Hope* Debate'.

73   Shail, 'Introduction: Cinema in the Era of "Trouble and Strife"', p. xviii.

74   Petley, 'The Lost Continent'.

75   Higson, *Waving the Flag: Constructing a National Cinema in Britain*, p. 4.

76   Higson, *Waving the Flag: Constructing a National Cinema in Britain*, pp. 4–5.

77   Harper and Smith, 'Introduction', p. 6.

78   For more on Ken Russell, see Atkins, *Ken Russell*; Hanke, *Ken Russell's Films*; Wilson, *Ken Russell, A Director in Search of a Hero*; Gomez, *The Adaptor as Creator*; Phillips, *Ken Russell*; Flanagan (ed.), *Ken Russell: Re-viewing England's Last Mannerist*. For more on Nicolas Roeg, see Feineman, *Nicolas Roeg*; Lanza, *Fragile Geometry: The Films, Philosophy and Misadventures of Nicolas Roeg*; Sinyard, *The Films of Nicolas Roeg*; Izod, *The Films of Nicolas Roeg*; Salwolke, *Nicolas Roeg: Film By Film*; Sanderson, *Don't Look Now*; MacCabe, *Performance.*

79   Rolinson, 'The Last Studio System', p. 165.

80   For more on British television in the 1970s, see Forster, '1970s Television: A Self-conscious Decade'.

81   Woodward , 'I Was There? Rugby, National Identity and Devolution in 1970s Wales', Culture, Change and Continuity symposium, Aberystwyth University, 15 September 2011.

82   For more on Scotland on film, see Petrie, *Screening Scotland.*

83   Lev, *American Films of the 70s: Conflicting Visions*, p. xvi.

84   Bordwell and Thompson, *Film History: An Introduction*, p. 697.

85   Lev, *American Films of the 70s: Conflicting Visions*, p. 6.

86   Lev, *American Films of the 70s: Conflicting Visions*, p. xvii.

1

Equality or bust:
sexual politics

Everyone's raving about sex – Twice nightly!

Advertisement on the side of a red double-decker bus,
Carry On Loving (Gerald Thomas, 1970)

Big Dick and B.U.M. Productions: *Eskimo Nell*

Eskimo Nell (Martin Campbell, 1974) is a ribald British sex comedy. But it is also a film about film-making in 1970s Britain. Michael Armstrong (who wrote the script and had written and directed the 1969 Tigon horror film *The Haunted House of Horror*, aka *Horror House*) plays a young director, Dennis, just out of film school. We see him descend the grand steps of a neo-classical building which houses the Film Academy. This is a fictional establishment which nevertheless speaks of real developments taking place in the industry. During the early part of the decade it was possible to train as a film-maker within a 'school'-type environment in Britain for the first time. The National Film School was set up in 1971 at the old Beaconsfield Studios in Buckinghamshire (a facility previously used by the Crown Film Unit and the British Lion Film Corporation). Colin Young was the School's first Director, and its twenty-five initial students included Bill Forsyth (*Local Hero*), Ben Lewin (*Ally McBeal*), and Mike Radford (*Il Postino*).[1]

During the post-credits sequence of *Eskimo Nell*, as the lyrics of an incongruous country-and-western-style song tell the back story in a jaunty way, we see Dennis enter the London offices of major US film companies United Artists and Columbia-Warner in an attempt to secure work. The film was shot entirely on location in London (both exteriors and interiors), and there is the palpable sense of a grubby city living through an economic and cultural crisis. Initially, Dennis is not successful in obtaining work, but as he wanders, disheartened, around Wardour Street, Soho, he spots a small sign by a modest doorway and enters. Here he finds the offices of the sleazy B.U.M. Productions, a small, independent production company run by Benny U. Murdoch (Roy Kinnear), which evidently specialises in seedy sex films.

Eskimo Nell was directed by Martin Campbell, who had just directed *The Sex Thief* (1973), and eventually went on to make the BBC television drama series *Edge of Darkness* (1985), and other notable films such as the blockbuster *The Mask of Zorro* (1998), and the James Bond films *GoldenEye* (1995) and *Casino Royale* (2006). He was also one of the producers of *Black Joy* (Anthony Simmons, 1977), an early film about black British culture (discussed in Chapter 4), and an associate producer on *Scum* (Alan Clarke, 1979). *Eskimo Nell* was produced by the infamous Stanley Long, who was, according to Simon Sheridan, the 'godfather of British cinema sex'.[2] During his early career, Long worked as a photographer, before moving on to produce 'glamour' home movies for the 8mm market. In addition to later making a name for himself as the producer of films such as *Eskimo Nell*, Long directed three sex comedy films in the 1970s: *Adventures of a Taxi Driver* (1975), *Adventures of a Private Eye* (1977), and *Adventures of a Plumber's Mate* (1978).

Eskimo Nell features well-respected British actors such as Roy Kinnear and Christopher Timothy, and another future household name, Christopher Biggins. Kinnear was a versatile British actor who worked throughout the 1970s. Like many British actors of his generation, Kinnear's career began in the theatre. He joined Joan Littlewood's influential Theatre Workshop at the Theatre Royal, Stratford East in London in 1959. And he later secured roles in a number of films directed by his good friend Richard Lester, including *A Hard Day's Night* (1964); *Help!* (1965); *A Funny Thing Happened On the Way to the Forum* (1966); *How I Won the War* (1967); *The Bed-Sitting Room* (1969); *Juggernaut* (1974); *Royal Flash* (1975); and the *Musketeer* series of films of the 1970s and 1980s. Overall, Kinnear's wide-ranging work of the period also speaks of the vicissitudes of 1970s British film production. For example, he appears in the Hammer horror film *Taste the Blood of Dracula* (Peter Sasdy, 1970) alongside Christopher Lee; in the Dickensian musical drama *Scrooge* (Ronald Neame, 1970); in the Children's Film Foundation films *Egghead's Robot* (Milo Lewis, 1970) and *Raising the Roof* (Michael Forlong, 1972); and in the David Puttnam-produced drama *Melody* (aka *S.W.A.L.K.*) (Waris Hussein, 1971). He features in *The Alf Garnett Saga* (Bob Kellett, 1972), a big-screen version of the popular television sitcom, *Till Death Us Do Part* (Norman Cohen, 1969); in the British thriller *Madame Sin* (David Greene, 1972) alongside US stars Bette Davis and Robert Wagner; and in the saucy comedy *The Amorous Milkman* (Derren Nesbitt, 1974). Kinnear also voices Pipkin in the animated feature *Watership Down* (Martin Rosen, 1978), and appears in *The Princess and the Pea* (1979), directed by Don Boyd – who attended the London Film School in 1968 and subsequently produced and directed a range of films during the period.[3] But Kinnear also worked transnationally. He plays Veruca Salt's father in *Willy Wonka & the Chocolate Factory* (Mel Stuart, 1971), a US musical produced by Warner Bros., based on a novel by Roald Dahl (Welsh born, of Norwegian parents), and shot in Bavaria, Germany. And he appears in the Australian comedy *Barry McKenzie Holds His Own* (Bruce Beresford, 1974). In addition to this, Kinnear also became a well-known face on British television, appearing in episodes of *That Was the Week That Was* (BBC, 1962–63), *Doctor at Large* (LWT, 1971), *Man About the House* (Thames, 1973–76), *The Avengers* (ABC/Thames, 1961–69), *George and Mildred* (Thames, 1976–79), *The Dick Emery Show* (BBC, 1963–81) and *The Goodies* (BBC/LWT, 1970–82).[4]

In *Eskimo Nell*, Kinnear's Benny U. Murdoch is a breast-obsessed sleaze-ball who proudly displays a poster of Doris Wishman's *Deadly Weapons* on his office wall. Dennis's friend and screenwriter Harris Tweedle (Christopher Timothy) is a naive, virginal innocent with a penchant for penguins. Harris has a girlfriend, Hermione (Katy Manning), whose mother is Lady Longhorn (Rosalind Knight), an upper-class family values campaigner and the chairwoman of the Society for Moral Reform. She tells Harris and Dennis, 'I represent a vast minority of people in this country' who want to see 'a total ban on anything other than nice, wholesome stories'. To raise finance, Murdoch must woo three backers, each of whom has a very different vision for the film. Exploitation supremo Big Dick (Gordon Tanner) wants a hardcore porn film; homosexual accountant Vernon Peabody (Jeremy Hawke) wants a cross-dressing musical starring his drag queen toy-boy, Johnny (Raynor Burton); and the philanthropic Ambrose Cream (Richard Caldicott) wants a kung-fu musical starring his latest find, Millicent Bindle (Prudence Drage). Interestingly, all three initial backers for the film insist on their own 'star' playing the lead role in return for the funds that they promise to provide. When the funding arrives, Benny takes the cash and flees, leaving Dennis and Harris having to make three films to satisfy all three backers, but also having to find more funding to be able to do this. They find some way of pulling this off, obtaining financial assistance from Lady Longhorn for their 'wholesome film'. But as the date of the premiere arrives, the film cans get mixed up, and the porn film is subsequently screened for Lady Longhorn and an upper-class audience which includes the Queen.

Though *Eskimo Nell* is primarily a sex comedy, issues of good taste and low morals are immediately placed at the heart of the narrative in a knowing way. The film opens with a short pre-credits sequence in which the camera pans well-stacked library shelves. On the soundtrack, backed by swelling strings, a well-spoken narrator speaks of how, across the years, cinema has adapted 'classics from the annals of world literature'. As the camera pans along bound copies of novels – *Little Women*, *Rebecca*, *Jane Eyre* – a suspicious, tatty-looking copy of *Eskimo Nell* is pulled from the shelves. At a later cocktail party held by Lady Longhorn, the members of the Society for Moral Reform discuss how to stop seedy films reaching British screens. *Eskimo Nell* certainly seems to suggest that 'filth' is very much bound up with low culture, and, as such, with the world of the working class. Lady Longhorn haughtily opines that an adaptation of the nineteenth-century epic poem 'Eskimo Nell' might be 'Just what the public needs – something nice and wholesome', where the public is taken to be the masses; in other words, the uneducated lower classes. But, in a sequence cross-cut with this one – in which the planned film and its potential audience are characterised in very different ways – sex-film producer Benny

Murdoch tells Harris that the film should open with 'bleeding great tits', thus marking himself out as lower class, vulgar, and cynical about attempts to make a film that might appear to be artistic in any way. Back in the drawing room with Lady Longhorn, Dennis tries to market the project, eulogising about its potentially high-cultural value and the ways in which it might appeal to good taste; pointing out that he has visions of Eskimos wandering through a frozen white landscape. Indeed, throughout *Eskimo Nell*, Dennis and Harris – who are clearly sensitive, educated, middle-class young men – obviously display artistic ambitions. But these ambitions are in danger of getting out of control. At the film shoot, for example, Dennis behaves like a pretentious art house director, offering Jeremy (Christopher Biggins) direction, by telling him 'You symbolise the dialectical collection of opposites coming to a listless distance from reality.' At one point, Harris admits to not going to the pictures much, but that he did see *Nanook of the North* (Robert Flaherty, 1922); a confession that demonstrates a playful awareness of British film history. Having said this, Harris says *Nanook* wasn't very good because it 'didn't have any penguins in it'.

In its evocation of working-class, end-of-pier sauciness and its employment of crude double entendres, *Eskimo Nell* distinctly echoes some aspects of the mid-to-late period (late 1960s and early 1970s) 'Carry On' series of films. For example, at the celebratory dinner after the first screening of the 'wholesome' version of the film, Lord Coltwind (Jonathan Adams) tells Lady Longhorn and the assembled diners that the film is 'Something you can take the whole family to without being worried in any way. Pure escapism, that's what going to the cinema is all about. Not all this pornography and sex distorting young minds. I know, I've studied pornography over the years and I know what effect it can have on you.' This dialogue is delivered in a performance punctuated by facial tics and lusting eyes which clearly suggests repressed sexuality. As such, Adams' performance is reminiscent of the work of 'Carry On' actors Peter Butterworth and Kenneth Connor in the famous film cycle. Lord Coltwind's behaviour here is certainly similar to that of Mayor Frederick Bumble (Kenneth Connor) in *Carry On Girls* (discussed later in this chapter), who also appears to suggest, on the surface at least (to retain a sense of decorum) that he is disgusted by open displays of permissiveness. But at the same time, it is clear that he is secretly turned on by lascivious sexual activity. The figure of Lord Coltwind in *Eskimo Nell* unambiguously recalls the real-life campaigner Lord Longford, a deeply religious aristocrat (whose name is also, of course, echoed in that of Lady Longhorn) who conducted a crusade in an attempt to outlaw pornography in Britain during the 1970s (the Longford Report was published in 1972). But Longford was accused of being a hypocrite for touring the very Soho sex clubs that he sought to close down.[5]

Eskimo Nell is a farce. The narrative derives most of its comedy from improbable and unlikely situations; mistakes made that might cause embarrassment; physical humour and absurdity. Thus, *Eskimo Nell* can be read in terms of a long history of British farces which stretches back through the well-known work of Noël Coward and Oscar Wilde to Shakespeare's *The Comedy of Errors* and Chaucer's fourteenth-century *The Canterbury Tales*. Like many farces, *Eskimo Nell* features a narrative which develops at an increasingly frantic pace, and climaxes with a chase scene. The film also demonstrates other generic qualities of farces. It foregrounds transgressive behaviour, and features characters who behave in often infantile and irrational ways. But, in addition to this, the film is shot through with eccentricity and a surreal sense of mischief which, on occasion, comes surprisingly close to the 1970s work of the Monty Python team and Spike Milligan. Indeed, writing about *Eskimo Nell* in *Monthly Film Bulletin*, Clyde Jeavons put it that 'the film's infectious air of gleeful vengeance and genuine satirical bite give it, against all the odds, a rare claim as a British comedy of the Seventies that is both funny and relevant'.[6]

Eskimo Nell, like *Nobody Ordered Love* and *Long Shot*, also acknowledges its own position as a successfully produced British film in a difficult period, and, as such, as a minor miracle in a time of crisis for the British film industry. So, while *Eskimo Nell* is a film which was evidently made with a clear audience in mind, it is also – despite the crude and filthy aspects of the narrative and its necessary displays of flesh – an inventive, cine-literate film. It would not be beyond the realms of feasibility to consider it alongside other films about film-making, such as *Le Mepris* (Jean-Luc Godard, 1963) and *Singin' in the Rain* (Gene Kelly and Stanley Donen, 1952). Indeed, Diane

Langton's performance as the half-witted actress Gladys Armitage in *Eskimo Nell* bears the distinct hallmarks of Jean Hagen's squeaky-voiced portrayal of the asinine movie star Lina Lamont in *Singin' in the Rain*.

But having said that, many would no doubt argue that *Eskimo Nell* essentially remains a low-cultural text. Leon Hunt points out that three genres remain particularly important in British film production during the 1970s, albeit in often hybrid forms; these are horror, comedy, and sexploitation.[7] Indeed, this would appear to chime with I.Q. Hunter's view that this was a period 'when exploitation was one of the few thriving areas of indigenous cinema'.[8] But Hunter goes further, suggesting that 'Low-budget sex comedies, "permissive" dramas, sex education films (known in the trade as "white-coaters") and sexploitation documentaries sustained the British film industry in the 1970s.'[9] Bearing in mind the prevalence of low-budget British horror, sex and comedy films, but widening his view to include other cultural forms, Leon Hunt writes of the 1970s as a decade of low culture. He points out that 'Popular culture of the 1970s has largely been excavated as an orgy of unsoundness, both an uneasy "coming to terms" with feminism and "permissiveness", and what looks like a sort of last major assault in the face of impending ideological policing.'[10] He further advocates that the 'low' can be distinguished 'both as a doubly marginalised district within the popular and as an ostensibly irrecuperable textual community'.[11] The central organising theme of his fascinating book, *British Low Culture* (1998), is 'permissive populism';[12] a 'popular appropriation of elitist 'liberationist' sexual discourses'.[13] Here Hunt sees the 1970s as a 'cruel parody' of the 1960s.[14] And, interestingly, this is the 'male heterosexual *fin de siècle*'.[15] He makes a strong argument for the critical reconsideration of 'low' cultural texts, and, to his credit, has no reservations about 'asserting their importance'. As he puts it, 'At the end of the day, value cannot be separated from use, and all of these objects have a capacity to produce knowledge of one sort or another.'[16] But, as we have seen, *Eskimo Nell* is a complex film which self-reflexively subverts and resists its low-cultural status.

One aspect of so-called British 'low culture' that Hunt concentrates on in his book is television comedy. A veritable plethora of television comedy spin-offs was produced for British cinemas in the 1970s. These films traded on the successful characters developed in a range of television shows, and did so in the knowledge that films featuring these much loved figures would no doubt prove successful at the box office (in Britain, at least). *On the Buses* (Harry Booth, 1971) was the highest-grossing British film in Britain in 1971. *Steptoe and Son* (Cliff Owen, 1972) was also a big box office hit. Other films of this strain include *Dad's Army* (Norman Cohen, 1971), *Bless This House* (Gerald Thomas, 1973), *The Likely Lads* (Michael Tuchner, 1976), *Porridge* (Dick Clement, 1979) and *George and Mildred* (Peter Frazer-Jones, 1980).[17] A number of these spin-offs foreground an end-of-pier attitude to sex, or, at the very least, refer to sexual behaviour as a kind of latent, underground activity which is in danger of exploding into mainstream British culture. As Simon Sheridan points out, 'For many Britons the concept of a national sexual identity is a strictly comical affair.'[18] It is certainly the case that a large number of British films from the late 1960s through to the end of the 1970s – including *Eskimo Nell* and numerous 'Carry On' films – deal with sex in a comic and often absurd fashion.[19]

Carry on Mary: *Carry On Girls*

The late 1960 and early 1970s saw the gradual easing of censorship in Britain.[20] For example, taking advantage of the abolition of the censorship powers of the Lord Chamberlain, Kenneth Tynan opened the notorious sex revue *Oh! Calcutta!* in London in the summer of 1970. But a variety of pro-life organisations also emerged at this time, which contested the liberalisation of censorship laws.[21] Lord Longford, in his *Report on Pornography* (1972), admitted that Tynan's revue made him realise there was need for an inquiry into pornography, and that he should mount a public campaign against its influence.[22] The 'moral majority' dimension of the Longford Report became a major aspect of the public face of new conservatism during the 1970s, with its emphasis on the family, moral standards and 'Victorian values' that Margaret Thatcher later propelled to the heart of government social policy.[23]

Women's liberation groups submitted their views to the Longford Committee thus: 'Anything which treated women as objects, particularly where fantasy is used to portray them as male-dominated, was to be deplored and advertising which used sexual overtones to sell products to either sex was almost as offensive as pornography.'[24] This discourse was grist to the mill for many British film-makers. For example, *Don't Just Lie There, Say Something!* (Bob Kellett, 1973) satirised Longford's campaign through the figure of Sir William Mainwaring-Brown (Leslie Phillips), a government spokesman for an anti-pornography bill. So, cinema effectively mediated the concerns of campaigners, while at the same time appealing to the desires of audiences interested in what was on offer in this new culture of permissiveness.

In *Eskimo Nell*, Lady Longhorn is battling an increasingly permissive society. Through this figure, the film is clearly engaged in satirising the activities of the campaigner Mary Whitehouse, who proved to be an influential figure in 1970s culture.[25] Whitehouse – in her trademark horn-rimmed glasses and colourful frocks – was a middle-class schoolteacher from the West Midlands driven by a traditionalist, Anglican mindset. She was a member of the evangelical Christian group Moral Re-Armament (MRA), ran the National Viewers' and Listeners' Association, and regularly appeared on the BBC's *Woman's Hour*, where she extolled the virtues of British women who believed in a Christian way of life.[26] Along with Malcolm Muggeridge, she co-founded the Festival of Light movement, which organised a 'Rally Against Permissiveness': an event that saw women in their thousands converge on Trafalgar Square in London in the late summer of 1971. Evidence of the ways in which Whitehouse infiltrated the popular imagination can be found widely in British films of the period. Perhaps unsurprisingly, she appears in a variety of guises in sex films, including as Mary Tighthouse in *The Love Pill* (Ken Turner, 1971), as Mary Watchflower in *I'm Not Feeling Myself Tonight!* (Joseph McGrath, 1975), and as Norma Blackhurst in *Hardcore* (James Kenelm Clarke, 1977).[27] Whitehouse was also lampooned on television in 'Gender Education', a 1971 episode of *The Goodies* which features a character, Desiree Carthorse, the head of the Keep Filth off Television Campaign (played by Beryl Reid), who asks the Goodies to make a sex education film.[28] They oblige, making 'How to Make Babies by Doing Dirty Things'.

Mary Whitehouse also appears, in spirit, in *Carry On Girls*, in the shape of the busy-body character Augusta Prodworthy (June Whitfield). *Carry On Girls* (1973) was the twenty-fifth film in the 'Carry On' cycle.[29] Critics have tried to re-evaluate the cultural impact of these films, primarily because low comedy has, on the whole, been culturally undervalued.[30] The 'Carry On' films were clearly influenced by the series of comedies produced by Ealing Studios during the late 1940s and 1950s, but they more obviously celebrate the working class, and, as such, were aimed at a primarily working-class audience. There were earlier antecedents, too. The 'Carry On' series bears the hallmarks of the British traditions of the music hall, and specifically acts such as Max Miller, George Formby and Will Hay.[31]

Carry On Camping (Gerald Thomas, 1969) is generally taken to be the film which evidences a significant shift in tone of the 'Carry On' cycle at the level of representations of sex. As Andy Medhurst points out, 'After Barbara Windsor's brassiere had at last burst ... where was the humour in teasing about the possibility of such an occurrence?'[32] But even with the increased incidence of such events during the 1970s (Margaret Nolan goes braless in *Carry On Girls*, for example), 'Carry On' films were increasingly at odds with the perceived demand for nudity and sex on screen.[33] They certainly did not cater for the sex film audience. But they did continue to indulge in mild titillation. As such, the mid-1970s films of the cycle were given AA certificates, thus diminishing their potential audiences in cinemas to the over-fourteens. These, it seems, were no longer family films. The audience for 'Carry On' films, then, effectively fell apart. Films such as *Carry On Girls* appear to move towards increased sexual display, but at the same time retain a firm foothold in older, less sexualised cultural traditions. Thus, according to Leon Hunt, this is a film which 'fragments fascinatingly before our eyes'.[34] As such, *Carry On Girls* and other later films of the cycle remain intriguing historical documents that offer telling representations of the myriad tensions pulling at British society and culture during the period. The falling away of the 'Carry On' films in the late 1970s (before being resurrected temporarily in 1992 with *Carry on Columbus*) can be put down to the exponential rise of the British sex film – witness, for example, the extraordinary success of *Come Play With Me* (Harrison Marks, 1977) and the *Confessions* films, which featured nudity. So it is more than a little ironic, then, that the final film of the series (before *Columbus* in 1992) was *Carry On Emmannuelle* (1978), which functions as a parody of Just Jaekin's notorious 1974 French soft-core sex film.[35]

Carry On Girls is set in the (fictional) sleepy English seaside town, Fircombe. The film opens with shots of rain lashing the drab promenade, and a mock-up thermometer outside Fircombe Town Hall which provides evidence of the low temperature; a gag that distinctly recalls the final shots of the Ealing comedy *Passport to Pimlico* (Henry Cornelius, 1949). At a council meeting, Councillor Sidney Fiddler (Sid James) raises the idea of holding a beauty contest in order to boost tourism in the struggling town. The Mayor, Frederick Bumble (Kenneth Connor), supports the scheme, while at the same time barely concealing the fact that this contest might provide an opportunity for him to go some way towards satisfying his repressed sexual urges. But the feminist Councillor Augusta Prodworthy (June Whitfield) is outraged that the town could exploit women in this way, and storms out of the meeting in disgust. The motion is carried in Augusta's absence, and Sidney asks his friend, the London-based publicist Peter Potter (Bernard Bresslaw), to assist with the organisation of the contest. Sidney's long-suffering girlfriend, Connie Philpotts (Joan Sims), runs the hotel on the seafront in which the beauty contestants stay. Here sequences occur in which Connie's older residents, including the Admiral (Peter Butterworth), find themselves overrun by scantily-clad young women, and witness a staged fight between the swimsuit-wearing beauty-queen biker, Hope Springs (Barbara Windsor), and the bikini-clad Dawn Brakes (Margaret Nolan). Meanwhile, the Mayor's wife, Mildred (Patsy Rowlands), joins Prodworthy's bra-burning movement, and takes part in the plot to stop the Miss Fircombe contest on the pier. Prodworthy's feminist gang puts 'Operation Spoilsport' into action, sabotaging the final contest with water, mud and itching powder, in a sequence that clearly recalls the infamous Miss World contest held at the Albert

Hall in London in November 1970 which saw the presenter, Bob Hope, attacked by agitators hurling smoke bombs and flowers – an action which 'catapulted radical feminism into the public consciousness'.[36]

Carry On Girls was made during a period of rapid change for many British women. Germaine Greer's book *The Female Eunuch* (1970) was perhaps the most important text published at this time, signalling the rise of modern feminism. In her book, Greer argues that women had become marginalised and oppressed, but that they were also complicit in this marginalisation and oppression. Other key publications of the period include *Patriarchal Attitudes* (Eva Figes, 1970) and *Woman's Estate* (Juliet Mitchell, 1971). In this climate of new, radical ideas, women were seizing the opportunity to protest. The Equal Pay Act 1970 became law (but it did not come into force until 1975). In 1971, marches on International Women's Day mobilised around demands for equal pay, education and job opportunities, free contraception, abortion on demand, and twenty-four hour nurseries. In 1972, Britain's first feminist magazine, *Spare Rib*, was launched, and Virago Press was set up by Carmen Callil in 1973 with the aim of publishing women writers. *Cosmopolitan*, a magazine aimed at young, upwardly-mobile, professional women, was launched in 1972. In some ways, during the 1970s, many more women began to see the freedoms usually associated with the 1960s. The Sex Discrimination Act 1975 was passed, and the Social Security Act 1975 enhanced pension provision and job security for women who sought to leave work to raise families.[37] Moreover, the Domestic Violence and Matrimonial Proceedings Act 1976 responded to fears concerning violence to women being meted out by brutish husbands in an alarming number of British households.

Evidence of the socio-cultural shifts brought about by the rise of feminism in Britain during this period can be found across film genres. For example, the horror film *The Deadly Females* (Donovan Winter, 1976) features a gang of 'hit women' based in a west London antiques shop, controlled by Joan (Tracy Reed), a bored housewife who at one stage exclaims 'We live in the savage Seventies.' This film plays on a number of contemporary concerns (mention is made of Irish Republican Army (IRA) attacks and the murder of a Bunny

Girl), but it also clearly offers a comment on contemporary femi-nism. In *The Corpse* (aka *Crucible of Horror*) (Viktors Ritelis, 1971), a mother and daughter, Edith (Yvonne Mitchell) and Jane Eastwood (Sharon Gurney), unite against the domineering, sadistic patriarch in their family, Walter (Michael Gough), by planning to murder him. And elsewhere, the James Bond film *The Spy Who Loved Me* (Lewis Gilbert, 1977) displays knowing nods to 1970s feminism, not least through the playful representation of the female Agent Triple XXX (Barbara Bach), while at the same time retaining elements of the misogyny traditionally associated with the enduring film cycle.

Writing at the time of the release of *Carry On Girls*, Gareth Jones argued that the writer Talbot Rothwell was 'Thriving as ever on the sexual repressions of his audience'.[38] But while the film facilitates mild titillation, as a historical text *Carry On Girls* is also alive to profound shifts in British culture during the period, especially at the level of sex, gender, and class. Sid Fiddler (Sid James) is an unreconstructed male. 'That's the way to deal with women – treat 'em rough,' he tells Peter (Bernard Bresslaw) on the telephone, before being caught by Connie (Joan Sims). He is clearly very fond of Connie, but evidently does not want to commit to her. He tells her 'Anything for you.' 'Anything but marriage,' she replies. But, married or not, these are working-class characters who have evidently made something of themselves – a town councillor and a hotel owner. Augusta Prodworthy, the Mary Whitehouse-type character, is well-spoken and proper. Her sense of decorum appears to have strong, upwardly mobile, class-based resonances. In some ways, with her blonde hair, force of will and strength of character, we might retrospectively read her as a proto-Thatcher-type figure. After all, she has designs on becoming the first female mayor of Fircombe. The old admiral (Peter Butterworth) might well be a war veteran, but here he is marked as a dirty old man who gets his comeuppance at the hands of Hope Springs (Barbara Windsor), who responds to his bottom pinching in a lift by returning the compliment, teasing him: 'So you want to play, do you?' As a jeans-wearing biker but also a busty beauty queen, Hope is clearly conflicted when it comes to her gendered identity. But she is one of the most positive, forward-thinking characters in the film (as her name suggests).

Overall, though, most of the characters in *Carry On Girls* appear to be struggling with permissiveness. But others clearly have the ability and, eventually, the desire to embrace the sexual spirit of the time. One of the final contestants in the beauty contest is Peter Potter's girlfriend, Paula Perkin (Valerie Leon). Initially, Paula appears to be a demure, bespectacled, virginal young woman. The sexual revolution has evidently passed her by. When they say their goodbyes on a station platform before Peter (Bernard Bresslaw) travels down to Fircombe, he makes his excuses for keeping her in the dark about the planned beauty contest: 'I couldn't trust myself to ask you to come with me. I'd only burst into your bedroom and try to make love to you or something.' Paula replies, 'You know I wouldn't let that happen.' It is clear that they are planning to marry, but that Peter remains sexually unfulfilled. Other couples in the film are clearly sexless, too, including the Mayor (Kenneth Connor) and his wife, Mildred (Patsy Rowlands), whom he likens to a 'compost heap'. But, interestingly, Paula (Leon) manages to bring about her own personal sexual revolution; crossing the divide from sexless prude to sex bomb; making her own way to Fircombe, entering the beauty competition (donning a swimsuit), and thus encouraging men to gaze at her statuesque body, much to the apparent amazement and excitement of her fiancé, Peter. Suddenly, it seems that Peter's dreams are going to come true. But there are limits to what he himself will do. When asked to dress up in women's clothes in order to enter the beauty competition as a publicity stunt, Peter declares to Sid 'I'm not changing sex for you or anybody else.'

Valerie Leon is also an actor whose career speaks of the fragmented nature of British film production during the period. She appears in a wide range of films, television shows and advertisements, many of which have developed cult status. She features in several 'Carry On' films, two James Bond films, in the satire *The Rise and Rise of Michael Rimmer* (Kevin Billington, 1970) with Peter Cook, and in the sex comedy *No Sex Please – We're British* (Cliff Owen, 1973), working again with Margaret Nolan. Furthermore, Leon plays a major role in the Hammer horror film *Blood from the Mummy's Tomb* (Seth Holt, 1971), and appeared in television shows such as *The Goodies*. Some of these texts have since become 'cult', primarily because of their perceived awfulness, and Leon's perfor-mances arguably speak of this awfulness in some ways. Indeed, her dialogue has been dubbed on at least one occasion (including in *Carry On Girls*, by June Whitfield). But nostalgia has also developed for her statuesque proportions, her 'pre-political correctness' onscreen persona, and a series of performances marked by a measured classiness. Her cult persona is perhaps best exemplified by her appearances in a series of 1970s television advertisements for Hai Karate aftershave in which she played a tall, dark, powerful woman who finds herself irresistibly drawn to any (usually small) man who happens to be wearing the product. It was these memo-rable performances that led to her being cast in *Revenge of the Pink Panther* (Blake Edwards, 1978), which features a sequence where she performs as a leather-clad dominatrix. As Paula in *Carry On Girls*, Leon signals the fact that young women now have it within their power to explore their sexuality, even if, for her, this initially involves the contradictory act of offering herself up for display at a sexist beauty contest.

Do you play? Permissiveness

As *Eskimo Nell* and *Carry On Girls* serve to demonstrate, shifts in gender politics are worked through in highly complex and often seemingly contradictory ways in a number of British films of the 1970s. Indeed, in many films, traditional, conservative views on masculinity, femininity and sex are often brought into conflict with discourses of permissiveness. For example, *The Lovers!* (Herbert Wise, 1972), starring Richard Beckinsale as Geoffrey and Paula Wilcox as Beryl, is a big screen adaptation of a British television series (Granada, 1970–71) about a courting couple. In its light-hearted examination of views on sex before marriage, the film (like the television series) speaks of the ways in which traditional family values were seemingly coming under threat from the new socio-cultural mores which generally placed an emphasis on individual fulfilment. Geoffrey evidently cannot wait to get involved in the passionate world of the permissive society. But this film effectively takes a conservative position on these socio-cultural shifts, because

Beryl has other ideas – making her boyfriend wait until they are married, when, she hopes, in return for sexual favours, he might prove to be a good husband. This depiction of the temptations of permissiveness can be read as a mediation of specific historical developments that occurred during the late 1960s and early 1970s. After all, the Family Planning Act was passed in 1967, and by 1973 the contraceptive pill was available on the National Health Service to all British women. Dominic Sandbrook tellingly points out that 'It was in the early 1970s, not the 1960s, that young single women began taking the Pill.'[39] The wider availability of 'the pill' in the early 1970s certainly appeared to mark a turning point in sexual behaviour, and in ways people talked and thought about sex.[40]

But, in British cinema, the permissive society was by no means always something to be celebrated. One film from the beginning of the decade worth considering here is *Permissive* (Lindsay Shonteff, 1970), one of a handful of so-called 'groupie' films of the period, such as the Stanley Long-produced *Groupie Girl* (aka *I am a Groupie*) (Derek Ford, 1970). *Permissive* follows the journey of a lone young woman, Suzy (Maggie Stride), to London. Initially, this provincial innocent finds she does not fit in with the 'scene'. But she meets a friend, Fiona (Gay Singleton), and tags along with her, witnessing uninhibited sexual activity at groovy gatherings. However, this is a bleak portrayal of a city coming down from the apparent highs of the 1960s. Eventually, Suzy, like Fiona, finds herself becoming a groupie for the rock band, Forever More. So her journey towards permissiveness is far from happy. *Goodbye Gemini* (aka *Twinsanity*) (Alan Gibson, 1970) mines similar territory, seeing fraternal twins Jacki (Judy Geeson) and Julian (Martin Potter) who, free from the control of their father (who is away on business) and their housekeeper (who they purposefully trip on some stairs), begin to explore a London in which sex and drugs are seemingly central to the everyday lives of people of their age group. But there is a palpable sense of strangeness concerning the way that permissiveness is portrayed in this film. As the twins witness the 'freedoms' on display, they are accompanied by Jacki's teddy bear, Agamemnon, which, bizarrely, they treat as a father figure. Furthermore, the twins have psychotic tendencies, and Julian evidently has sexual designs on his sister.[41]

The changes to the sex life of the British nation, as mediated in films of the 1970s, often appear to bring about severe tensions within the institutions of marriage and the family. Moreover, individuals who enter freely into monogamous relationships are sometimes seen to find much more than they bargained for. For example, Hammer's *Straight on Till Morning* (Peter Collinson, 1972) stars Rita Tushingham as Brenda, a young, single woman from Liverpool who goes south to London, telling her mother 'I'm going to find a father for the baby', when in fact we discover that she is not pregnant. As Brenda arrives at Earls Court underground station, she appears to be a weak figure, unsure of herself. In the big city, she too (like Suzy in *Permissive*, and Jacki and Julian in *Goodbye Gemini*) sees young people engaging in seemingly unemotional, promiscuous sex. But Brenda meets Peter (Shane Briant), an indolent figure who lives in a mews cottage and drives a Jaguar E-Type. As is the case in many film representations of dwellings in 1970s Britain, his flat is furnished with a curious mixture of the old and the new, featuring as it does sleek and shiny modern furniture and hi-fi equipment alongside dusty antiques and a grandfather clock – a microcosm of a nation torn between past, present and future. As a rich young man, Peter does 'nothing'. He has no purpose. He allows Brenda to stay with him. While initially sharing his domestic space with her, he suddenly declares 'Cleaning up is a woman's job', and from this point on Brenda transforms into a disturbed vision of a bourgeois housewife. What we see here, then, is the potential horror of a bad marital relationship, in which individuality is cruelly stifled. Peter's behaviour becomes more and more unstable, to the extent that he kills both his dog and Brenda's previous flatmate, Caroline (Katya Wyeth), with a Stanley knife, recording the sounds accompanying these horrifying acts on his reel-to-reel tape recorder. So, as a representation of a relationship between two young people in modern Britain, *Straight on Till Morning* finds little to celebrate.

The socio-cultural shifts of the early 1970s led many more people to seek sexual gratification. Evidence of this can be found across a wide range of cultural texts of the period, such as in the incredibly successful publication *The Joy of Sex* (Alex Comfort, 1972). But sex was often sought outside monogamous relationships. David Hockney, the subject of the documentary film *A Bigger Splash*

(Jack Hazan, 1973), painted *Mr and Mrs Clark and Percy* (1970–71), which depicts the fashion designer Ossie Clark and his wife Celia Birtwell shortly after their wedding, and features symbolism which hints at infidelity.[42] And a number of British films of the period strongly suggest that many married couples would rather have performed the range of sexual positions detailed in Comfort's book with individuals other than their own husbands or wives.

In *The Romantic Englishwoman* (Joseph Losey, 1975), Glenda Jackson plays Elizabeth Fielding, the discontented wife of successful novelist Lewis (Michael Caine). Writing about Glenda Jackson's portrayal of this young, unhappily married woman, Melanie Williams notices a 'scene of marital discord … Accumulated images of material comfort, sexual liberation and liberal compassion only throw into relief the overwhelming spiritual lack at the heart of the heroine's bourgeois life'.[43] Elizabeth decides to travel to Baden-Baden in Germany, where she meets Thomas (Helmut Berger). She returns to her husband in England, but the paranoid Lewis appears convinced that she has had an affair while away, and this imagined fling finds its way into the book he is currently working on. When Thomas subsequently turns up in England, he is invited to stay in the couple's spare room, and Lewis tries to find out what is going on between him and his wife. Meanwhile, Elizabeth wonders what it would be like to have the kind of freedom that Thomas appears to enjoy, and she considers what she would stand to lose if she were to walk out on her husband in order to enjoy a life free of responsibilities to others.

Another film that places a marriage in crisis at the heart of the narrative is *Zee & Co.* (aka *X, Y and Zee*) (Brian G. Hutton, 1972), which also stars Michael Caine. This film starts with a slow-motion game of table tennis between the principal characters, Zee Blakeley (Elizabeth Taylor) and her successful architect husband Robert (Caine), which bears comparison to power-play set-pieces seen in the collaborative film projects of Joseph Losey (director) and Harold Pinter (screenwriter): *The Servant* (1963), *Accident* (1967), and *The Go-Between* (1970). Indeed, in *Zee & Co.*, sexual politics are worked through as a series of games that speak of burning jealousies. The Blakeleys have a life of parties and conspicuous consumption, and share a house filled with gaudy late-1960s and early-1970s fashions and furnishings. Theirs is a life of sad, troubled 1970s socialites – all cigarettes and soda siphons, facelifts and faith healers. Indeed, a drunken haze envelops their lives, facilitating a palpable sense of solipsism and self-hatred. Their marriage is clearly fragmenting. Robert initially settled down to a life of married commitment with Zee, but he is evidently still a 'naughty boy'. Indeed, Zee calls him a 'peacock'. When Stella (Susannah York) catches Robert's eye at a party, they begin an affair under Zee's nose. Zee – a 'shrewish wife', according to Tom Milne[44] – asks Stella at one stage, 'Do you play?' It turns out that Zee and Robert are 'interdependent', as they tell Stella. But it seems that this arrangement works rather better for the husband than the wife. 'You love the uncertainty,' Zee tells Robert. Zee struggles with Robert's infidelities to such a degree that she later attempts suicide. She finally uses Stella's lesbian past to torment her rival, and dares Robert to join them in a threesome. Recent shifts in gender politics in Britain as such certainly inform the film, as in a sequence at a party when Zee tells Stella, 'We should have brought our embroidery' when they walk into the testosterone-filled territory of the snooker room. Robert and Zee are seemingly unable to have children, and this might be a cause of their unhappiness. But, as the narrative develops, it becomes clear that it is Stella who must suffer as a result of the extramarital sexual relationships that take place. We might come to the conclusion that, in the end, this is a conservative film, as the young woman is being punished for coming between the bickering, middle-aged husband and wife.

The Romantic Englishwoman and *Zee & Co.* are just two examples of films which display one of the recurring representational themes of the period: relationships in crisis. A considerable number of films feature couples experiencing severe problems in communication, or who have split up or divorced. This is perhaps unsurprising, considering the fact that, by the late 1970s, Britain had the highest divorce rate in Europe.[45] Many films of the decade tell stories of marital infidelities, or of characters who find themselves having to deal with the temptation of sex outside a stable relationship. As such, these 'relationship in crisis' films are indicative of increased permissiveness. During this period it was commonplace (and indeed much more socially acceptable) to be single, or to concern oneself with seeking one's own happiness, rather than serving a partner or bringing up children.[46] This socio-cultural trend clearly informs *Sunday Bloody Sunday*, in which Glenda Jackson's Alex Greville is, according to Melanie Williams, 'the definitive single woman of the early 1970s – gulping down instant coffee made hastily from the hot tap, trying to break free from bourgeois proprieties and monogamous commitment but feeling the lure of them nonetheless'.[47]

Interestingly, troubled marriages (or seemingly strong marriages which hold dark secrets) often appear in British horror films of the period. For example, in the Amicus-produced portmanteau film *The Vault of Horror* (Roy Ward Baker, 1973),[48] 'The Neat Job' features Terry-Thomas as an obsessively neat, middle-aged man, Arthur, who marries a younger woman (his friend's daughter), Eleanor (Glynis Johns). Eleanor moves into his 1970s-styled bachelor pad, and starts to take control of his space, nagging the older man incessantly. Arguments develop over where things should be kept, and how tidy the rooms should be. These escalate to the point where Eleanor attacks Arthur with a hammer, and kills him. She subsequently cuts up his body and stores the separate parts in neat jars – as he would have liked it.

The 'An Act of Kindness' tale in another Amicus portmanteau, *From Beyond the Grave* (Kevin Connor, 1973), features Ian Bannen as Christopher Lowe, a bored man in a loveless marriage to the nagging Mabel (Diana Dors). Lowe befriends an old soldier, Underwood (Donald Pleasence), and eventually starts an affair with his daughter, Emily (Angela Pleasence). On one occasion, Emily produces a doll of Lowe's wife, Mabel, and asks him whether or not she should cut it. When he agrees, she proceeds, and blood drips from the doll's mouth. Lowe rushes home to find Mabel dead. He then marries Emily. But at the wedding reception, instead of cutting the cake, she plunges the knife into the decorative groom, and Lowe falls down dead.

Similar goings-on at a wedding occur in the Pete Walker film *Schizo* (1976), which sees William Haskin (Jack Watson) travelling south to London from a drab Teeside, infiltrating the wedding reception of Samantha (Lynne Frederick) and carpet factory boss Alan (John Leyton), and depositing a bloody knife next to the wedding cake. It turns out that Haskin had previously murdered

Samantha's mother. In some senses this appears to be a dark film about the near schizophrenia displayed by married couples.[49] But disturbed marriages appear elsewhere in horror films of the period.

In *Frightmare* (Pete Walker, 1974), Edmund and Dorothy Yates (Rupert Davies and Sheila Keith) are a late-middle-aged married couple living in a remote rural cottage. The film suggests that all might not be well, even in the oldest and most successful of unions. Edmund is a chauffeur, and we witness his evident love for Dorothy. But we later discover that she is a cannibal, and this throws Edmund's devotion to her into stark relief. Here, marriage is essentially seen to be a 'mental institution'. Other marriages and relationships in crisis can be seen in *Fright* (Peter Collinson, 1971), featuring Honor Blackman, George Cole, Ian Bannen, Susan George, and Dennis Waterman, and *Dominique* (Michael Anderson, 1980) starring Cliff Robertson and Jean Simmons.

A number of horror films of the 1970s depict families in crisis, or tensions developing between generations. According to Andrew Tudor, early 1970s films share 'a clear diagnosis of the origins of psychosis in a psychosexual and familial context, an emphasis reinforced by the period's growing permissiveness in matters of on-screen sex and nudity'.[50] Furthermore, Kim Newman points out that 'Hammer's psycho-thrillers tend to revolve around the theme of trouble within the family'.[51] The institution of the family can function in representational form as a microcosm of society, then; 'one which through its internal dynamics registers broader social problems.'[52]

Very much in this vein, *Mumsy, Nanny, Sonny & Girly* (aka *Girly*) (Freddie Francis, 1970) is an allegorical horror/comedy film about the breakdown of a nuclear family, which is seen to be a result of the type of social-cultural shifts being brought about by increased permissiveness in British society. Set in a large country house, the film features members of a bizarre, wealthy English family whose names are synonymous with the roles they play: Mumsy (Ursula Howells), Nanny (the nanny, Pat Heywood), Sonny (the son, Howard Trevor), and Girly (the daughter, Vanessa Howard).[53] The family evidently takes pleasure in making contact with outsiders, and subsequently 'playing' with them before murdering them. Another British family horror of the period is *What Became of*

Jack and Jill? (Bill Bain, 1972), an Amicus-produced film based on a generation gap which sees two young lovers, Johnny (Paul Nicholas) and Jill (Vanessa Howard), plotting to murder Jill's wealthy grandmother (Mona Washbourne), so they can inherit her money. *The Fiend* (aka *Beware My Brethren*) (Robert Hartford-Davis, 1972) features Tony Beckley as Kenneth, a young man who works as a swimming baths attendant and night security guard, but who has a powerful, controlling mother (Birdy Wemys), and who feels driven to kill a number of young women. And in *The Night Digger* (aka *The Road Builder*) (Alastair Reid, 1971), an old, blind widow, Edith Prince (Pamela Brown), keeps her middle-aged daughter Maura Prince (Patricia Neal) at home in a bizarre master/servant relationship. This curious film features a screenplay by Roald Dahl (adapted from a novel by Joy Cowley – *Nest in a Falling Tree*) and a score by Bernard Herrmann (best known for his work with Alfred Hitchcock). All these films can be read within the context of a socio-cultural hangover caused by the revolutions in youth culture seen in the 1960s.

According to Peter Hutchings, the 1970s was a period during which the horror genre arguably gained 'some maturity and artistic integrity as well as a sense of social responsibility'.[54] Interestingly, for Hutchings, the 1970s saw the arrival of 'something called modern horror'.[55] This was a period, then (in British cinema but also in the USA and Europe) when the idea first really developed that horror films 'could provide a meaningful engagement with key social and political issues of the day'.[56] Across a range of these films, issues of shifts in gender relations, hostility to figures of authority, generational conflicts, and the breakdown of family lives are prevalent. British films such as *The Sorcerers* (Michael Reeves, 1967); *Witchfinder General* (Michael Reeves, 1968); *Taste the Blood of Dracula* (Peter Sasdy, 1969); *Blood on Satan's Claw* (Piers Haggard, 1970); *Scream and Scream Again* (Gordon Hessler, 1970); *Hands of the Ripper* (Peter Sasdy, 1971); and *Demons of the Mind* (Peter Sykes, 1971) all depict young people being assaulted, tortured or killed 'by monstrous older figures'.[57] Hutchings further notices a series of 'anti-father' horror films, such as *The Abominable Dr Phibes* (Robert Fuest, 1971); *Dr Phibes Rises Again* (Robert Fuest, 1972); and *Theatre of Blood* (Douglas Hickox, 1973).

British horror films set in a British past also often deal with the psychological effects of life in a traditional family unit or structure.[58] Hutchings notices a group of 1970s British horror films which concentrate on the relationships between fathers and their children, where the father often tries to prevent his children from becoming adults.[59] These include *And Now the Screaming Starts* (Roy Ward Baker, 1973), which has a lord of the manor, Sir Henry Fengriffen (Herbert Lom), dominating a house across generations. And in *The Creeping Flesh* (Freddie Francis, 1972), *The Hands of the Ripper* (Peter Sasdy, 1971), and *Demons of the Mind* (Peter Sykes, 1971), a 'general absence of normative heterosexual relations can be seen to derive from the father's refusal in each film to share his power with any other male'.[60] Hutchings also discusses three 'maternal dramas' of the early 1970s: *Blood From the Mummy's Tomb* (Seth Holt, 1971), *Countess Dracula* (Peter Sasdy, 1970), and *Dr Jekyll and Sister Hyde* (Roy Ward Baker, 1971). *Blood From the Mummy's Tomb*, 'identifies the nuclear family as an institution which favours male authority', but also 'aligns itself with much feminist thought of the day'.[61] This film certainly sees the total collapse of Margaret Fuch's (Valerie Leon) family. In *Countess Dracula*, Countess Elisabeth Nodosheen (Ingrid Pitt) displays an awareness of 'the relation between fantasies of maternal power and the familial and social roles assigned to women in a patriarchal society'.[62] And *Dr Jekyll and Sister Hyde* (Roy Ward Baker, 1971) is a Hammer horror that places issues of gender and sexuality at the heart of the narrative. Dr Jekyll (Ralph Bates) is a scientist searching for the 'elixir of life', which he discovers in female hormones. Taking these hormones causes him to have a temporary sex change, turning him into Sister Hyde (Martine Beswick). Interestingly, while Jekyll 'hasn't been himself of late', Sister Hyde, when she appears, is evidently a sexually voracious creature. *Dr Jekyll and Sister Hyde* thus features transsexual behaviour, but, according to Hutchings, can also be recognised as a maternal drama.[63]

As Sue Harper and Justin Smith have demonstrated, a number of films of the 1970s are preoccupied with transformations in masculinity.[64] Films such as *A Clockwork Orange* (Stanley Kubrick, 1971); *The Wicker Man* (Robin Hardy, 1973); *That'll Be the Day*

(Claude Whatham, 1973); and *Stardust* (Michael Apted, 1974) are 'preoccupied by what men are or might be'.[65] Furthermore, during the 1970s, shifts in gender politics were also evidenced in images of androgyny and bisexuality across popular culture.[66] Harper and Smith notice a number of what they term 'boundary-walkers' in British films of the period.[67] As we have seen, androgyny operates in *Dr Jekyll and Sister Hyde*, but also in *Performance* (Donald Cammell and Nicolas Roeg, 1970), for example, which features characters of often ambiguous sexuality or gender. A less well-known film, *I Want What I Want* (John Dexter, 1971), tells the story of a secret cross-dresser, Roy (Anne Haywood), who becomes a transsexual woman named Wendy. And *Girl Stroke Boy* (Bob Kellett, 1971) sees well-to-do Lettice Mason (Joan Greenwood) and her husband George (Michael Horden) bemused by the androgynous identity of their son's (Clive Francis) mysterious guest from the West Indies, Jo Delaney (Peter Straker).

Homosexuality was decriminalised in England and Wales with the passing of the Sexual Offences Act 1967. The first demonstration of the Gay Liberation Movement was in November 1970, and *Gay News* was published from 1971.[68] So it is not surprising that gay culture became much more visible in films and television of the 1970s.[69] Gay life was examined in the film work of Derek Jarman, whose *Sebastiane* (1976) – co-directed with Paul Humfress – was arguably the first British film to depict a positive view of homosexuality. And Ron Peck's film *Nighthawks* (1978) was effectively the first British film to depict the gay community realistically. But homosexuality also emerged in mainstream cinema and television, even if it was often represented in coded form, as in the figure of Cecil Gaybody (James Logan) in *Carry On Girls*, and in performances elsewhere by regular 'Carry On' stars, Charles Hawtrey and Kenneth Williams. We might also think here of the career of Frankie Howerd, who appeared in the films *Up Pompeii* (Bob Kellett, 1971), *Up the Chastity Belt* (Bob Kellett, 1971), and *Up the Front* (Bob Kellett, 1972), as well as on television. The television presenter Larry Grayson was in his prime during the 1970s, fronting *Shut That Door* (ATV, 1972–77) and *The Generation Game* (BBC, 1978–82). And John Inman's Mr Humphreys was bringing camp to a department store in the sitcom *Are You Being Served?* (BBC, 1972–85).

But some British films of the 1970s choose to tell the stories of characters who could not, for whatever reason, flourish in a new, permissive sexual climate. *Little Malcolm and His Struggle Against the Eunuchs* (aka *Little Malcolm*) (Stuart Cooper, 1974) stars John Hurt as Malcolm Scrawdyke, a delusional Northern art student who, on expulsion from college, seeks revenge on what he sees as the castrated multitudes. With a small group of followers, he sets up a quasi-fascist, revolutionary organisation called the Party of Dynamic Erection. But ultimately it is Malcolm who proves to be impotent; unable to act when Ann (Rosalind Ayres) asks him, 'How would you like to fuck me?' Faced with an attractive young woman who has sexual urges and is clearly prepared to act on them, Malcolm's emasculation is complete. Filmed on location in a cold, damp, run-down Oldham, *Little Malcolm* demonstrates that certain boyish, introspective, immature young men are clearly struggling with the cultural shifts brought about by the sexual revolution.

So, British films of the 1970s demonstrate that a highly complex range of ideological discourses are in operation during the decade concerning shifts in attitudes to sexuality and gender. Taken together, these texts speak of a battleground of ideas. Homosexuality is becoming more visible and less obviously marked as a perverse act. Young men are often represented as sex-mad or sexually inadequate (and tortured as a result). Young women are often represented as sexually inactive or sexually aware and even promiscuous (sometimes, at the same time, in the same film). Films often exploit lesbianism, or offer the female body up for the male gaze while also embracing aspects of contemporary feminist ideas. But serious film-making artists also explore issues of sexual exploitation. For example, Stephen Dwoskin's film *Dyn Amo* (1972) operates as a 'comment on human exploitation', in which four girls appear in turn on a satin-covered bed in a grim strip club.[70] Through the utilisation of tense close-up shots, this film teases out the horrors evident in such sexualised performances. Each of the four girls is presented less realistically than the one who went before, and the last girl experiences what is tantamount to torture in a sequence which becomes expressionistic in character. Other film-makers working in the 1970s would represent shifts in the sex life of Britain while, at the same time, examining other aspects of a fragmenting nation. It is to those film-makers I shall now turn.

Notes

1 A. Walker, *National Heroes*, p. 216. For more on Colin Young, see Petrie, 'Interview with Colin Young'.
2 Sheridan, *Keeping the British End Up: Four Decades of Saucy Cinema*, p. 231.
3 See North, 'Don Boyd: The Accidental Producer'.
4 Roy Kinnear also appears in *On a Clear Day You Can See Forever* (Peter Coe, 1970); *The Firechasers* (Sidney Hayers, 1970); *Alice's Adventures in Wonderland* (William Sterling, 1972); *The Pied Piper* (Jacques Demy, 1972); *That's Your Funeral* (John Robins, 1973); *The Cobblers of Umbridge* (TV) (Ned Sherrin, 1973); *Three for All* (Martin Campbell, 1975); *One of Our Dinosaurs is Missing* (Robert Stevenson, 1975); *The Adventures of Sherlock Holmes' Smarter Brother* (Gene Wilder, 1975); *Not Now, Comrade* (Ray Cooney, 1976); *Herbie Goes to Monte Carlo* (Vincent McEveety, 1977); *The Last Remake of Beau Geste* (Marty Feldman, 1977); *Hound of the Baskervilles* (Paul Morrissey,1978); *The London Connection* (aka *The Omega Connection*) (Robert Clouse, 1979); and *Mad Dogs and Cricketers* (Nicholas Parsons, 1979).
5 Lord Longford's obituary by Peter Stanford, *The Guardian*, 6 August 2001.
6 Jeavons, 'Eskimo Nell', p. 274.
7 Hunt, *British Low Culture: From Safari Suits to Sexploitation*, p. 30.
8 Hunter, 'Take an Easy Ride: Sexploitation in the 1970s', p. 3.
9 Hunter, 'Take an Easy Ride: Sexploitation in the 1970s', p. 3.
10 Hunt, *British Low Culture: From Safari Suits to Sexploitation*, p. 8.
11 Hunt, *British Low Culture: From Safari Suits to Sexploitation*, p. 8.
12 Hunt, *British Low Culture: From Safari Suits to Sexploitation*, p. 2.
13 Hunt, *British Low Culture: From Safari Suits to Sexploitation*, p. 2.
14 Hunt, *British Low Culture: From Safari Suits to Sexploitation*, p. 2.
15 Hunt, *British Low Culture: From Safari Suits to Sexploitation*, p. 5.
16 Hunt, *British Low Culture: From Safari Suits to Sexploitation*, p. 15.
17 Street, *British National Cinema*, pp. 97–9.
18 Sheridan, *Keeping the British End Up: Four Decades of Saucy Cinema*, p. 10.
19 Other sex comedies or films that foreground sexual activity include: *Can You Keep It Up For a Week?* (Jim Atkinson, 1974); *Come Play with Me* (George Harrison Marks, 1977); *Confessions from a Holiday Camp* (Norman Cohen, 1977); *Confessions of a Driving Instructor* (Norman Cohen, 1976); *Confessions of a Pop Performer* (Norman Cohen, 1975); *Confessions of a Window Cleaner* (Val Guest, 1974); *Home Before Midnight* (Pete Walker, 1978); *Intimate Games*

(Tudor Gates, 1976); *It's a 2' 6" Above the Ground World* (aka *The Love Ban*) (Ralph Thomas, 1972); *Keep it Up, Jack!* (Derek Ford, 1973); *Percy* (Ralph Thomas, 1971); *Perry's Progress* (aka *It's Not the Size That Counts*) (Ralph Thomas, 1974); *Sex Play* (aka *Games Girls Play*) (Jack Arnold, 1974); *Stand Up, Virgin Soldiers* (Norman Cohen, 1977); *Under the Doctor* (Gerry Poulson, 1976); *The World Is Full of Married Men* (Robert Young, 1979); *Not Now, Darling* (Ray Cooney, 1973); *Not Now, Comrade* (Harold Snoad and Ray Cooney, 1976); *Au Pair Girls* (Val Guest, 1972); *Penelope Pulls It Off* (Peter Curran, 1975); *The Playbirds* (Willy Roe, 1978); and *Rosie Dixon – Night Nurse* (Justin Cartwright, 1978).

20 For more on censorship of 1970s British cinema, see Barber, *Censoring the 1970s*.
21 Moore-Gilbert, 'Introduction: Cultural Closure or Post-avantgardism?', p. 5.
22 Laing, 'The Politics of Culture: Institutional Change in the 1970s', p. 53.
23 Laing, 'The Politics of Culture: Institutional Change in the 1970s', p. 54.
24 Longford Committee (1972), cited in Laing, 'The Politics of Culture: Institutional Change in the 1970s', p. 54.
25 Turner, *Crisis? What Crisis? Britain in the 1970s*, p. 135.
26 Sandbrook, *State of Emergency*, p. 460.
27 Sheridan, *Keeping the British End Up: Four Decades of Saucy Cinema*, p. 16.
28 Sandbrook, *State of Emergency*, p. 460.
29 Other 'Carry On' films made running up to and during the 1970s were *Carry On Up the Khyber* (1968); *Carry On Camping* (1969) (the most successful British film of that year at the British box office); *Carry On Loving* (1970); *Carry On Up the Jungle* (1970); *Carry On Henry* (1971); *Carry On at Your Convenience* (1971); *Carry On Abroad* (1972); *Carry On Matron* (1972); *Carry On Dick* (1974); *Carry On Behind* (1975); *Carry On England* (1976); *That's Carry On* (Gerald Thomas, 1977); and *Carry On Emmannuelle* (1978).
30 Medhurst, 'Carry On Camp', p. 19.
31 Gerrard, 'What a Carry On! The Decline and Fall of a Great British Institution', p. 37.
32 Medhurst, 'Music Hall and British Cinema', p. 183.
33 Street, *British National Cinema*, p. 97.
34 Hunt, *British Low Culture: From Safari Suits to Sexploitation*, p. 39.
35 Gerrard, 'What a Carry On! The Decline and Fall of a Great British Institution', p. 43.
36 Sandbrook, *State of Emergency*, p. 375.
37 Moore-Gilbert, 'Introduction: Cultural Closure or Post-avantgardism?', p. 9.
38 Jones, 'Carry On Girls', p. 245.
39 Sandbrook, *State of Emergency*, p. 10.
40 Sandbrook, *State of Emergency*, p. 426.

41 It is important to remember here that the British film industry underwent a shift in the late 1960s and early 1970s as a liberalisation of censorship took place. But this shift was felt more clearly by films that apparently had artistic integrity; films that were to be treated 'with respect'. So, films such as *A Clockwork Orange* (Stanley Kubrick, 1971), *Straw Dogs* (Sam Peckinpah, 1971), and *Last Tango in Paris* (Bernardo Bertolucci, 1972) were all passed controversially by the British Board of Film Censors. See Phelps, 'Film Censorship', p. 45. For more on film censorship, see Barber, *Censoring the 1970s*.

42 Sounes, *Seventies: The Sights, Sounds and Ideas of a Brilliant Decade*, pp. 16–28.

43 M. Williams, 'Staccato and Wrenchingly Modern: Reflections on the 1970s Stardom of Glenda Jackson', p. 45.

44 Milne, 'Zee & Co.', p. 83.

45 Sandbrook, *State of Emergency*, p. 30.

46 Sounes, *Seventies: The Sights, Sounds and Ideas of a Brilliant Decade*, p. 11.

47 M. Williams, 'Staccato and Wrenchingly Modern: Reflections on the 1970s Stardom of Glenda Jackson', p. 51.

48 Roy Ward Baker was one of the most prolific directors of British horror films, working on *Scars of Dracula* (1970); *The Vampire Lovers* (1970); *Dr Jekyll and Sister Hyde* (1971); *Asylum* (1972); *And Now the Screaming Starts!* (1973); *The Legend of the 7 Golden Vampires* (aka *The 7 Brothers Meet Dracula*) (1974); and *The Monster Club* (1980).

49 During the 1970s, as well as *Schizo* (1976), Walker also directed *Man of Violence* (aka *Moon*) (1970); *Cool it Carol!* (1970); *Die Screaming, Marianne* (1971); *Four Dimensions of Greta* (1972); *The Flesh and Blood Show* (1972); *Tiffany Jones* (1973); *House of Whipcord* (1974); *Frightmare* (1974); *House of Mortal Sin* (1975); *The Comeback* (1978); and *Home Before Midnight* (1979).

50 Tudor, *Monsters and Mad Scientists: A Cultural History of the Horror Movie*, p. 58.

51 Newman, 'Psycho-thriller, qu'est-ce que c'est?', p. 76.

52 Hutchings, *The Horror Film*, p. 182.

53 During the period Francis remained busy, directing the films such as *Trog* (1970); *Tales From the Crypt* (1972); *The Creeping Flesh* (1972); *Tales that Witness Madness* (1973); *Son of Dracula* (1974); *Craze* (1974); *The Ghoul* (1975); and *Legend of the Werewolf* (1975). But he had also worked in television and as a cinematographer on *Women in Love* (Ken Russell, 1969), and *The Elephant Man* (David Lynch, 1980).

54 Hutchings, *The Horror Film*, p. 170.

55 Hutchings, *The Horror Film*, p. 170.

56 Hutchings, *The Horror Film*, p. 170.

57 Hutchings, *The Horror Film*, p. 175.

58 Hutchings, *Hammer and Beyond*, p. 167.

59 Hutchings, *Hammer and Beyond*, p. 173.

60 Hutchings, *Hammer and Beyond*, p. 175.
61 Hutchings, *Hammer and Beyond*, p. 169.
62 Hutchings, *Hammer and Beyond*, p. 169.
63 Hutchings, *Hammer and Beyond*, p. 171.
64 Harper and Smith, *British Film Culture in the 1970s: The Boundaries of Pleasure*, p. 147.
65 Harper and Smith, *British Film Culture in the 1970s: The Boundaries of Pleasure*, p. 148.
66 M. Williams, 'Staccato and Wrenchingly Modern: Reflections on the 1970s Stardom of Glenda Jackson', p. 49.
67 Harper and Smith, *British Film Culture in the 1970s: The Boundaries of Pleasure*, pp. 147–53.
68 Harper and Smith, *British Film Culture in the 1970s: The Boundaries of Pleasure*, p. 139.
69 Sandbrook, *State of Emergency*, p. 404.
70 Rayns, 'Dyn Amo', p. 7.

2

On the road:
British journeys

ERIC: So, what're you doing then? On your holidays?
CARTER: No, I'm visiting relatives.
ERIC: Oh, that's nice.
CARTER: It would be... if they were still living.

Get Carter (Mike Hodges, 1971)

In *No Sex Please – We're British* (Cliff Owen, 1973), a suburban bank clerk, Brian Runnicles (Ronnie Corbett), accidently receives a delivery of pornographic material meant for a sex shop. He fails to get rid of the films, and, after a number of farcical attempts, they end up in the hands of his boss, the anti-pornography campaigner, Mr Bromley (Arthur Lowe), who inadvertently screens them to a gathered audience of ornithologists. Films such as *No Sex Please – We're British* – adapted from the successful stage comedy of the same name by Alistair Foot and Anthony Marriott – clearly evidence the socio-cultural tensions of the age fuelled by an increased visibility of sex in places (such as suburban high streets) where it had not been so visible before. Pornography was a relatively young industry at the beginning of the early 1970s.[1] Its widespread visibility, at least, was a new phenomenon. By 1975, the porn boom in Britain saw twelve major soft-core publishers distributing material through 400 wholesalers to an estimated 20,000 sex shops across the nation.[2] Andrew Higson points out that pornographic films 'were really only more extreme versions of a fascination with sexuality and with the body as object of display that pervaded most aspects of 1970s cinema'.[3] Sex, it seems, was suddenly all over British films. But this was not a straightforward development. Indeed, by featuring a farcical narrative concerning a consignment of pornographic films, while also, at the same time, providing mild titillation for its male audience in the form of actresses Valerie Leon and Margaret Nolan performing as scantily-clad prostitutes, *No Sex Please – We're British* further evidences the sexual tensions pulling at an increasingly fragmented British society.

But, interestingly, allusions to pornography were not just the domain of low-budget British film comedies in the early 1970s. For example, *Get Carter* (Mike Hodges, 1971) stars Michael Caine as Jack Carter, a gangster who travels from London to Newcastle in order to investigate events surrounding his brother's death. He discovers that his niece, Doreen (Petra Markham), has been forced into appearing in a pornographic film. Chris Petit's film *Radio On* (1979) is also obliquely concerned with a pornography racket, this time in Bristol. And Lindsay Anderson's *O Lucky Man!* (1973) makes it clear that a love of porn exists beneath the veneer of contemporary British respectability. It is *Radio On* and *O Lucky Man!* I shall be exploring primarily in this chapter. But here I am interested more specifically in how they operate as 'journey films' which develop distinctive visions of a fragmenting nation and its people.

Luck and judgement: *O Lucky Man!*

A wide-eyed young coffee salesman is met by a middle-aged man in the foyer of a respectable provincial hotel in northern England. The older man leads the younger man out, past the reception desk, through back rooms, and into a private party. Here the two men are greeted by a scantily-clad young woman who offers them smoking jackets. They make their way through a throng of people, past a busy bar. A pornographic film is being screened. This is followed by a live sex show featuring a young black man and two young white women. We witness the wide-eyed, bawdy reactions of the policemen, journalists and businessmen present, which say much about the highly complex contemporary British attitudes to pornography and sexual activity. In this sequence, Lindsay Anderson's hugely ambitious *O Lucky Man!* echoes distinctly the type of 'nudge nudge, wink wink' discourse regarding sex which was satirised by *Monty Python's Flying Circus* (BBC, 1969–74) in a 1969 sketch entitled 'Candid Photography' – which also appears in the film *And Now For Something Completely Different* (Ian MacNaughton, 1971). This type of behaviour is also characteristic of films such as *No Sex Please – We're British*. And it infuses many 'Carry On' films; specifically a sequence in *Carry On at Your Convenience* (Gerald Thomas, 1971) in which Vic (Kenneth Cope) and Bernie (Bernard Bresslaw) follow Myrtle (Jaki Piper) and Lewis (Richard O'Callaghan) into a cinema and watch the beginning of an 'educational' nudie film which has evidently been passed by the censor. In these representational moments, then, sex rears up into 1970s British life, to a mixture of genuine excitement, jokey derision, embarrassment, and disgust.

In the hotel sequence in *O Lucky Man!*, Arthur Lowe plays Mayor Johnson, the middle-aged man who guides the principle protagonist, Travis (Malcolm McDowell), into the secret party; asking him, with a knowing wink, 'Do you like you-know-what?' In early 1970s Britain, then, sex is evidently something that everybody suddenly knows about or has an opinion on. But this is not yet a culture in which sex ('you-know-what') can always be discussed openly and honestly. In light of this, the sex life of early 1970s Britain that *O Lucky Man!* depicts is certainly not far away from that seen in *No Sex Please – We're British*, or, for that matter, *Eskimo Nell* and *Carry On Girls*. This is also evident in the ways in which the film portrays women. As Andrew Higson advocates, the women in *O Lucky Man!* are 'all-engulfing, sexually voracious figures'.[4] As such, Rachel Roberts as Gloria Rowe and Mrs Richards; Mary Macleod as Mrs Ball and the Vicar's wife; and Helen Mirren as Patricia can be read alongside Barbara Windsor's Hope Springs in *Carry On Girls* and Diane Langton's Gladys Armitage in *Eskimo Nell* as women who seemingly threaten (but also excite) male figures with their sheer force of feminine sexual energy.

While the representation of gender relations in the film is certainly instructive, Lindsay Anderson's *O Lucky Man!* operates primarily as a savage critique of the state of the nation. In this chapter I want to approach *O Lucky Man!* as a film that documents the journey of the central protagonist – a road journey across Britain (or, indeed, across a vision of Britain), placing it alongside another film about a 'British' journey – Chris Petit's *Radio On* (1979). I want to argue that both films offer intriguing visions of a nation struggling with a fragmenting sense of identity. This is a Britain being ripped apart by modernisation and change; a Britain that appears unsure as to whether it should look to the future or remain nostalgic for the past; unsure as whether it should look to Europe, to America, or inward; and unsure as to how it might negotiate its way in an increasingly complex world.

After the critical success of Anderson's *If...* (1968), Malcolm McDowell began to write a script called 'Coffee Man' about his experiences as a coffee salesman travelling the length and breadth of Britain. The screenwriter David Sherwin developed the story, seeing it as a potential satire in the style of Voltaire's *Candide* or Swift's *Gulliver's Travels*. Director Lindsay Anderson thought the story had similarities to Thornton Wilder's *Heaven is My Destination*, Franz Kafka's *Amerika*, and John Bunyan's *The Pilgrim's Progress*.[5] *O Lucky Man!* was produced by Albert Finney's Memorial Films. David Sherwin, Anderson and McDowell formed a company called SAM (an acronym of their surnames) and secured a budget of $1.5 million from Warner Bros.[6] *O Lucky Man!* would be the American company's first British film for a number of years.[7] Anne Head noted, at the time the film appeared, that Anderson was the only British director acceptable to the Americans to make a film with a British subject.[8] Shooting began in March 1972, and continued on location in and around London and across Kent, Yorkshire, Buckinghamshire and Scotland. Anderson enlisted Jocelyn Herbert as designer, Miroslav Ondříček as cameraman, and David Gladwell as editor (Gladwell subsequently directed *Requiem for a Village*, discussed in Chapter 6). Malcolm McDowell plays Mick Travis again (last seen in *If...*). The young actor had become a generational icon through his starring roles in his previous collaboration with Anderson and Stanley Kubrick's *A Clockwork Orange* (1971). The supporting cast in *O Lucky Man!*, according to Raymond Durgnat, were 'Chameleon character actors ... The Many Faces of the Faceless English: Alec Guinness, Peter Sellers, Benny Hill, Dick Emery'.[9] These actors often play multiple roles; a conceit which 'draws attention to the art of acting as such and disturbs the illusion of dramatic representation'.[10] The characters in the film also have a 'cartoon-like' quality, and are generally not given emotional or psychological depth.[11] But the film is no less powerful because of this. Indeed, in this way it shows us the shallow nature of much of contemporary life.

One actor who appears in *O Lucky Man!* in a number of roles is Arthur Lowe. One of Lowe's early roles was in the Ealing Studios classic *Kind Hearts and Coronets* (Robert Hamer, 1949). But he remains best known for playing Captain Mainwaring in the hugely successful British television comedy series *Dad's Army* (BBC, 1968–77). A film version of this series was released in cinemas in 1971 (directed by Norman Cohen). When the *Dad's Army* television series ended in 1977, Lowe remained very much in demand on television, securing significant roles in shows such as *Bless Me Father* (LWT, 1979–81) and *Potter* (BBC, 1979–83). However, his career in cinema remained interesting and generically varied. The fact that Lowe worked in art films, comedies, sex comedies, mysteries and horror films again speaks of the essentially fragmented nature of 1970s British film production. For example, Lowe appears in *If...* (Lindsay Anderson, 1968); the realist adaptation of a stage play, *Spring and Port Wine* (Peter Hammond, 1969); the satires *The Bed-Sitting Room* (Richard Lester, 1969) and *The Rise and Rise of Michael Rimmer* (Kevin Billington, 1970); and adaptations of television sitcoms, *Dad's Army* (Norman Cohen, 1971) and *Man About the House* (John Robins, 1974). But he also appears in the comedy adaptation of Spike Milligan's war memoirs, *Adolf Hitler: My Part in His Downfall* (Norman Cohen, 1974); the epic black comedy/art film *The Ruling Class* (Peter Medak, 1972); and the horror film *Theatre of Blood* (Douglas Hickox, 1973), among others. Lowe also made a large number of television commercials. His last film role was in Lindsay Anderson's *Britannia Hospital* (1982). He died in April of that year.[12]

O Lucky Man! premiered in London on 2 May 1973. It had been selected for the Cannes Film Festival in March, but did not receive an award. It was reported in the trade paper *Variety* that the film had been cut from 175 to 166 minutes at the request of Warner Bros. for release in the USA in June. Lindsay Anderson went as far as to suggest that he had approved the cuts, and that this would be his 'final, approved and definitive version'.[13] But there has been considerable debate concerning the different edits of the film. Charles Silet claims that the film was cut from 186 to 166 minutes, as does Allison Graham.[14] Paul Cornelius argues that the film was originally 187 minutes long, and that Warner Bros. cut it to 166 minutes, but that a 177-minute version was also in circulation. Erik Hedling has analysed these discrepancies carefully, and argues that the film actually existed in four different edits – a 186-minute edit shown at a press screening in London; a 174-minute edit premiered in London and shown at Cannes; a 166-minute-long version distributed by Warner Bros. (this is the version kept by most archives); and a 177-minute-long cut which, he argues, 'follows the original most closely'.[15] It is tempting to read these discrepancies in edits as evidence that this is a truly fragmentary text about a fragmenting nation.

On the release of *O Lucky Man!* a number of critics were less than kind about the film. According to Gordon Gow, in *Films and Filming*, this 'robust satire' was 'inordinately long'.[16] It was 'some intellectual's idle exercise designed for the casual entertainment of the uselessly educated', according to Jeff Millar in *Film Heritage*, who further argued that the film was 'deliberately passionless'.[17] Gow pointed out that the misanthropic message of the film seemed to be that 'Man is lucky if he muddles through life's whirligig.'[18] The narrative structure of the film was also criticised. In a paper delivered at a Brecht event at the 1975 Edinburgh Film Festival, Alan Lovell argued that 'As the film progresses this pilgrim's progress less and less seriously structures the film in an effective way.'[19] Having said this, other critics have since been more sympathetic to Anderson's achievement. For example, Erik Hedling advocates that *O Lucky Man!* 'is a highly self-reflexive film in the typical mode of its time, though taking the device further than most British films'.[20] He notes that viewing the film, one can detect the influence of figures as diverse as Humphrey Jennings, Thomas Grey, Samuel Taylor Coleridge, Adam Lindsay Gordon, William Blake, Sergei Eisenstein, John Ford, and Preston Sturges (the film displaying demonstrable similarities to Sturges's 1941 film, *Sullivan's Travels*).[21] Whatever its artistic merits or failures, *O Lucky Man!* stands as an intriguing historical document which, in its ambitious sweep, offers a curious, prescient and often disturbing vision of a nation falling apart at the beginning of the 1970s.

'Luck' became an organising principle for the narrative.[22] This luck is most obviously the luck (or indeed the lack of it) of McDowell's wide-eyed Mick Travis. But the film is also concerned with the luck of Britain as a nation. Indeed, over the course of Travis's travels, Britain is seen to be a nation in the cultural doldrums of a post-countercultural era; a nation suffering economic depression; a nation nostalgic for older, seemingly simpler times; a nation struggling to come to terms with its diminished status in the world as its empire continues to fall apart. Moreover, it is seen to be still divided by class and plagued by inequality and injustice, run by corrupt and inept institutions. So, *O Lucky Man!* represents Britain in a 'state of change'.[23] In other words, this is a state-of-the-nation film; a film that depicts a nation in the midst of a profoundly disturbing identity crisis. Indeed, the film was released into a nation that saw its reputation sinking to new lows. This was perhaps best exemplified by the fact that the dictator Idi Amin (who had seized power in formerly British Uganda in 1971) had the temerity to write to Prime Minister Edward Heath in order to assure him that Uganda might help the British through 'the alarming economic crisis' befalling the country.[24]

O Lucky Man! has a pre-credits sequence that features black and white footage of coffee workers in the fields of South America. So, from the very first shots of the film, coffee is set up as a symbol of capitalism and the growing consumer society. Capitalism (and Britain's relationship with capitalism) thus takes centre stage.[25] This is further emphasised in the post-credits sequence in the film, which is concerned primarily with the development of sales techniques, showing Gloria Rowe (Rachel Roberts) schooling young recruits to Imperial Coffee in how to handle potential customers and close a deal. Travis starts out as a salesman. This is an appropriate occupation for a man who will end up travelling the length of early 1970s Britain. But during the narrative, Travis moves through various strata of British culture and life – the leisure industry; the Church; the Army; the Air Force; the Government; the legal system; business; and, finally, the entertainment industry. As such, the film operates as a critique of these wide-ranging institutions and the potential ramifications of their continued control over British life.

Like so many British films of the period, *O Lucky Man!* is a generic hybrid. At times it feels like a social realist film, while at other times it feels like a fantasy, a horror film, a comedy, a musical, and a thriller. As such, *O Lucky Man!* is a film which is as fragmented in generic and formal terms as the nation it purports to represent. The visions of Britain that *O Lucky Man!* serves up are often grim and troubling. An example is the notorious sequence which takes place at the Millar Research Clinic. Here, volunteers are paid to donate their bodies for scientific experiment. Travis tries to negotiate an increased fee for himself, and is then prepared for his operation. But, apparently changing his mind, he decides to escape from the facility, and (in a scene that would work in any number of British horror films of the period from the Hammer, Amicus or Tigon studios) stumbles into another private room, where he finds a man whimpering in bed. Lifting the blankets, Travis discovers that this man has had his head grafted on to the body of a pig. Despite the horrors that are being perpetrated at this clinic, the head of the institution which carries out this kind of activity, Professor Millar, extols the virtues of science and its power to shape a better future.

British horror films of the 1970s exploit similar territory. For example, the Amicus film *Scream and Scream Again* (Gordon Hessler, 1970), starring Christopher Lee, Peter Cushing and Vincent Price, features a jogger who suffers a heart attack and blackout during his daily run. He wakes up in what initially appears to be a hospital bed. A nurse tends him, putting a pipe into his mouth. But he subsequently realises that something is badly wrong. Pulling back the covers he finds that one of his legs is missing. He screams and blacks out again. When he wakes again, he finds that both legs are missing. It turns out that he is a victim of Dr Browning (Vincent Price), who, although he has the legitimacy of a British government research contract, is trying to create a race of zombies.

Capitalism, class, privilege and corruption are interrelated in the Britain of *O Lucky Man!* and, as such, the nation it depicts is still a long way from being a meritocracy. While Travis initially displays ambitions to get to the 'top', Patricia (Helen Mirren) is already there – the daughter of a wealthy father (and establishment figure), Sir James Burgess (Ralph Richardson). Sir James becomes involved in a business opportunity that develops in the fictional African country, Zingara, run by a brutal dictator, Dr Munda (Arthur Lowe in blackface). This project is effectively a twisted example of unethical modern capitalism. Burgess sells Dr Munda a consignment of PL45 ('honey'), a chemical his forces can spray on rebel areas to facilitate the slow and horrible death of anybody who comes into contact with it. The Royal Air Force is involved in supplying this deadly cargo. Travis is sent by Sir James to make sure the drums of 'honey' are loaded on to the planes at a secret location. But Travis is later set up by Sir James when the police raid a meeting with Dr Munda and others present at the aristocrat's house. As Travis is arrested, Sir James haughtily tells the assembled party that 'The dividing line between the House of Lords and Pentonville jail is very, very thin.' Travis is sentenced to five years in prison. Central to this sequence appears to be the idea that British corporations might be investing in post-colonial territories and financing attacks on large numbers of men, women and children which involve the use of chemical weapons. But, as they are run by establishment figures, these corporations are effectively above the law. There are discernable echoes of coeval US activities in Vietnam here.

Overall, then, there is a distinct feeling of a sickness at the heart of British culture in *O Lucky Man!* The film offers a misanthropic vision of a fragmenting nation. Indeed, summing up at Travis's trial, the judge says: 'Society is based on good faith; on a commonly accepted bond. It is the inflamed greed of people like you, Michael Travis, that has led to the present breakdown of our society.' Travis responds: 'My Lord, I did my duty. I only wanted to be successful. I did my best.' Travis is essentially punished for wanting to succeed in modern capitalist Britain on modern capitalist Britain's terms. But he fails, because he was, is, and always will be an outsider. He does his time in prison, and re-emerges as a well-read, optimistic, Marxist humanist. But even then he is punished – savaged by the homeless people he tries to help in the East End of London. Interestingly, Erik Hedling argues that Travis has moved from being a revolutionary in *If...* (1968) to being a conformist in *O Lucky Man!*[26] And in some senses *O Lucky Man!* is a revisionist film, in that it takes a more 'bilious' view of life than is visible in *If...* (1968).[27] While the Travis of 1968 can smell potential revolution in the air (with the riots in Paris occurring at that moment, and the counterculture still at its height), the Travis of *O Lucky Man!* instead moves through a world that is coming to terms with the apparent failure of the revolutionary movements of the 1960s. In some ways this feels like a world in which little or nothing has changed. Well-bred and well-connected older men still hold all the aces. But this representation of Britain in *O Lucky Man!* clearly echoes the real nation, which saw increasing occurrences of high-visibility corruption in the early 1970s, such as the Poulson–Maudling affair.[28] This was a period in Britain, after all, during which Edward Heath's government was engaged in secret talks with the Irish Republican Army (IRA), and which saw the pollution scandal unfolding at Rio Tinto Zinc's smelter at Avonmouth. As Dominic Sandbrook puts it, 'By this point corruption had become one of the clichés of national cultural life'.[29] A so-called 'new capitalism' was also visible in the television shows *Plane Makers/ The Power Game* (ATV, 1963–69), *Mogul/ The Trouble Shooters* (BBC, 1965–72), and *The Brothers* (BBC, 1972–76).[30] Moreover, 'Tiny' Rowland's activities with the London and Rhodesian Mining Company (Lonrho) exemplified an apparently new style of doing business (and thus getting ahead) in Britain.[31] Through the figure of Sir James and others, *O Lucky Man!* evidences a seemingly corrupt nation.

But there are some positive aspects to the nation as it is depicted in the film. The young people in *O Lucky Man!* other than Travis (who are not connected to the upper-class establishment) at least have music as a means to express their angst and world-weariness. Hope is portrayed elsewhere in the film too, such as during the sequence in which the Vicar's wife (Mary Macleod) and children look after Travis in his hour of need. There is undoubtedly comedy in the film, too. Interestingly, Frank Cunningham sees Travis as a figure who 'must realize the wisdom of the great Romantic revolutionary Blake: he must create systems of his own lest he be enslaved by those of other men'.[32] But it is not clear at the end of the film (when Travis effectively auditions for a role in the film in which he has just appeared) whether he has come to any such realisation. The film thus remains ambiguous. But Travis's last smile for the camera, and the ensuing joy of the party that closes the film, offer a ray of hope in an otherwise grim depiction of a nation. There is fun to be had. As a satire, *O Lucky Man!* draws on the 'comic mode'.[33] In its wildest and most surreal moments the film also echoes the work of the Monty Python team.

But, despite the traces of hope and humour in the film, at distinct moments in *O Lucky Man!* the narrative moves towards the territory of the disaster movie genre, such as during the sequence that occurs after Travis is caught, interrogated and tortured at the mysterious government facility, when he and other individuals run from burning buildings. Peter Hutchings asks whether there is a 'meaningful apocalyptic theme' running through 1970s British culture.[34] He argues 'it is not unthinkable that British disaster fictions from the 1970s might in some instances be articulating in a covert or unconscious manner a socially and historically specific sense of despair and negativity'.[35] Overall, Hutchings believes that British films of the period that deal in apocalypse operate 'as a site for a series of transactions organized around both cultural and commercial factors'.[36] Narratives that channel fear of apocalypse (or, at the very least, ecologically disastrous situations) can be found across a range of films and television shows. For example, US-produced but shot in Britain, the apocalyptic film *No Blade of Grass* (Cornel Wilde, 1970) tells the story of a mysterious virus which affects crops such as wheat and rice. John Custance (Nigel Davenport) is an architect who decides to leave London with his family to travel north to his brother's farm to escape food riots and seek safety. But the journey becomes dangerous, as the group are met with hostility from haggard, hungry people. *Doomwatch* (BBC, 1970–72) is a television series that features a government-backed scientific agency tasked with investigating environmental and ecological threats. A film version of *Doomwatch* appeared in 1972 (directed by Peter Sasdy) (discussed in Chapter 7). Moreover, the comedy film *Rentadick* (Jim Clark, 1972), starring James Booth, Richard Briers and Julie Ege, tells the story of attempts made by a detective agency to protect an experimental new nerve gas which can cause paralysis.

On television, *Doctor Who* (BBC, 1963–89) saw the figure of the Doctor (Jon Pertwee) often preventing threats to the existence of humanity.[37] 'Doctor Who and the Silurians' (1970) is a serial that tells the story of creatures awakened by activities of an experimental nuclear power research centre built into a network of caves under a moor. And the serial 'The Green Death' (1973) features a threat that develops from toxic waste deposited by a chemical factory in South Wales.[38] The television series *The Changes* (BBC, 1975) imagines a future on earth when humanity destroys all machines and reverts to a pre-modern state. And *Survivors* (BBC, 1975–77) is an eco-catastrophe drama, devised by Terry Nation (who had written *Doctor Who* serials), about a group of people who have survived a plague known as 'the Death'. Such apocalyptic themes were also prevalent in the worlds of contemporary British history and literature. For example, historian Peter Laslett's *The World We Have Lost* (1965) mourns the loss of an England before the ravages of progress had stained life and landscapes. And Richard Adams' bestselling novel *Watership Down* (1972) tells the story of anthropomorphic rabbits embarking on a journey to find a new, safe home, when their warren is threatened with destruction. An animated film adaptation of the novel, directed by Martin Rosen, appeared in 1978. Increased coverage of environmental issues was also witnessed in the media during the 1970s. Books were published, including *Can Britain Survive?* (Edward Goldsmith, 1971), *A Blueprint for Survival* (Edward Goldsmith and Robert Allen, 1972), *The Death of Tomorrow* (John Alexander Loraine and R. D. E. Rumsey, 1972), and *Small is Beautiful* (E. F. Schumacher, 1973). Furthermore, Gordon Rattray Taylor's *The Doomsday Book* (1971) is an apocalyptic text warning of a population crash caused by overcrowding, pollution, and a disturbed balance of nature.[39]

But there were optimistic, positive responses to such themes, even if they operated on a microcosmic (as opposed to a national or global) level. For example, *The Good Life* (BBC, 1975–78) is a sitcom about a likeable, happily married couple, Tom (Richard Briers) and Barbara (Felicity Kendall), who try to live self-sufficiently by turning their suburban semi-detached house into a smallholding, much to the chagrin of their upwardly mobile neighbours, Margot (Penelope Keith) and Jerry Leadbetter (Paul Eddington). And the popular children's' television series *The Wombles* (BBC, 1973–75), based on characters created by Elisabeth Beresford, tells the stories of furry creatures who live on Wimbledon Common and survive by recycling human detritus – 'making good use of the things that we find', as the theme song by Mike Batt puts it.[40] A film, *Wombling Free*, followed in 1977, directed by Lionel Jeffries, who during this period also directed *The Railway Children* (1970), *The Amazing Mr. Blunden* (1972), *Baxter!* (1973), and the live action/animated hybrid film *The Water Babies* (1978).

It seems that in 1970s Britain, people were often suspicious of scientific advances, while at the same time being eager for new technologies that might make modern life a little bit easier to cope with. Synthetic or artificial products were increasingly coming on to the market – often, it seems, before being fully tested for safety. For example, nutritional substitutes such as the soya products TVP (textured vegetable protein), Protena and Kesp (created by Courtaulds) were used by the catering industry as cheaper alternatives to meat. Courtaulds also manufactured synthetic fabrics using methods that remained industrial secrets; and made Planet cigarettes, which consisted of a mixture of tobacco and cellulose derived from eucalyptus and wattle trees.[41] This, effectively, is the nation depicted in *O Lucky Man!* As Alexander Walker argues, 'In such a world, Anderson asks, is it really unthinkable for a loony man of science to be experimenting on people in the hope of turning them into more adaptable pigs? Since pigs have a better survival value than humans, is it really blameworthy?'[42]

As is the case in Brechtian epic theatre, Lindsay Anderson is often clear about the fact that he is presenting an illusion to the viewer. Naturalism is carefully avoided. But having said this, *O Lucky Man!* is constructed around a number of location-shot sequences, and references are clearly made to the contemporary socio-cultural and political concerns of Britain. For example, as Travis drives through the English countryside, a radio announcer speaks of shootings in Belfast, and thus places anxieties concerning Irish nationalism and terrorism very much within this vision of a fragmenting Britain. So, while the film is Brechtian in many ways, such as in its use of the device of having Alan Price's group periodically turn up like a Greek chorus,[43] it is also particularly unsettling precisely because it presents what often feels like a very 'real' Britain. The bizarre places Travis visits, the strange characters with whom he comes into contact, and the comedy and horror of much of what he experiences, feel all too familiar, and thus believable. But this is also a film that feels dream-like. After all, characters often blur and blend into other characters, and rational aspects of human behaviour often appear to be absent. Interestingly, Anderson has pointed out in interviews that he was influenced by Zen Buddhism.[44] And some have noticed that the film resembles a cinematic koan (a nonsensical or paradoxical question which might facilitate meditation).[45] As such, *O Lucky Man!* can be read as a puzzle that reflects the puzzle of modern Britain.

After *O Lucky Man!*, Anderson went on to make *In Celebration* (1974) and *Britannia Hospital* (1982), a film which would signal even more clearly the aesthetic influence of popular British genre films such as the 'Carry On' series and the Hammer horrors. But, notwithstanding his ability to draw on and echo popular culture in his work, Anderson liked to be seen as a poet.[46] As such, his 1970s films might best be placed alongside contemporary British films by the likes of Bill Douglas, Terence Davies, and Barney Platts-Mills.[47] But it should also be remembered that, as well as being a significant film director, Anderson was also a critic, and an important figure in British theatre who had a long association with the Royal Court Theatre (where he was co-Artistic Director between 1969 and 1972). So it could also be said that *O Lucky Man!* also comes from a British dramatic tradition which continued to inform much intelligent film-making of the 1970s (whether this was through adaptations of dramatic material or through examples of playwrights or theatre directors directing films), including Lindsay Anderson's own *In Celebration* (1974), but also *A Day in the Death of Joe Egg* (Peter Medak, 1970); *Perfect Friday* (Peter Hall, 1970); *Three Sisters* (Laurence Olivier and John Sichel, 1970); *The Homecoming* (Peter Hall, 1973); *Butley* (Harold Pinter, 1974); *Akenfield* (Peter Hall, 1974); *Hedda* (Trevor Nunn, 1975); *Equus* (Sidney Lumet, 1977); and *The Life Story of Baal* (Edward Bennett, 1978). Arguably, the 1970s were golden years for British theatre (including radical and fringe groups), and the Royal Shakespeare Company (RSC) in particular.[48] But other film-makers and artists also emerged.

I'm up on the Westway, in and out the lights: *Radio On*

Perhaps it is no more than a co-incidence that Mick's surname, 'Travis', evokes *travers*, the French for 'from one side to another'. Raymond Durgnat observed that *O Lucky Man!* gives us 'The travel-ing life: post-Marx, post-Pudovkin, post-Brecht, post-Godard'.[49] We could go as far as to call this a British road movie; a film made possible, in some ways, by the emergence of a motorway system during the 1960s that facilitated easier and faster access to wider parts of the country.

I want to move on now to consider another film of the 1970s which has been termed a road movie – Chris Petit's feature-length film *Radio On* (1979). There is no significant plot to *Radio On* as such. A man, Robert (David Beames), finds out that his brother is dead, and decides to drive from London to Bristol to find out what happened. His brother's death might or might not be linked to a pornography racket (he never finds out, and nor do we). Beames plays Robert as a cold, removed creature, without any emotion or real sense of purpose. His is a seemingly pointless, elliptical exist-ence. Much of the film sees him driving in his battered old Rover on ancient and modern English roads.

At the release of *Radio On* in 1979, the film was met with some incredulity, but also a sense of optimism for what it might signal in terms of a possible British cinema of the future. Geoffrey Nowell-Smith argued perceptively that it was 'a film without a cinema'.[50] Richard Combs saw it as a 'tentative starting point for a possible British cinema (American movies, remodelled in Europe then refitted here?)'.[51] On the welcome release of the film on DVD in 2008, a new generation of critics engaged with the film. Sukhev Sandhu poetically put it that *Radio On* operates as 'A greyscale anthropology of a former colonial superpower'.[52] It is clear that *Radio On* is a film that evokes strange, liminal, late-1970s British landscapes characterised by darkness, slowness, emptiness and ennui.

Radio On had a budget of £80,000. It was financed by the British Film Institute Production Board plus a loan from the National Film Finance Corporation (NFFC). But it was an international co-production. Half of the budget for the film was provided by

Road Movies Filmproduktion, a company run by German director Wim Wenders. In terms of its formal qualities, *Radio On* certainly bears comparison with the road films of Wenders, especially in terms of how far 'digression becomes an end in itself'.[53]

If *Radio On* is a road movie, the road effectively leads nowhere. But Petit himself has tried to challenge this reading, pointing out, in an article he wrote on the film some thirty years after it appeared, that the English road movie is a 'contradiction in terms'.[54] He writes that 'Most contemporary cinema doesn't really cover the world we drive through or explore the phenomenon of driving: the state of driving and driving's state of mind, the road and going on the road, logging our daily landscapes, the stuff against which we unconsciously measure ourselves, those way-stations and haunts of migratory drift.'[55] Petit also mentions the fact that 'Driving always struck me as the most unreal thing, especially motorway driving with its illusion of stasis and speed, the driver passive and immobile while everything else around moves. In a pointless world, mobility becomes a point. Driving, like cinema, is a form of projection' and 'Driving twins with cinema, another form of projection.'[56] While in many ways they are very different films, *O Lucky Man!* and *Radio On* share a fascination with the notion of the journey – the picaresque or existential journey of a lone traveller. They also share the conceit of using popular music as a structuring device. Both films acknowledge the underground presence of pornography in Britain. And, like *O Lucky Man!*, *Radio On* effectively resists rational interpretation.

But there are specific similarities between the films. Twice, *O Lucky Man!* features brief shots of cars driving along the elevated Westway in west London. In *Radio On* we see Robert driving in his car, almost a decade later, on the same road but in the opposite direction, out of the city. The Westway operates as a symbolic location in both films. Built between 1964 and 1970, this 2.5-mile stretch of elevated dual carriageway was designed to carry traffic into and out of London along the A40 from Paddington, and to relieve congestion around Shepherd's Bush. The road cuts through Victorian terraces and much older streets and buildings. This, then, is an archetypally modern thoroughfare, which pays little or no attention to the historical or topographical nature of its surroundings. As such, it signals a 1960s vision of a newly modern, forward-thinking, urban Britain; a Britain which is nevertheless struggling to free itself from its past. The Westway also provides a clear link between *Radio On* and the work of the British author, J. G. Ballard, who, in his novel *Concrete Island* (1974), creates a character, Robert Maitland, an architect who finds himself trapped on a concrete island between the Westway and the M4 motorway in west London. Robert has to survive on anything he can find in his crashed Jaguar. *Radio On* feels distinctly Ballardian in other ways too; not least in its interest in the psychologically transformative nature of modern technology; the iconography of technological commodities; the spread of a US-style consumer culture; and cold, passionless characters. Furthermore, the merging of inner and outer landscapes in *Radio On* is also reminiscent of Ballard's *Crash* (1973) and *High Rise* (1975). Indeed, in *Radio On*, on hearing of his brother's death, Robert remains completely unemotional. He displays a Ballardian numbness throughout the film.

There are other clear similarities between *O Lucky Man!* and *Radio On*. For example, as Travis drives his car in *O Lucky Man!*, we hear a radio announcer speak of shootings in Belfast. In *Radio On*, Robert hears similar stories on his car radio several years later. One of the most troubling sequences in *Radio On* occurs when a Scottish squaddie lets himself into Robert's car and talks about his reasons for joining up and what he has witnessed in Ulster. He spits 'fuck all else to do where I come from. There's no work, no prospects, nothing'. Here, then, the Irish troubles which came to be at the heart of 1970s British politics forcibly enter the life of a numb, distant, emotionless character. The effect is jarring and powerful. But there is a slowness to *Radio On* that differs from the jaunty, playful rhythm of movement developed in *O Lucky Man!* Indeed, there are long sections in Petit's film when apparently little or nothing happens. Often, as spectators, we are doing not much more than watching (or, indeed, listening to) time pass. This is reinforced by the sound of ticking clocks which recurs throughout the film. In this way, *Radio On* evokes a nation characterised by slow and steady decay.

Whereas *O Lucky Man!* has a fiercely critical eye trained on Britain as a nation (and the myths that facilitate the construction of Britain as an 'idea'), *Radio On* depicts a Britain in which ideas of Britishness, if not absent, are problematised at every turn. To do this, *Radio On* engages with the relationship between filmic space and landscape, but also, more specifically, the relationship between film 'setting' and a rich, hybridised popular culture which operates as a kind of imaginative landscape. Indeed, Petit's film constructs a highly complex, fragmented imaginary landscape (or set of landscapes).[57] The film develops a hybridised cultural space which is informed by evocative visual and sonic signs – grainy images of urban locations (such as the Westway in London, and the Bristol Hippodrome) and other richly symbolic or historical spaces (such as Silbury Hill), set against an innovative, transnational, post-punk musical soundtrack. But the imaginary landscape of the film is also replete with American iconography – pictures of Cadillac tail fins; Wimpy bars; an Apollo pinball machine; an early computer arcade game ('Tumblers'); the music of 1950s rock 'n' roll stars; and other transnational (usually European, and specifically West German) cultural references. So, melding Martin Schäfer's black-and-white photography of southern England with American cultural icons and US, European and British music on the soundtrack, *Radio On* serves to radically deconstruct Britain and Britishness as an idea.

Like Lindsay Anderson's *O Lucky Man!*, *Radio On* features a musical soundtrack which works to provide a loose structure for the narrative. Indeed, most of the energy of the film is provided by the music, as well as other rhythmic sounds such as passing cars. The central importance of music in Petit's film is particularly evident in the extraordinary opening sequence of the film, in which David Bowie's six-minute song 'Heroes/Helden' unfolds in its entirety over shots taken with a handheld camera which travels slowly through a mysterious, dark flat at night. Indeed, the music in the film is effectively given main billing in the title sequence. This music tends to have a German or American flavour. It features tracks from Bowie's Berlin album *Low* (1977) as well as *'Heroes'* (1977) (and it is worth pointing out that David Beames as Robert looks not unlike like *'Heroes'*-era Bowie). But some of the music featured in the film is pure Americana, or at the very least celebrates US culture, such as the British musician Ian Dury's 'Sweet Gene Vincent', which

plays over shots of factory workers on a production line. The futuristic sounds of synthesizer music also feature heavily too, alongside
ambient tracks such as Robert Fripp's 'Urban Landscape'.

At the beginning of the film, Robert sits in his car and opens an
envelope from his brother, in which he finds three music cassettes –
all albums by the German electronic group Kraftwerk. Chris Chang
argues that this group play diegetic, extra-diegetic and symbolic
roles in the film.[58] During the opening sequence, the camera stops
to allow us to read a mysterious note pinned to a wall of the flat:
'We are the children of Fritz Lang and Werner von Braun. We are
the link between the '20s and the '80s. All change in society passes
through a sympathetic collaboration with tape recorders, synthesizers and telephones. Our reality is an electronic reality.' In its use
of the sounds of synthesizer music in the construction of a hybrid
cultural landscape, *Radio On* very much evokes a pop cultural trend
that could be noticed taking place in Britain in the late 1970s. In
June 1979, Tubeway Army's 'Are Friends Electric?' shot to No.1 in
the popular music chart, signalling the genesis of the synth-pop era
in Britain which would see big hits from the likes of Ultravox, The
Human League, Heaven 17, Depeche Mode and Visage; many
of which would draw on European Romantic cultural traditions.
Interestingly, the Tubeway Army's Gary Numan developed a star
image very reminiscent of Bowie's alien persona in *The Man Who Fell
to Earth* (Nicolas Roeg, 1976). And Numan's big hits, such as 'Cars'
were not dissimilar in formal terms to Bowie's so-called 'Berlin'
trilogy. But a key influence on this movement was Kraftwerk, whose
1978 song 'The Model' subsequently became a big hit in 1982. In
Britain, the emergence of synthesizer music effectively signalled a
break from the influence of American rock 'n' roll and the blues,
but also from British folk cultural traditions. Furthermore, much
early synth-pop felt cold and emotionless, evoking a kind of urban
paranoia, and bringing to mind, once again, J. G. Ballard's visions
of brutalist desolation. In some ways, *Radio On* can be read as a text
that resonates with these cultural developments. Synthesized music
plays a significant role in the construction of the imaginary cultural
landscape in the film, such as during the memorable sequence in
which we join Robert in his old Rover car on the M4, and listen to
the stuttering rhythms of Kraftwerk's 'Radioactivity'.

Interestingly, Robert himself is seemingly ambivalent about modern technologies and modernity in general. After all, interior shots of his 1950s two-tone Rover with 'real wood dashboard'[59] make it appear to be a mode of travel from another era, more suited to ancient English roads than the motorways. Perhaps this is the reason why, when driving to Bristol, rather than continue west on the M4 motorway, Robert decides to exit at junction 12 (the exit for Theale) and continue on the old A roads. In some ways he seems keen to reconnect with an older vision of England. Indeed, his journey takes him past the prehistoric man-made chalk mound, Silbury Hill. As such, the film engages in a kind of prolonged psychogeography of one particular road, the A4. Sting's garage worker tells Robert that, after a gig at the Bristol Hippodrome, the American rock 'n' roll star Eddie Cochran died following car crash on the A4 in April 1960, with fellow singer Gene Vincent in the car. In London, we see the art-deco-style Gillette factory (designed by Sir Banister Flight Fletcher and built in 1936/7) lit up at night on the A4 Great West Road at Brentford. Robert drives along the Westway, past looming residential tower blocks which operate as powerful metaphors for the failure of modernity – 'the shattered ideals of the post-war consensus'.[60] The 'Free Astrid Proll' graffiti on a wall in west London brings awareness of terrorist activity in West Germany to the streets of the English city (Proll was a founding member of the Baader–Meinhof gang). And the Bristol Hippodrome operates as the film's Holy Grail.[61] Along this road, modern architecture is effectively employed to de-familiarise urban Britain and, as such, to destabilise traditional ideas of Britishness. The Grovesnor Hotel near Temple Meads Station in Bristol and its nearby flyover (since demolished) feature in a pictorial sequence which displays a kind of romantic Americana reminiscent of the work of the US artist Edward Hopper (who died in 1967). A 1930s-built art deco house is featured in a later sequence in the film, located on the A4 Bath Road at Brislington Hill. The effect of this exploration of an old road across southern England is to offer a richly evocative vision of the country at the end of the 1970s which does not always chime with popular contemporary mythologies of Englishness.

In their lack of clarity or sense of closure, the ambivalent last scenes of *Radio On* serve to locate the film within (or at least alongside) the British avant-garde. Robert drives his old Rover into a quarry and leaves the car on the 'edge', with its doors open, seemingly with nowhere else to go. The car here can be read as emblematic of an old England now on the edge of an abyss of uncertainty. The film ends with Robert at the Blue Anchor Bay railway station on the North Somerset Railway (near Minehead). From what is visible to us on screen, it remains unclear whether he decides gets on a train and head back east. Michael O'Pray argues that, 'If by the end of the 1970s the old avant-garde was collapsing, then the art cinema proper in Britain barely existed at all.'[62] But *Radio On* arguably speaks of the possibility of an enduring crossover between art film and the avant-garde in British film-making which might have developed subsequently. After all, the film features several very long takes, and dialogue does not appear until the eleventh minute. And, while the film has a narrative of sorts (and this narrative unfolds in a linear fashion), the amount of information available to the viewer remains absolutely minimal. Chris Chang rightly points out that *Radio On* is a film 'thoroughly steeped in its own absences, negations, and abysmal voids'.[63]

O'Pray argues that 'In the 1970s it makes sense to distinguish between avant-garde cinema, oppositional or independent cinema and art cinema – and even between a low-budget subsidised art cinema and a much more commercial and mainstream art cinema.'[64] But by the end of the decade (when *Radio On* appeared), it became far more difficult to make such clear-cut distinctions. O'Pray notices key differences between the 1970s films *Berlin House* (Malcolm Le Grice, 1970), *Performance* (Donald Cammell and Nicolas Roeg, 1970), *Sebastiane* (Derek Jarman and Paul Humfress, 1976), and *The Song of the Shirt* (Jonathan Curling and Sue Clayton, 1979). *Berlin House* is only a few minutes in length, was made very cheaply on 16mm film, and distributed by the London Film-Makers' Co-op to a narrow range of venues.[65] *Sebastiane* is a feature-length colour film made on a budget of tens of thousands of pounds, largely from private sources. *Performance* is a commercial, mainstream film funded and distributed by Warner Bros. and starring a major rock star, Mick Jagger, even if formally – in its employment of radical montage and complex time patterns – it feels like a European art film. *The Song of the Shirt* is a product of oppositional cinema, funded by the British Film Institute, the Arts Council, and Greater London Arts. This is a feature-length film which was intended to be educational. But it is also political, and evidences the type of theoretical positions being espoused by the *Screen* film journal during the 1970s.[66]

Radio On offers further proof that British experimental film-makers were involved in wide-ranging activities during the decade.[67] As we have seen, Derek Jarman became a prominent figure, making not only *Sebastiane* (with Paul Humfress, 1976) but also films such as *In the Shadow of the Sun* (1972/80) and *Jubilee* (1978). According to O'Pray, Jarman's work straddles and amalgamates art cinema and the avant-garde, in that while he worked on short, super 8mm films, he also showed a multi-projection, three-screen film work at London's Institute of Contemporary Arts (ICA) in their 'Festival of Expanded Cinema', and made feature-length films.[68] Peter Greenaway also produced wide-ranging work during the 1970s, including films such as the short *Vertical Features Remake* (1978), the longer *A Walk Through H* (1978), and the feature-length *The Falls* (1980), which was followed by *The Draughtsman's Contract* (1982).

So, a rich British vein of avant-garde film-making activity was evident during the 1970s, which had a 'spontaneous and heterogeneous' quality.[69] This could be seen in particular in the output of the London Film-Makers Co-op (founded in 1966), and, specifically, in the work of artists such as Malcolm Le Grice – such as his trilogy *Blackbird Descending* (1977), *Emily* (1978), and *Finnegan's Chin* (1981); William Raban – such as his *View* (1970), *Colours of This Time* (1972), *Broadwalk* (1972), and *River Yar* (with Chris Welsby, 1972); US-born Stephen Dwoskin – such as *Times For* (1971), *Dyn Amo* (1972), *Behindert* (1974), *Central Bazaar* (1976), *The Silent Cry* (1977), and *Tod und Teufel* (1973); and Gill Eatherley's multi-screen films such as *Pan View* (1972), *Shot Spread* (1972), *Clod Argument* (1973), and *Doubles Round* (1973).

Feminist avant-garde film-making blossomed in the 1970s too, as evidenced in films such as *Penthesilea: Queen of the Amazon* (Laura

Mulvey and Peter Wollen, 1974); *Riddles of the Sphinx* (Peter Wollen and Laura Mulvey, 1976); *Amy!* (Peter Wollen and Laura Mulvey, 1980); and Sally Potter's *Thriller* (1979). By the late 1970s, women film-makers had left the London Film-Makers' Co-op to set up their own production and distribution units, such as Circles and Four Corners.[70] Other groups working successfully during the 1970s included the Berwick Street Film Collective, the London Women's Film Group, Cinema Action, and Liberation Films.[71] This was also an era during which The Other Cinema, Polit Kino, Cine Gate, 24 Frames, and the Short Film Service were all active.[72]

Avant-garde film-making in Britain also incorporated a range of work which became known as 'structuralist–materialist'. At the centre of this movement was Peter Gidal. These film-makers attempted to avoid what they saw as the illusionism of films, and happily rejected narrative in favour of a focus on the material qualities of film itself – its grain, light and movement.[73] But a number of other celebrated film-makers working during the 1970s did so outside the rubric of structuralist aesthetics. These included Jeff Keen, Margaret Tait, and Chris Welsby.[74] Welsby developed a keen interest in filming landscapes. Evidence of this can be found in *Seven Days* (1974), which employs a carefully placed static camera to record shifts of sun and clouds in the sky. Tait was a Scottish film-maker with an interest in landscapes, the natural world, and the poetic possibilities of film, as seen in *Ariel* (1974). As such, some distinct formal and thematic connections can be made between the work of Welsby, Tait and Petit's *Radio On*.[75] Furthermore, Jeff Keen's work was influenced by Dada, surrealism and popular culture. He drew on Disney cartoon characters, horror magazines of the 1950s, pornography and B-movie trailers – themes reminiscent of those also operating in *Radio On*. *Mad Love* (1972–78) employed collage-based techniques and performance. Interestingly, Michael O'Pray argues that Keen's work of the period 'plugs into a tradition of English eccentricity bordering on bad taste found in the *Carry On* series, Michael Powell and Ken Russell'.[76]

Wish you were here: British travellers in *And Soon the Darkness, Incense for the Damned* and other places

Like *O Lucky Man!* and *Radio On*, a number of 1970s British films are constructed around the notion of journeys. These journeys often facilitate an examination of the state of the nation. But other films feature characters travelling away from or outside Britain. Many of these films evidence suspicions of foreigners and, as such, display a distinct pessimism about the European project. For example, *And Soon the Darkness* (Robert Fuest, 1970) – written by Brian Clemens and Terry Nation – tells the story of Cathy (Michele Dotrice) and Jane (Pamela Franklin), two young nurses from London taking a cycling holiday together in rural France. The film was shot on location and at Elstree Studios, and distributed by EMI. The opening shot shows the two young women riding away down a tree-lined French road, with flat fields stretching out to the horizon. Cathy spots a local young man (Sandor Elès) in a café, and becomes interested in him. She is clearly sexually active, whereas Jane is evidently not interested in forming acquaintances with young men on this trip. As the narrative progresses, the friends have a disagreement, and Jane leaves Cathy behind by the roadside when she decides to sunbathe. Jane subsequently spends much of the rest of the film trying to relocate her friend, and later discovers her dead body. Cathy had been on a 'bad road', according to middle-aged café owner, Madame Lassal (Hana Maria Pravda). She was warned about being 'on the road alone'. So there is the distinct suggestion in this film that young British women should not take the road to sexual and spiritual freedom. As such, we might come to the conclusion that Cathy is essentially being punished for being interested in sex as a young, unmarried, single woman. The film ends with a sudden downpour – a washing away of sin. But the apparently exotic 'otherness' of the French setting of *And Soon the Darkness* facilitates this examination of morality. Rural France is an 'elsewhere' here; a space of immorality and sexual violence.

In other films of the period, European locales become spaces of sexual danger or sexual freedom. For example, *Incense for the Damned* (aka *Blockbusters*) (Robert Hartford-Davis, 1971) is a horror/

thriller hybrid made by Titan International which tells the story of a young Oxford University don, Richard Fountain (Patrick Mower), who disappears while on a research trip to Greece. His friends, Tony Seymore (Alexander Davion) and Bob Kirby (Johnny Sekka) fly out with Richard's fiancée Penelope (Madeleine Hinde) to search for him, and spend time in picturesque fishing villages and ancient ruins while trying to deduce his whereabouts. But Richard has travelled on to the island of Hydra, where he has fallen under the spell of a beautiful, mysterious vampire, Chriseis Konstantanini (Imogen Hassall), who has a penchant for sado-masochistic sexual orgies. It turns out, as Tony Seymore (Davion) puts it, that 'Richard came to Greece in search of some sort of freedom'. Major Longbow (Patrick Macnee) replies 'they say this climate works wonders for that sort of thing'. It also turns out that Richard was known to be a virgin before travelling from Oxford to Greece, and that he evidently feared entering into a dull, passionless marriage to Penelope, the daughter of Dr Goodrich (Peter Cushing). Instead, he is drawn to the type of hot-blooded Mediterranean sexual freedom embodied by the dark, wild figure of Chriseis.

These films appeared in a nation that was going through 'seismic change' in its holiday habits in the early 1970s.[77] Companies such as Horizon had become successful package holiday operators by the end of the 1960s. The BBC launched its *Holiday* television programme in 1971. ITV followed with *Wish You Were Here* in 1974. In 1971, four million holidays abroad were taken by British tourists. By 1981, the figure was eighteen million.[78] Some holidaymakers reported that going away made them see their native land in a new light.[79] But a range of British films of the 1970s find humour in the activities of provincial Britons who travel abroad. The most obvious example of this is *Carry On Abroad* (Gerald Thomas, 1972), in which the familiar team is shipped to foreign shores on a four-day package holiday to an unfinished hotel in Elsbels. In this film, the warm Mediterranean comes to operate as a space in which repressed British characters can attempt to engage in the types of activities they clearly feel would be frowned upon in their cold, grey home town. Stanley Blunt (Kenneth Connor) is clearly keen to attempt to have sex with his long-uninterested English wife,

Evelyn (June Whitfield). But a handsome young Spaniard (Ray Brooks) gets her in the mood. The film thus depicts locals as openly sexual creatures, seemingly free from the pressures individuals are traditionally placed under in British society. But locals are also marked as unscrupulous, lazy, feckless and corrupt. The hotel falls apart around the British guests, while the venal hotelier, Pepe (Peter Butterworth), tries to pretend all is well. But the mythological British bulldog spirit shines through the ensuing destruction.

Are You Being Served? (Bob Kellett, 1977), a film version of another successful television sitcom, mines similar territory, having employees of the Grace Brothers department store get away from Britain for a few days, and seeing them make crude gags about food and foreign toilet habits. And *Three For All* (Martin Campbell, 1975), a musical comedy featuring Adrienne Posta, Lesley North, Cheryl Hall, Paul Nicholas, Robert Lindsay, Richard Beckinsale and Graham Bonnet (the future lead singer of rock group Rainbow), tells the story of young women who follow their boyfriends (a British rock group) to Spain. This film features the kind of goings-on one might expect on such a trip. This is just one of a number of films of the 1970s that features British rock and pop music and musicians. It is to these films that I now want to turn my attention.

Notes

1   Sandbrook, *State of Emergency*, p. 440.
2   Sandbrook, *State of Emergency*, p. 442.
3   Higson, 'A Diversity of Film Practices: Renewing British Cinema in the 1970s', p. 233.
4   Higson, 'A Diversity of Film Practices: Renewing British Cinema in the 1970s', p. 234.
5   Hedling, *Lindsay Anderson: Maverick Film-Maker*, pp. 113–14.
6   Hedling, *Lindsay Anderson: Maverick Film-Maker*, p. 115.
7   A. Walker, *National Heroes*, p. 50.
8   Hedling, *Lindsay Anderson: Maverick Film-Maker*, p. 115.
9   Durgnat, '*O Lucky Man* Or: The Adventures of a Clockwork Cheese', p. 39.
10 Hedling, *Lindsay Anderson: Maverick Film-Maker*, p. 131.
11 Izod *et al.*, 'What Is There to Smile At? Lindsay Anderson's *O Lucky Man?*', p. 219.

12 During this period Arthur Lowe also appeared in *The Bawdy Adventures of Tom Jones* (Cliff Owen, 1976), *The Lady Vanishes* (Anthony Page, 1979), and *Sweet William* (Claude Whatham, 1980).

13 *Variety*, 13 June 1973.

14 A. Graham, *Lindsay Anderson*, p. 168.

15 Hedling, *Lindsay Anderson: Maverick Film-Maker*, p. 118.

16 Gow, 'O Lucky Man!', p. 45.

17 Millar, 'O Lucky Man!', pp. 36–7.

18 Gow, 'O Lucky Man!', p. 45.

19 Lovell, 'Brecht in Britain – Lindsay Anderson (on *If...* and *O Lucky Man!*)', p. 70.

20 Hedling, *Lindsay Anderson: Maverick Film-Maker*, p. 142.

21 Hedling, *Lindsay Anderson: Maverick Film-Maker*, pp. 136–42.

22 A. Walker, *National Heroes*, p. 51; Hedling, *Lindsay Anderson: Maverick Film-Maker*, p. 114.

23 A. Walker, *National Heroes*, p. 50.

24 Turner, *Crisis? What Crisis? Britain in the 1970s*, p. 23.

25 Hedling, *Lindsay Anderson: Maverick Film-Maker*, p. 114.

26 Hedling, *Lindsay Anderson: Maverick Film-Maker*, p. 119.

27 A. Walker, *National Heroes*, p. 52.

28 See Sandbrook, *State of Emergency*, pp. 506–15.

29 Sandbrook, *State of Emergency*, p. 515.

30 Sandbrook, *State of Emergency*, p. 521.

31 Sandbrook, *State of Emergency*, pp. 524–7.

32 Cunningham, 'Lindsay Anderson's *O Lucky Man!* and the Romantic Tradition', p. 260; Hedling, *Lindsay Anderson: Maverick Film-Maker*, p. 119.

33 Lovell, 'Brecht in Britain – Lindsay Anderson (on *If...* and *O Lucky Man!*)', p. 70.

34 Hutchings, 'The Power to Create Catastrophe: The Idea of Apocalypse in 1970s British Cinema', p. 110.

35 Hutchings, 'The Power to Create Catastrophe: The Idea of Apocalypse in 1970s British Cinema', pp. 111–12.

36 Hutchings, 'The Power to Create Catastrophe: The Idea of Apocalypse in 1970s British Cinema', p. 116.

37 Sandbrook, *State of Emergency*, p. 205.

38 Sandbrook, *State of Emergency*, pp. 205–6.

39 Sandbrook, *State of Emergency*, p. 181.

40 Turner, *Crisis? What Crisis? Britain in the 1970s*, p. 55.

41 Turner, *Crisis? What Crisis? Britain in the 1970s*, p. 47.

42 A. Walker, *National Heroes*, p. 52.

43 Gow, 'O Lucky Man!', p. 46.

44 Hedling, *Lindsay Anderson: Maverick Film-Maker*, p. 123.

45 Lavery, '*O Lucky Man!* and the Movie as Koan', pp. 35–40.

46 Dixon, *Re-Viewing British Cinema*, p. 173.

47 Patterson, 'Films We Forgot to Remember', p. 6.

48 Sandbrook, *State of Emergency*, p. 42.

49 Durgnat, '*O Lucky Man* Or: The Adventures of a Clockwork Cheese', p. 39.

50 Nowell-Smith, 'Radio On', p. 30.

51 Combs, 'Ich bin ein Englander, or Show Me the Way to Go Home', p. 136.

52 Sandhu, 'Border Zones', p. 11.

53 Combs, 'Radio On', p. 54.

54 Petit, 'Road Movies: Germany–England/England–Germany', p. 40.

55 Petit, 'Road Movies: Germany–England/England–Germany', p. 40.

56 Petit, 'Road Movies: Germany–England/England–Germany', p. 40.

57 Pym, 'Radio On', p. 234.

58 Chang, 'Event Horizon: Chris Petit's *Radio On* Returns from the Ether', p. 16.

59 Pym, 'Radio On', p. 234.

60 Sandbrook, *State of Emergency*, p. 190.

61 Pym, 'Radio On', p. 234. For more on *Radio On*, see Hoyle, '*Radio On* and British Art Cinema'.

62 O'Pray, 'The British Avant-Garde and Art Cinema from the 1970s to the 1990s', p. 184.

63 Chang, 'Event Horizon: Chris Petit's *Radio On* Returns from the Ether', p. 16.

64 O'Pray, 'The British Avant-Garde and Art Cinema from the 1970s to the 1990s', p. 179.

65 The London Film-Makers' Co-op was founded in 1966. It provided production resources and a cultural centre for avant-garde cinema.

66 O'Pray, 'The British Avant-Garde and Art Cinema from the 1970s to the 1990s', p. 180.

67 Fowler, 'Multiple Voices: *The Silent Cry* and Artists' Moving Image in the 1970s', p. 73.

68 O'Pray, 'The British Avant-Garde and Art Cinema from the 1970s to the 1990s', p. 178.

69 Dickinson, *Rogue Reels*, p. 48.

70 O'Pray, 'The British Avant-Garde and Art Cinema from the 1970s to the 1990s', p. 183.

71 See Harvey, 'The "Other Cinema" in Britain: Unfinished in Oppositional and Independent Film, 1929–1984'.

72 Fowler, 'Multiple Voices: *The Silent Cry* and Artists' Moving Image in the 1970s', p. 73.

73 See Allen, 'Moving Images and the Visual Arts in 1970s Britain'.

74 O'Pray, 'The British Avant-Garde and Art Cinema from the 1970s to the 1990s', pp. 182–3.

75 For more on 1970s British experimental film-making, see Rees, *A History of Experimental Film and Video*; Dickinson, *Rogue Reels*, pp. 41–61; Allen, 'Moving Images and the Visual Arts in 1970s Britain'.

76 O'Pray, 'The British Avant-Garde and Art Cinema from the 1970s to the 1990s', p. 182.

77 Sandbrook, *State of Emergency*, p. 141.

78 Sandbrook, *State of Emergency*, p. 142.

79 Sandbrook, *State of Emergency*, p. 143.

3

The songs remain the same:
pop, rock and war children

Remembering World War Two

The Second World War continued to cast a long shadow across British culture during the 1970s.[1] As we have seen, the hit television comedy series *Dad's Army* (BBC, 1968–77) centres on the experiences of a group of men in a Home Guard unit. A film version was made in 1971 (directed by Norman Cohen), which also remembers the war years fondly as a period of cohesive communities, strong national identity, and a proud British spirit. Jeffrey Richards notices that 'There is nostalgia, embodied in the use in the television series of popular songs of the period to link the scenes.'[2] But this is nostalgia 'not so much for the war as a time of shortage, destruction and loss but as a period of shared effort and sacrifice, common purpose and good neighbourliness and justified struggle against a wicked enemy'.[3] The success of *Dad's Army*, and its subsequent endurance in British cultural life, certainly offers evidence that the British often look to a shared idea of a national past for a collective sense of identity that is apparently missing in the present. The popularity of the BBC television series *Colditz* (BBC, 1972–74) also speaks of this.

British acts of remembrance for the war occurred across a wide range of films during the 1970s. For example, the first film in the Scottish film-maker Bill Douglas's celebrated trilogy, *My Childhood* (1972), begins with the sound of an air-raid siren. In a Scottish mining village in 1945, Jamie (Stephen Archibald) befriends Helmuth (Karl Fieseler), a German prisoner of war engaged in agricultural labour. Helmuth becomes a kind of surrogate father figure for the boy in the absence of his own father. But Helmuth leaves before the end of the film, leaving Jamie distraught. In *Overlord* (Stuart Cooper, 1975), events of the Second World War are viewed within an inventive formal structure which mixes archival shots of the war (held by the Imperial War Museum) with contemporary black-and-white footage of fictional events. Cooper's filmed sequences are effectively documentary-realist in style. The film was shot by Johnny Alcott (better known for his work with Stanley Kubrick), and some of the images are staggering in their beauty and power, such as the poetic shots of meticulous wartime preparations. Interestingly, some of the archival footage is set up to appear as though it is a dream being experienced by the principle protagonist, a soldier named Tom (Brian Stirner). There is also a strange sense of calm displayed in the film, though – of knowing, and of resignation to, one's fate.

Other British films of the period employ the war as a backdrop. For example, *Soft Beds, Hard Battles* (Roy Boulting, 1974) features Peter Sellers playing multiple roles in a film set in Paris (mostly in a brothel) during the Second World War. *The Blockhouse* (Clive Rees, 1973), filmed in Guernsey, also stars Peter Sellers, and tells the story of labourers held by German soldiers who take shelter in a German bunker on D-Day, but remain trapped there for years afterwards. The war appears in British cinema in the 1970s in other unusual places, too. For example, *The Beast in the Cellar* (aka *Are You Dying, Young Man?* and *Young Man, I Think You're Dying*) (James Kelley, 1970), a Tigon horror film about a pair of elderly sisters (Beryl Reid and Flora Robson) who, thirty years previously, trapped their brother in the cellar to avoid him being conscripted. Now psychotic, he manages to escape, and subsequently goes on a murderous rampage. *Let's Get Laid* (James Kenelm Clarke, 1977) is a comedy featuring Robin Askwith as a soldier returning from the war who gets mixed up in a farcical series of mistaken identities. And *The Custard Boys* (Colin Finbow, 1979), set during late summer in Norfolk in 1942, tells the story of a teenage evacuee who forms a firm friendship with a Jewish German boy.[4] Furthermore, the British rock group Pink Floyd released their double album *The Wall* album in November 1979. This LP record, and the subsequent Alan Parker film, *The Wall* (1982), starring Bob Geldof, places the

Second World War very much at the centre of a narrative which depicts the experiences of the rock star protagonist, Pink (clearly representative of the bassist and lyricist Roger Waters). Alan Parker had already worked in British cinema during the 1970s, directing *Bugsy Malone* (1976) and *Midnight Express* (1978), both of which saw the involvement of David Puttnam at the production stage. In this chapter I shall primarily explore two films that Puttnam produced during the 1970s – *That'll Be the Day* (Claude Whatham, 1973) and *Stardust* (Michael Apted, 1974), and examine the ways in which they speak of a rich relationship that was developing between British film-making and music during the 1970s.

Here is a nice bit of nostalgia: *That'll Be the Day*

David Puttnam and Ray Connolly were two kids born during the Second World War who, as adults in the 1970s, seemingly shared a need to engage with memories of the Britain in which they grew up. Together they wrote and produced two films that depicted aspects of their own visions and recollections of the memorable post-war period – *That'll Be the Day* (Claude Whatham, 1973) and *Stardust* (Michael Apted, 1974). Both films feature David Essex in the lead role of Jim MacLaine. And both films were produced by David Puttnam and Sandy Lieberson (as Goodtimes Enterprises), with financial backing from Nat Cohen's Anglo-EMI Films.

That'll Be the Day captures the development of Jim MacLaine from his rejection as a child by his soldier father (James Booth) after his return from the war, through to his working-class adolescence under the guidance of his matriarchal mother (Rosemary Leach). She is a strong, conservative figure who advocates the benefits of hard work. Nevertheless, Jim emerges as an itinerant who dreams of pop stardom. On a whim, he decides to leave school before taking his A-level exams (thus forfeiting any chance of going to university and rising through the middle classes), and ends up drifting around seaside resorts and fairgrounds. The film depicts a nation typified by damp, old boarding houses and drab streets, peopled by grey-haired, inward-looking individuals. But this is also a world of wide-eyed youth.

The sequel, *Stardust*, follows the progress of the now guitar-playing Jim into a band which eventually enjoys huge success in the mid-1960s, through to Jim's global superstardom as a solo artist in the late 1960s, and on through his subsequent slide into reclusiveness, drug addiction, and madness. Both films highlight the influential nature of American popular culture (and popular music in particular) in Jim's imaginative development, as well as that of his British contemporaries. Indeed, an early scene in *That'll Be the Day* features a telling shot of a queue outside the Rex cinema. We see Jim's face reflected in a glass case in which a poster of James Dean is displayed. A girl – who turns out to be his future wife, Jeanette (Rosalind Ayres) – says to a friend 'Hey, there's Jim.' There appears to be ambiguity operating in this statement – does she mean MacLaine or Dean? Clearly, Jim dreams of being a Dean-like figure. And, interestingly, James Dean seems to have struck a chord with the young Ray Connolly, who, after working with Puttnam on the Jim MacLaine films, went on to direct the documentary *James Dean: The First American Teenager* (1975).

Connolly wrote the *That'll Be the Day* screenplay in six weeks, working very closely with Puttnam.[5] It was based loosely on the Harry Nilsson song '1941', which appears on the *Pandemonium Shadow Show* LP (1967). The Jim MacLaine character was evidently based on the young Puttnam, while his teenage best friend – the straight, middle-class university student Terry (Robert Lindsay) – was seemingly more like Connolly.[6] It was Puttnam's idea to have his own father's return from the war incorporated into the film. He even cast his young son, Sasha, as the child he himself had been.[7] Puttnam approached Claude Whatham to direct *That'll Be the Day* after Michael Apted had initially turned him down.[8] Roy Baird acted as executive producer and Gavrik Losey was installed as production manager.

That'll Be the Day is an example of the type of clever, independent film-making that often proved successful in Britain during the 1970s.[9] Its success was bound up with Puttnam's shrewd acknowledgement of ongoing cultural developments in the West, as well as his insights into the state of the movie industry in general. In his published history of cinema on both sides of the Atlantic, *The Undeclared War* (1997), Puttnam argues that at the beginning of the

1970s Hollywood was in 'crisis', primarily because a new popular culture had emerged, driven by bands such as The Beatles and The Rolling Stones. At that time, the men who ran the major Hollywood studios were in their sixties, while most of their audience were in their teens or twenties. Successful companies such as Warner Bros., MCA, and Disney weathered the depression in film-making by engaging in a form of 'horizontal integration' – defraying costs across a range of activities, with spin-offs into soundtracks, books, toys, and marketing.[10] It seems that Puttnam himself quickly saw the benefits of such an approach. Putting films into production such as *That'll Be the Day* (Claude Whatham, 1973), *Stardust* (Michael Apted, 1974), and *Slade in Flame* (aka *Flame*) (Richard Loncraine, 1975) – featuring the pop group, Slade – Puttnam recognised the possibilities that existed for producers to pioneer complex film packages by exploiting tie-ins to other media. He also noticed the ways in which profitable films could be organised around successful popular music artists, and thus showed that British cinema could remain viable, even in difficult times, if it aligned itself strategically within a growing multi-media entertainment market.[11] Furthermore, Puttnam sought to keep costs under control – a lesson he learned on *Melody* (aka *S.W.A.L.K.*) (Waris Hussein, 1971), when Gavrik Losey suggested that he should employ location shooting wherever and whenever possible.[12]

The first sequence in *That'll Be the Day* is shot in soft focus in low light, and serves to evoke a vision of a distant (but seemingly still present) past. This sequence features no extra-diegetic or diegetic music, but the voice of Jim's mother has been treated with reverb in post-production. The sequence also features other telling sounds, including a clock chiming loudly. We hear a steam train in the distance, and then the noise of Jim's father's footsteps echoing off a row of modest terraced houses at night. Though the visuals here in some ways recall the British social realist tradition, the soundtrack serves to problematise this in formal terms, by suggesting a memory. The sequence certainly captures widely-shared memories of the austerity characteristic of the war years and the subsequent period.

As the film-makers were interested in keeping costs down, but also achieving a level of realism and authenticity, shooting took place on location on the Isle of Wight, just off the south coast of

England (primarily at a holiday camp in Puckpool, Ryde). Gavrik Losey persuaded the owner of the holiday camp to rent the whole site out to the crew during the quiet winter period.[13] Sequences in the film were also shot at the Sandown High School, Shanklin Pier, and Billy Manning's Amusements at Southsea, on the mainland. The coffee bar featured was located at 22 Cross Street, Ryde, and the roller skating rink scene was shot at Brambles Holiday Camp, Freshwater. The location shooting helps to facilitate the nostalgic feel of the film. As Tony Rayns wrote in *Sight and Sound* soon after the film was released, 'the only difficulty encountered in establishing the "period" setting had been persuading the local extras to cut their hair'.[14]

In *That'll Be the Day*, it is in the carnivalesque spaces of the coast, situated on the periphery of mainstream British culture, that Jim MacLaine sees a chance to renew himself. One key three-minute sequence in the film takes place on location at a fairground at night, and features no dialogue. The camera follows Jim and two girls around this site. The colours of the fairground are striking – all pinks, bright yellows, and lilacs. But the fluorescent lights also lend the sequence an oneiric quality, suggesting a distance from present-day reality, and thus facilitating the location of this activity within an imaginary British past. Here, as elsewhere in the film, the bright lights of US consumer culture are set against a resolutely cold, grey, and wet vision of England. Jim and the girls wander about, with popular songs playing on the soundtrack. We hear a range of tracks in quick succession, including Del Shannon's 'Runaway'. Again, this music is filtered through reverb, lending the whole sequence the dreamy quality of a distant memory. But the music also serves to construct a rich, imaginative landscape which sees the optimistic warmth of an emergent US popular culture seemingly flood into cold, austere Britain. The rock 'n' roll songs used on the soundtrack here (and subsequently released on the 2-LP soundtrack by Ronco Records) come to have a talismanic hold over Jim, and over the film as a whole. The third side of the LP features oldies, including 'That'll Be the Day' (Norman Petty, Buddy Holly, and Jerry Allison) performed by Bobby Vee, and 'What Did I Say' (Ray Charles) performed by Billy Fury. The fourth side features new material, including Viv Stanshall's 'Real Leather Jacket', Eugene

Wallace's 'Slow Down', and Stormy Tempest (a group put together for the film, which included David Essex) performing 'What in the World (Shoop)'.[15] These songs provide a distinct rhythm and structure to the film.

But the songs originally had not been considered be a central aspect of the film. It was only when Puttnam failed to persuade Nat Cohen's Anglo-EMI to put up the whole budget that he struck a deal with Ronco Records for the soundtrack LP.[16] Puttnam has suggested in an interview more recently that '*That'll Be the Day* was funded effectively by its album.'[17] He also remembers that it was television advertising for the LP that really brought about the box office success of the film. Ronco sold more than 600,000 copies, and it went on to yield a net profit of over £400,000 against costs of less than £300,000. But the deal with Ronco had a profound effect on the formal properties of the film. Ray Connolly told Alexander Walker that this deal meant having to create openings in the film for fifteen seconds of music here and there.[18] Indeed, *That'll Be the Day* features only two short bursts of non-diegetic score, and uses pop songs as non-diegetic music only once.[19] Choices of music for the film were overseen by Neil Aspinall (once a Beatles road crew member) and Keith Moon of The Who, who was cast in the film (and its sequel, *Stardust*) as drummer J. D. Clover.

According to Pauline Reay, the pop music compilation score was established in the US film *American Graffiti* (George Lucas, 1973).[20] But clearly, at the same time, the British film *That'll Be the Day* was doing something very similar. Kevin Donnelly notices that *That'll Be the Day* was 'the first British example of founding a film upon a collection of old songs from different artists that would be sold on a soundtrack'.[21] Certainly, *American Graffiti* is a film that bears direct comparison to *That'll Be the Day* in numerous ways. Both appeared in 1973; both look back in time to tell the stories of youths making their way in the 1950s; and both feature rock 'n' roll soundtracks which draw upon the vast resources of popular recordings from that period. But Puttnam's previous film, *Melody* (aka *S.W.A.L.K.*) (Waris Hussein, 1971) also uses popular music in a way that guaranteed it a decent level of success at the box office. This film features Bee Gees songs, to which Puttnam had secured the rights, and 'Teach Your Children', a popular song by the transnational folk-rock super group Crosby, Stills and Nash. Puttnam continued to mine the potential of popular music in subsequent film projects. On his next film, *The Pied Piper* (Jacques Demy, 1972), the producer cast the folk artist Donovan in the lead role of the Piper of Hamelin. The singer also provides songs for the film, which was critically panned, but went on to become moderately successful at the box office (especially in Japan).[22] Puttnam had recognised the enduring power of popular music in post-war British culture, then, and the rich cultural complexities brought about by a transatlantic Anglo-American musical dialogue. This was a path-breaking creative development from a resourceful film producer which subsequently showed the way to other independent producers.[23] Indeed, in the latter half of the 1970s and into the 1980s, an increased synergy and cross-promotion developed between the film and music industries, both in Britain and elsewhere.[24]

The casting of *That'll Be the Day* clearly exploited the bankability of British pop and rock stars, many of whom had made their names in the glory years of the 1960s. Others were enjoying contemporaneous success. David Essex, playing Jim, was fresh from a stage performance in the popular *Godspell*. The former Beatle, Ringo Starr, offered a memorable performance as Mike. Billy Fury was cast as Stormy Tempest. These casting decisions profoundly affected the overall tone of the film, facilitating a level of intertextual complexity which draws on the rich, ongoing history of popular music. Interestingly, pop and rock stars were receiving far more offers to take acting roles in films in the late 1960s and 1970s than they had done in the early 1960s.[25] Examples of such performances include John Lennon in *How I Won the War* (Richard Lester, 1967); Ringo Starr in *The Magic Christian* (Joseph McGrath, 1969); Mick Jagger in *Performance* (Donald Cammell and Nicolas Roeg, 1970) and *Ned Kelly* (Tony Richardson, 1970); Roy Harper in *Made* (John Mackenzie, 1972); Roger Daltrey in *Tommy* (Ken Russell, 1975), *Lizstomania* (Ken Russell, 1975), and *McVicar* (Tom Clegg, 1980); David Bowie in *The Man Who Fell to Earth* (Nicolas Roeg, 1976); Sting in *Quadrophenia* (Franc Roddam, 1979) and *Radio On* (Chris Petit, 1979); and Art Garfunkel in *Bad Timing* (Nicolas Roeg, 1980). Adam Faith, who appears in *Stardust* as Mike, the roadie for the Stray Cats and Jim's constant companion, was 'the first British pop star successfully to transpose his career from pop star to actor'.[26] Faith had, after all, appeared in films such as *Beat Girl* (Edmond T. Gréville, 1959) and *Mix Me a Person* (Leslie Norman, 1962). Overall, then, the success of *That'll Be the Day* was very much built on the exploitation of established star images and the ability of pop stars to 'translate stage charisma into screen presence', as Kevin Donnelly puts it.[27]

That'll Be the Day is steeped in nostalgia for a British past. At the time of the release of the film, the *Variety* critic 'Hawk' wrote: 'Here is a nice bit of nostalgia'.[28] 'Hawk' also thought that the film had 'a superior period feel evident in details of setting, action and dialogue'.[29] In *Films and Filming*, Julian Fox also noticed the realistic feel of the vision of the past depicted in the film: 'Sitting through *That'll Be the Day* is like looking through the wrong end of a telescope.' Fox further suggested that the film 'takes on the awe-inspiring aspects of a historical document'.[30] However, while it looked to the past, *That'll Be the Day* was a film very much in touch with present times and present concerns. Christopher Booker (1980) and Bart Moore-Gilbert (1994) have both advocated that a cult of nostalgia was discernable in the 1970s.[31] British film and television, in particular, increasingly turned to nostalgic representations of the past.[32] But perhaps this was nothing new. Gary Whannel points out that 'The notion of a golden age recently eroded has been a significant part of the English cultural sensibility for at least one hundred years, but it wells to the surface with particular prominence at times of cultural fragmentation and recomposition.'[33] As we have seen, the 1970s in Britain was one such period of fragmentation; a period during which the nation appeared to be coming to terms with the changes brought about by the extraordinary revolutions of the 1960s. After all, as Christopher Booker puts it, 'One of the main reasons why the Seventies had such an air of hangover, of aftermath, was that a psychological climax had been passed which could never be worked up to with the same frenzied excitement again.'[34]

But there was some excitement to be had by British music fans in the early 1970s. The year *That'll Be the Day* appeared on British cinema screens (1973) was a year of transition in the history of British rock music. Progressive rock was reaching its peak. Pink

Floyd's seminal *Dark Side of the Moon* was released, enjoying phenomenal success. Yes attempted to consolidate their early 1970s appeal by releasing *Tales of Topographic Oceans*, a double LP featuring just one very long track on each of its four sides. Led Zeppelin was conquering America at the same time as releasing *Houses of the Holy*. The Who released *Quadrophenia*. Mike Oldfield's epic *Tubular Bells* was the first release on Richard Branson's new Virgin label. But British pop music was also hugely successful. Interestingly, bearing in mind the nostalgic feel of *That'll Be the Day*, one of the most visible musical genres of the early 1970s, 'glam', had a distinctly retro look and feel, which was evident in the images and sounds of bands such as Mud and Showaddywaddy – the latter being 1974 winners of the television talent show *New Faces* (ATV, 1973–78).[35] In 1973, Gary Glitter, primarily a UK singles artist, released his LP *Touch Me*. The glam rock band Slade consolidated their chart success in the UK by playing sell-out dates at London's Earls Court and appearing in the Puttnam-produced film *Slade in Flame* (aka *Flame*) (Richard Loncraine, 1975) – the 'Citizen Kane of rock musicals', according to British film critic Mark Kermode.[36] Roxy Music released *For Your Pleasure*, and Elton John released his double LP, *Goodbye Yellow Brick Road*, which features the nostalgic, glam-style hit, 'Crocodile Rock'. In the same year, glam rock group The Sweet had a huge hit in Britain with 'Ballroom Blitz'.[37] The success of the 1972 Wembley rock 'n' roll revival concert, as well as the release of David Bowie's *Pin Ups* and Bryan Ferry's *These Foolish Things* (both albums comprising entirely of cover versions) also speak of a backward-looking trend that was evident across much of the British music scene during the early part of the decade.[38]

A sense of nostalgia for the 1950s was not just the preserve of the British in the 1970s. Writing about *American Graffiti* (George Lucas, 1973), Paul Monaco highlights what he sees as a movement towards nostalgia in American films of the decade.[39] Fred Davis suggests that nostalgia can be understood as 'memory without pain'.[40] *American Graffiti* was released to considerable commercial success, perhaps because it served to evoke a pre-Vietnam period of seeming American innocence; a period during which gas-guzzling cars could be driven by young people without concern for rising oil prices or the fears for the environment which would typify much of the 1970s. Writing about the 'nostalgia film', Fredric Jameson identifies *American Graffiti* as a key example of *la mode retro*. This film, for Jameson, works as a postmodern pastiche; as a parody emptied of a sense of humour. It is a film which is 'about the past and about specific generational moments of that past'.[41] Indeed, Jameson suggests that Lucas's film inaugurated a new genre which set out to recapture 'all the atmosphere and stylistic peculiarities of the 1950s United States'.[42] In some senses, the same could be said for the depiction of US-influenced Britain in *That'll Be the Day*. Interestingly, according to Jameson, such films exemplify the inability of contemporary film audiences to 'focus on our present, as though we have become incapable of achieving aesthetic representations of our own current experience'.[43] They operate as 'an alarming and pathological symptom of a society that has become incapable of dealing with time and history'.[44] We might then read *That'll Be the Day* as a film that was successful, not just because of the clever marketing of its soundtrack LP, but because the songs in the film, and the realistic images captured by the film they accompany, served to allow audiences, for some precious moments, to forget about the trials and tribulations of the early 1970s in Britain, and to wallow in the imagined comforts of a simpler time. For one thing, the songs played in *That'll Be the Day* serve to fix the narrative in historical time.[45] As Ian Inglis puts it, 'compiled scores, and the external associations they encourage, direct the audience towards a specific musical and historical environment which helps to articulate and acknowledge the accompanying narrative'.[46] But our experience of the songs in this film feels more complicated than that.

The songs in *That'll Be the Day* certainly recall the 1950s/early-1960s era. But widely-known pop songs carry their own sets of feelings and associations, often developed through hearing them repeatedly.[47] As such, the songs in *That'll Be the Day* allow us to access a past which in some ways we already know, even if we did not experience it ourselves. Through their lyrical content and other sonic properties, these songs are profoundly visual; they evoke a range of visual images. In other words, these songs develop a synaesthetic force which, again, serves to further enhance the nostalgic tone of the film in which they appear. Because the songs in the film are so popular and so widely-recognised, they work to create imaginative spaces, and, as such, they effectively operate as sound territories (or phonotopes) which contain microcosmic, abstracted visions of the past. An example of this occurs during the sequence in the café, when Jim buys two girls Cokes. Shirley (Susan Holderness) asks him 'Got any money for the jukebox?' He responds in the affirmative, and she says 'You choose ... see what your taste's like.' When he subsequently picks a song, and the sound of an electric guitar fills the room, this has the effect of shifting the spatiality of the scene. The music, as it unfolds, creates a phonotope which serves to problematise the otherwise essential Britishness of this space. As Jim and Shirley talk about parochial things, such as what they will do on leaving school ('receptionist at County Motors', says Shirley), the music connects them to somewhere else. The song has the power to take those present in the sequence (but also in the audience) towards a rich idea of America.

In the earlier sequences of the film in particular, the phonotopes provided by US rock 'n' roll songs facilitate the development of the space that Jim imaginatively inhabits. It is clear that music is his world. But he is also driven by a desire to develop as a sexual creature. As we follow his sexual adventures, *That'll Be the Day* appears to take a view on sex which chimes with aspects of the permissive contemporary moment at the same time as it is nostalgic for a 'simpler' past.[48] According to his old friend, Terry (Robert Lindsay), when they meet again some time after leaving school, Jim has become a 'randy sod'. On the one hand, Jim is a misogynist who treats his lovers with little or no respect. All he is interested in is 'getting his end away' with 'birds' and 'tarts', according to Mike (Ringo Starr). Indeed, Jim rapes a schoolgirl at the fairground, and writes on the back of one lover with lipstick in order to signify her 'number' on his growing list of conquests. But one of his lovers, Sandra (Deborah Watling), appears highly disappointed with his sexual performance, asking him 'Do you always come so quickly?' This, of course, signifies her sexual experience relative to his at this moment, and arguably speaks of a post-pill world – the 1970s – rather than the early 1960s. During this sequence, a young baby can be heard crying in a neighbouring holiday chalet, suggesting the potential consequences of unprotected sex.

If *That'll Be the Day* is nostalgic for the culture and music scene (specifically the US music scene) of the late 1950s and early 1960s, it is also nostalgic for earlier, successful forms of British cinema. After all, as Alexander Walker argues, Jim MacLaine 'remained in the tradition of working- or lower middle-class lads from *Room at the Top* onwards: in other words, a bit of a bastard, but basically forgivable'.[49] Although shot in colour, the sections of the film which show the inability of the father to settle with his wife and child clearly demonstrate the influence of the working-class, kitchen-sink grittiness of the British New Wave films of the late 1950s and early 1960s. Specifically, the scene during which Jim's grandfather lies dying distinctly echoes *The Loneliness of the Long Distance Runner* (Tony Richardson, 1962). And the fairground fist-fight recalls *Saturday Night and Sunday Morning* (Karel Reisz, 1960). Moreover, sequences featuring dancers jiving in a hall clearly echo Lindsay Anderson's *This Sporting Life* (1963). Links can be made to other mid-1960s films, too. The Beatles loom large. Indeed, Sarah Street notices that *That'll Be the Day* demonstrates that the legacy of *A Hard Day's Night* (Richard Lester, 1964) was clearly 'a profound and lasting one'.[50] Richard Lester's film, of course, encouraged more film-makers subsequently to include pop music in their movies.[51]

Towards the end of *That'll Be the Day*, Jim has an epiphany by the pond in the park where his dad once took him as a child and where he told him he was leaving. Jim repeats history by doing the same – walking out on his young wife and baby. But he takes an electric guitar with him – a mythical object which he lifts off the wall of a music shop at the very end of the film in a shot that sets up the sequel, *Stardust*. When the shop assistant asks, 'Are you sure you'll be able to handle it?', Jim answers, 'I'll be alright.'

Manipulation and exorcism: *Stardust*

In a move that effectively links this film to *That'll Be the Day* in formal terms, *Stardust* (Michael Apted, 1974) begins with the rock and roll song 'Sweet Sixteen' playing over a shot of Jim MacLaine (David Essex) walking into a brightly-lit fairground at night. Again, as in *That'll Be the Day*, the fairground operates as a simulacrum of

American popular culture. Jim and his future manager and roadie, Mike (Adam Faith), witness live footage of John F. Kennedy's assassination on a small television set, placing the beginning of the film historically on 22 November 1963. They continue their conversation as they sit in American-style bumper cars. The story for *Stardust* was written by Puttnam and Connolly during a week spent in a rented house near Rome.[52] Alan Parker was their first choice to direct, but when he turned it down they approached their original first choice for *That'll Be the Day*, Michael Apted, who agreed. Nat Cohen at Anglo-EMI again supported the film. But *Stardust* was also the only film to be awarded a loan by the National Film Finance Corporation (NFFC) in the years 1973–74.[53] The total budget was just over £400,000.

Stardust follows the now-familiar rock trajectory of an individual from his/her initial excitement at being noticed and gaining a foothold in the music business, through to broader recognition and a growing fan base, and on through the subsequent conquering of America, followed by his/her fall from grace. Here we see Jim brought down by internal politics within his pop group, exploitation by big business, drug abuse, venality, and the type of overblown pretentiousness exemplified by the mid-1970s rock opera. Bearing all this in mind, it is fitting that key British rockers again play the members of the band (The Stray Cats) in the film, such as Dave Edmunds (Alex), Paul Nicholas (Johnny), and Keith Moon (once again playing J. D. Clover). Other major figures in the cast include Larry Hagman as the Texan tycoon, Porter Lee Austin – a part that saw him going on to secure the role of J. R. Ewing in the hugely successful US television soap *Dallas* (CBS, 1978–91). *Stardust* also features Ines Des Longchamps as Danielle, Karl Howman as Stevie, and future *Blue Peter* presenter Peter Duncan as Kevin. Brian Morris was again enlisted as art director, and his visual style, alongside the music on the soundtrack (produced and arranged by Dave Edmunds and David Puttnam), provides an almost seamless formal link between *Stardust* and the earlier *That'll Be the Day*.

In some ways, *Stardust* articulated a bleak national and generational mood when it opened in cinemas in October 1974. As Alexander Walker argues, 'The earlier film had been about innocence and temptation: this one was about manipulation and exorcism.'[54] Walker also points out that 'If *A Hard Day's Night* of ten years earlier had been a joyous release of Pop energy, *Stardust* was an implosion of disaffection.'[55] *Stardust* is certainly a film that takes a pessimistic view of the kind of 1960s dream of fame and fortune shared by Jim and many of his contemporaries. Indeed, the film suggests that any freedoms that fame and riches might bring will inevitably be taken away again by the demands of the capitalist system.

But *Stardust* begins by evoking an optimism felt by many in early-1960s Britain. The band's first lunchtime gig is in an underground space clearly reminiscent of the Cavern Club in Liverpool, where The Beatles originally cut their teeth. Later, as the band run out of the venue dressed in identical suits, images from Richard Lester's Beatles film *A Hard Day's Night* spring to mind. We later see television footage of the band, arriving, like The Beatles, in the USA, with legions of fans going berserk on the roofs of the airport terminal buildings. As he is interviewed by CBS on television, it is clear that Jim is now a more cerebral 'rock' figure than pop icon, echoing John Lennon's late-1960s conversion from rocker to avant-garde artist and activist. Jim's interview here provides a useful back story for those who might not have seen *That'll Be the Day*. But as he becomes an increasingly isolated figure, he chooses to work with classical musicians in the CBS studio rather than with his old mates in the band. And in a demonstration of late-1960s/early-1970s overblown, drug-fuelled pretentiousness, he writes an opera about women which, when performed, is transmitted via satellite to 300 million television viewers worldwide.

Puttnam repeated the trick of incorporating a number of songs in *Stardust*. Early in the film, songs can be heard playing on the radio in the group's van, such as 'It Might As Well Rain Until September' by Carole King, and 'Do You Want to Know a Secret?' by Billy Kramer and the Dakotas. When the film shifts to the USA and the late 1960s, we hear 'Monday, Monday' by The Mamas and the Papas. 'You've Lost That Loving Feeling' by The Righteous Brothers (1965) plays as Jim and his girlfriend drive a convertible down the Sunset Strip in Los Angeles. And Jefferson Airplane's 'White Rabbit' (1967) can be heard playing in the studio over the orgy scene when Jim's girlfriend overhears his sexual activities over the foldback speakers in the studio. Later, in his Spanish castle hideaway, Jim plays 'With a Little Help from My Friends' (1969) as interpreted by Joe Cocker – a song loaded with irony here. And Derek and the Dominoes' 'Layla' (1970) plays on the reel-to-reel tape machine as the TV crews arrive for Jim's final interview. All of these songs, working alongside Morris's production design, locate the action in historical time, and, as such, serve to bring the past into the present. Ronco Records again released a double soundtrack LP. Without the benefit of advertising, *Stardust* broke seventy-three of the eighty house records on the opening Saturday in England.[56] The film went on to make a net profit of in excess of £525,000.[57]

Stardust received a mixed response from critics in the USA. In *Variety*, 'Hawk' was generally positive, speculating that 'A potent factor in the success of "Day" was a carefully staged tv/music tie-in launch. It should prove equally useful this time.' The film was also 'strongly and inventively directed by Michael Apted'.[58] But in *Films and Filming*, Alexander Stuart argued that the film had 'a synthetic feel to it'.[59] Strangely placing *Stardust* alongside a British cinematic masterpiece released in the early 1970s, Stuart further suggested that '*Performance*, which was not directly about rock music, says far more about what happened in the 'sixties … than *Stardust* ever could.'[60] Writing in *Time Magazine*, Jay Cocks found the film 'fast, canny, tough-minded'.[61] Nigel Gearing argued that Jim 'has simply swapped anticipatory dreams for a beleaguered nostalgia'.[62] He also pointed out that 'As before, the dominant style is that of Fifties British "New Wave" – a fly-blown mode arguably appropriate to the earlier film's period recreation but effectively undercut here by otherwise energetic attempts to capture a subsequent, more exotic *Zeitgeist*.'[63]

Stardust, then, is a post-Beatles film about the pitfalls of global pop and rock superstardom. As such, it speaks of a culture in the 1970s in which global superstardom and the rock figure as consumer object properly became an idea. It thus resonates with similar themes to The Who's 1969 LP *Tommy* (adapted as a 1975 film by Ken Russell), and chimes with the real-life narratives of the doomed rockers Jimi Hendrix, Jim Morrison, and Janice Joplin, all of whom died young in the early 1970s after living fast in the late 1960s. But perhaps the clearest influence on the figure of Jim

MacLaine in his later manifestations in *Stardust* is David Bowie's flamboyant, sexually ambiguous alter-ego Ziggy Stardust, who was born to the rock world on the British singer's LP *The Rise and Fall of Ziggy Stardust and the Spiders from Mars* (1972). As Alwyn Turner points out, Bowie 'was the first rock artist to speak directly of the chaos that was modern Britain, to admit the failure of post-war dreams of progress and to offer instead an escape into fantasy'.[64] But in 1973, David Bowie killed off his 'Ziggy Stardust' alter-ego and introduced Aladdin Sane to his fans. While Bowie progressed from humble rock 'n' roll beginnings through the figures of Ziggy Stardust and Aladdin Sane; on through the plastic soul of *Young Americans* and his so-called 'thin white duke' (or 'Berlin') period towards further global success in the 1980s, Jim MacLaine's trajectory spirals out of control towards death. As such, the film moves out of the nostalgia mode which so obviously colours *That'll Be the Day*. As Jim is carried out of his Spanish castle after his final live interview, the dream of the 1960s is effectively carried out to an ambulance under a white shroud. Mike has the last word – 'It's a good story, innit!' But David Essex would return to the cinema, as a bus passenger in the US comedy *The Big Bus* (James Frawley, 1976), and later in a starring role in the British film *Silver Dream Racer* (David Wickes, 1980).

Both *That'll Be the Day* and *Stardust* exemplify the fact that there were growing industrial, commercial, and aesthetic links between popular music and British film-making during the 1970s.[65] Indeed, overlaps could be seen occurring between various forms of popular culture from the 1970s onwards.[66] This is evidenced in the many rock, pop, and concert films released during the 1970s. These films often feature British involvement at the level of production. They include *Let it Be* (Michael Lindsay-Hogg, 1970); *200 Motels* (Tony Palmer, Charles Swenson, Frank Zappa, 1971); *Born to Boogie* (Richard Starkey, 1972); *Yessongs* (Peter Neal, 1973); *The London Rock 'n' Roll Show* (Peter Clifton, 1973); *Never Too Young to Rock* (Dennis Abey, 1975); *Exodus – Bob Marley Live* (Keith Macmillan, 1978); and *The Song Remains the Same* (Peter Clifton, Joe Massot, 1976), which documents Led Zeppelin's highly successful 1973 US tour.

But the popularity of British rock music is evident in less obvious places in films of the period, too. For example, *Horror Hospital*

(Antony Balch, 1973) features Robin Askwith as Jason, a songwriter who is convinced a progressive rock band has stolen one of his songs. *The Music Machine* (Ian Sharp, 1979) is a film about a disco-dancing competition. And *That Summer!* (Harley Cokliss, 1979) is a youth film set in Torquay which spawned a successful soundtrack LP. Moreover, the maverick director, Ken Russell, also made a number of music-themed films during the decade, including *The Music Lovers* (1970), *Savage Messiah* (1972), *Mahler* (1974), and *Lisztomania* (1975). The late 1970s saw the rise of the provocative and confrontational punk subculture in Britain. Films which came out of this movement or documented its developments include *The Punk Rock Movie* (Don Letts, 1977), *Jubilee* (Derek Jarman, 1978), and *The Great Rock 'n' Roll Swindle* (Julien Temple, 1979).

A number of British-produced music films of the 1970s focus on black culture and music, or on music that displays the influence of immigrant culture on young, white artists. For example, *Reggae* (Horace Ové, 1970) is a documentary on the still-underground music genre at that time, featuring artists such as Toots and the Maytals, and Millie Small. This film, screened in cinemas and broadcast on BBC television, was the first feature-length film financed by black people in Britain.[67] *Roots Rock Reggae* (Jeremy Marre, 1977), produced by Harcourt Films, is a television film about the Jamaican reggae scene in the mid-1970s. And *Rude Boy* (Jack Hazan and David Mingay, 1980) is a part-fiction, part-documentary film that features footage of the reggae-influenced punk rock group The Clash performing at the 'Rock Against Racism' concert in London's Victoria Park in 1978, showing 'a Britain that was falling apart'.[68] Alexander Walker argued that *Rude Boy* documents 'a frightening and squalid vision of "Two Englands"'.[69] It is to films that specifically deal with racial divisions in a fragmenting 1970s Britain that I now want to turn.

Notes

1 Turner, *Crisis? What Crisis? Britain in the 1970s*, p. 152.
2 Richards, *Films and British National Identity: From Dickens to Dad's Army*, p. 360.

3   Richards, *Films and British National Identity: From Dickens to Dad's Army*,
    p. 360.

4   Other films of the decade that depict events in (or related to) the Second
    World War include *The McKenzie Break* (Lamont Johnson, 1970); *Murphy's
    War* (Peter Yates, 1971); *Adolf Hitler – My Part in His Downfall* (Norman
    Cohen, 1974); *England Made Me* (Peter Duffell, 1973); *The Double Headed
    Eagle* (Lutz Becker, 1973); *Voyage of the Damned* (Stuart Rosenberg, 1976);
    The Eagle Has Landed (John Sturges, 1976); *A Bridge Too Far* (Richard
    Attenborough, 1977); *Cross of Iron* (Sam Peckinpah, 1977); *Force 10 from
    Navarone* (Guy Hamilton, 1978); *The Passage* (J. Lee Thompson, 1978);
    Escape to Athena (George P. Cosmatos, 1979); *Hanover Street* (Peter Hyams,
    1979); and *Yanks* (John Schlesinger, 1979). *The Lady Vanishes* (Anthony
    Page, 1979) tells a story based in pre-war Nazi Germany, and *Inside
    Out* (Peter Duffell, 1975) reflects on Nazi gold looted during the war.
    Examples of First World War films include *Aces High* (Jack Gold, 1976),
    and the television film *All Quiet on the Western Front* (Delbert Mann, 1979).

5   Yule, *David Puttnam: The Story So Far*, p. 84.

6   Yule, *David Puttnam: The Story So Far*, p. 84.

7   Yule, *David Puttnam: The Story So Far*, p. 84.

8   Yule, *David Puttnam: The Story So Far*, p. 87.

9   Higson, 'A Diversity of Film Practices: Renewing British Cinema in the
    1970s', p. 221.

10 Puttnam, *The Undeclared War*, p. 264.

11 Higson, 'A Diversity of Film Practices: Renewing British Cinema in the
    1970s', pp. 221–2.

12 Gavrik Losey, interviewed by the author, 18 May 2007.

13 Gavrik Losey, interviewed by the author, 18 May 2007.

14 Rayns, 'Claude Whatham's Day', p. 84.

15 On the American release of *That'll Be the Day*, a version of Essex
    performing his own composition 'Rock On' replaced 'That'll Be the Day'
    over the end credits.

16 A. Walker, *National Heroes*, p. 71.

17 Lord Puttnam, interviewed by the author, 4 December 2007.

18 A. Walker, *National Heroes*, p. 71.

19 Donnelly, *Pop Music in British Cinema: A Chronicle*, p. 55.

20 Reay, *Music in Film: Soundtracks and Synergy*, p. 28.

21 Donnelly, *Pop Music in British Cinema: A Chronicle*, p. 56.

22 Yule, *David Puttnam: The Story So Far*, p. 62.

23 Reay, *Music in Film: Soundtracks and Synergy*, p. 21.

24 Reay, *Music in Film: Soundtracks and Synergy*, pp. 3–4.

25 Donnelly, *Pop Music in British Cinema: A Chronicle*, p. 54.

26 Donnelly, *Pop Music in British Cinema: A Chronicle*, p. 55.

27 Donnelly, *Pop Music in British Cinema: A Chronicle*, p. 56.

28 'Hawk', 'That'll Be the Day', p. 14.

29 'Hawk', 'That'll Be the Day', p. 14.

30 Fox, 'That'll Be the Day', p. 53.

31 Harper, 'Keynote Lecture: Don't Look Now? British Cinema in the 1970s Conference, University of Exeter, July 2007', p. 27.

32 Whannel, 'Boxed in: Television in the 1970s', p. 192.

33 Whannel, 'Boxed in: Television in the 1970s', p. 192.

34 Booker, *The Seventies: Portrait of a Decade*, p. 32.

35 Hunt, *British Low Culture: From Safari Suits to Sexploitation*, p. 18.

36 Mark Kermode, 'The Film Programme', BBC Radio 4, 6 April 2007.

37 For more on 1970s British music, see Allen, 'British Graffiti: Popular Music and Film in the 1970s'.

38 Edwards, 'On 1970s Music and Nostalgia', Culture, Change and Continuity in the 1970s symposium, Aberystwyth University, 15 September 2011.

39 Monaco, *Ribbons in Time: Movies and Society Since 1945*, p. 100.

40 Davis, *Yearning for Yesterday: A Sociology of Nostalgia*, p. 22.

41 Jameson, 'Postmodernism and Consumer Society', p. 116.

42 Jameson, 'Postmodernism and Consumer Society', p. 116.

43 Jameson, 'Postmodernism and Consumer Society', p. 117.

44 Jameson, 'Postmodernism and Consumer Society', p. 117.

45 Inglis, 'Introduction', p. 85.

46 Inglis, 'The Act You've Known for All These Years: Telling the Tale of The Beatles', p. 86.

47 Wright, 'Score vs. Song: Art, Commerce and the H Factor in Film and Television Music', p. 12.

48 Harper and Smith, *British Film Culture in the 1970s*, p. 195.

49 A. Walker, *National Heroes*, p. 72.

50 Street, *British National Cinema*, p. 143.

51 Reay, *Music in Film: Soundtracks and Synergy*, p. 28.

52 Yule, *David Puttnam: The Story So Far*, p. 89.

53 A. Walker, *National Heroes*, p. 217.

54 A. Walker, *National Heroes*, p. 76.

55 A. Walker, *National Heroes*, p. 78.

56 Yule, *David Puttnam: The Story So Far*, p. 94.

57 A. Walker, *National Heroes*, p. 79.

58 'Hawk', 'Stardust', p. 20.

59 Stuart, 'Stardust', p. 39.

60 Stuart, 'Stardust', p. 39.

61 Cocks, 'Stardust'.

62 Gearing, 'Stardust', p. 229.

63 Gearing, 'Stardust', p. 229.

64 Turner, *Crisis? What Crisis? Britain in the 1970s*, p. 25.

65 Inglis, 'Introduction', *Popular Music and Film*, p. 2.
66 Wright, 'Score vs. Song: Art, Commerce and the H Factor in Film and Television Music', p. 8.
67 Paul Ward; available at www.screenonline.org.uk/people/id/507421; accessed 21 September 2011.
68 A. Walker, *National Heroes*, p. 239.
69 A. Walker, *National Heroes*, p. 239.

4

Immigrant songs:
racial politics

Hunter and the hunted: *The Beast Must Die*

A camera mounted on a helicopter flying over mountainous terrain picks out a lone figure running away into the distance. The soundtrack features funky music – all wah-wah guitar pedals, rapid-fire hi-hats, and stabbing brass. The film cuts to shots of the helicopter pilot wearing sunglasses, scanning the terrain below. We see more hunters in a white Land Rover, chasing the man on the ground. It becomes clear that this man is black, and that he is being chased by white men. He runs into dark woods. Here he is captured on surveillance cameras. His grainy image is viewed on a screen by a grey-haired white man, who sends out instructions about his precise whereabouts to his pursuers. Eventually, the hunted man leaves the woods and stumbles, bedraggled, on to the manicured lawn of an impressive country house. A well-dressed group of people taking drinks *al fresco* watch him staggering towards them. But he is suddenly surrounded by the hunters, and shot. The people on the lawn run to his aid. But it turns out that he has not been shot with a bullet, but with a blank, and that the whole chase has been elaborately staged in order to test impressive security equipment in the house, which, it now becomes clear, is the home of the hunted man, Tom Newcliffe (Calvin Lockhart).

The Beast Must Die (Paul Dannett, 1974) was produced by Amicus and shot at Shepperton Studios. Newcliffe (Lockhart) invites a number of individuals to stay with him at his country mansion for the weekend, as he believes one of them to be a werewolf. As a keen hunter himself (hunting has apparently become his *raison d'être*, both in business and in pleasure), he seeks what he calls 'the biggest prize of all'. Newcliffe tells the designer of his surveillance equipment, Pavel (Anton Diffring), 'In this world you are either the hunter or the hunted.' But the 'neatly constructed'[1] opening sequence of the film described above appears to subvert 1970s audience expectations concerning the representation of blackness on screen. So, while this film was panned by the critics at the time of its release, it remains an interesting historical text in terms of the ways in which it plays with ideological expectations of representations of race. After all, the central protagonist is a young black man who appears to be a rich, powerful, legitimate businessman. But his status as such is never questioned. Indeed, despite the playful nature of the opening sequence, Tom's racial identity is never specifically mentioned or alluded to in the film.

The Beast Must Die was marketed as a horror film, but it clearly also draws from other genres. As such, the film is another example of a 1970s generic hybrid. In some senses, the narrative develops like a murder mystery. Indeed, the film features an innovative 30-second 'werewolf break' in which the audience is invited to mull over the clues they have seen and to attempt to deduce the identity of the werewolf. But in other ways *The Beast Must Die* clearly feels like a British take on US blaxploitation films such as *Sweet Sweetback's Baadasssss Song* (Melvin Van Peebles, 1971) and *Shaft* (Gordon Parks, 1971), primarily through its casting of Lockhart, but also through the stylistics of the music (composed by Douglas Gamley), which is so clearly evocative of the American genre. Tellingly, the film was entitled *Black Werewolf* for the US market. Indeed, blaxploitation had an impact on cinema to such a degree at this time that the James Bond film *Live and Let Die* (Guy Hamilton, 1973) also draws on stylistic aspects of the genre, especially in its New York sequences. *The Beast Must Die* features the British horror stalwart Peter Cushing, but also Charles Gray, who, in the 1970s, played James Bond's nemesis in *Diamonds Are Forever* (Guy Hamilton, 1971) as well as the Criminologist in *The Rocky Horror Picture Show* (Jim Sharman, 1975).

Though the opening sequence of the film and its casting of Lockhart make it an intriguing document concerning contemporary racial politics in British cinema (and the transatlantic influence of blaxploitation in particular), *The Beast Must Die* is not an example of a film which is clearly engaged in an examination of the immigrant experience in Britain. But, as I shall show in this chapter, other films of the period do deal with the struggle of immigrants in 1970s Britain who face racism and injustice, while at the same time attempting to forge a positive sense of identity. These films offer evidence of the ways in which Britain was becoming increasingly fragmented along racial lines, and document the widespread anxieties this caused. Here I shall be focusing primarily on British film representations of individuals of black heritage that appeared during the 1970s.[2]

Rivers of blood: stereotypes and revolution

Welcome to Britain (Ben Lewin, 1976), funded by the British Film Institute Production Board, is a documentary film about the ways in which immigrants and Commonwealth visitors were treated on arrival in Britain. This is just one of a number of interesting films that appeared in the 1970s which sought to engage with the immigrant experience. This was a tense moment in British history in terms of race, exemplified by an infamous series of events involving Enoch Powell, the backbench MP for a Wolverhampton seat, who saw mass immigration, or 'this injection of foreign bodies', as a principle cause of a lack of coherence in contemporary British identity.[3] Powell's ideas were crystallised in his notorious so-called 'rivers of blood' speech, given in Birmingham on 20 April 1968, in which he fiercely criticised Commonwealth immigration to Britain and the government's proposed anti-discrimination legislation. This speech lost him his position in the shadow cabinet, when he was subsequently sacked by Conservative party leader, Edward Heath, but the message appeared to strike an ominous chord. The historian Alwyn Turner argues that 'The fallout from that single speech changed British politics entirely.'[4] During a later election address in Wolverhampton in 1970, Powell further warned that immigration carried 'a threat of division, violence and bloodshed of American dimensions, and adds a powerful weapon to the armoury of anarchy'.[5] The image of Britain as a fragmenting nation at this time was thus further heightened by the highly visible racial divisions exploited by Powell and his apologists.[6]

By the beginning of the 1970s, a number of political developments and specific events served to highlight racial divisions. For example, while the Immigration Act 1971 felt like a positive step in securing rights for individuals moving to Britain, in effect it did little to reassure non-white communities.[7] Indeed, discrimination against blacks persisted well beyond the passing of the Race Relations Act 1976. Turner argues that 'The radicalization of race as a political issue in Britain was primarily the result of the growing strength of the National Front and the increasing levels of street violence; in the five years from 1976, there were some thirty-one racist murders of non-whites, primarily in east London and the Midlands.'[8] But the Anti-Nazi League was launched in response to these events, and staged counter-demonstrations on most of the occasions that the racist National Front took to the streets.

South Africa, which had become a republic in 1961 and left the British Commonwealth in 1968 (but which still had to negotiate the legacies of British colonial rule, rejoining the Commonwealth in 1994), provides the setting for two mainstream films of the period. The action adventure film *Gold* (Peter Hunt, 1974), starring Roger Moore and Susannah York, tells the story of criminal activity surrounding a South African goldmine, alongside a developing romance between Moore's and York's characters. And *The Wild Geese* (Andrew V. McLaglen, 1977) follows the adventures of a group of mercenaries played by Richard Burton, Richard Harris, Roger Moore, and Hardy Krüger.[9] According to Robert Stam and Louise Spence, this film glorifies the activities of white mercenaries and depicts the killing of Africans *en masse* as a means of fostering camaraderie between these men.[10] Both these films were heavily criticised at the time of their release for being shot in South Africa under the apartheid regime. Indeed, protestors picketed the London premiere of *The Wild Geese*.

So, if Britain was a nation going through an identity crisis in the 1970s, its fragmentary status had at least something to do with the politics of race, and, at the same time, the legacies of the empire. As such, it is no surprise that British films of the decade represent racial difference in telling ways. Thoughtful and challenging films appeared which concern themselves with the complexities of the immigrant experience (I shall discuss them in this chapter). But they are arguably outnumbered by films that represent 'Othered' communities in broadly negative or at least problematical terms. Indeed, films of this type are almost too numerous to mention. For example, though the film is clearly a satire, Lindsay Anderson's *O Lucky Man!* offers examples of representations of black people that arguably speak of the troubled racial politics of early 1970s Britain. We might remember the so-called 'chocolate sandwich' sex sequence at the party in the hotel, which features a black man and two white women, and Arthur Lowe's blackface portrayal of the venal Dr Munda. But other examples of films that feature often negative representations of blacks include *Gumshoe* (Stephen Frears, 1971), which stars Albert Finney as Eddie Ginley, a Liverpool comedian who dreams of becoming a private eye of the type usually found in pulp novels. This film features a now notorious sequence in which Ginley uses racist language in an argument with a black man.[11] Meanwhile, on television, the soap *Crossroads* (ATV/Central, 1964–88) introduced its first black character, Melanie Harper (Cleo Sylvestre) in January 1970. But she featured in a storyline that saw her trying to smuggle her boyfriend into the country illegally.[12] The comedy series *Rising Damp* (BBC, 1974–78) derived much of its comedy from the relationship between the landlord, Rigsby (Leonard Rossiter), and his well-spoken black lodger, Philip (Don Warrington). Moreover, infamous representations of racism frequently occurred in *Till Death Us Do Part* (BBC, 1965–68; 1970; 1972–76) and in *Love Thy Neighbour* (Thames, 1972–76). The BBC drama *Black Christmas* (Stephen Frears, 1977) – written by Michael Abbensetts and broadcast on 20 December – sees a black family and their white neighbour spend a troublesome festive period together. Most of the tension is generated by the family trying to come to terms with white British culture but also dealing with nostalgia for their West Indian heritage.

There were some more obviously positive representations of black people evident in films shot in Britain (or featuring British characters) in the 1970s. An example is Johnny Sekka's portrayal of Bob Kirby in *Incense for the Damned* (aka *Blockbusters*) (Robert Hartford-Davis, 1971), a film that sees a black man play a brave, likeable and heroic figure who, while searching for Richard Fountain (Patrick Mower) in Greece, fights off Penelope's (Madeleine Hinde) attackers, and tries to save Major Longbow (Patrick Macnee) as he hangs from a high cliff. And *A Warm December* (Sidney Poitier, 1972) tells the story of the recently widowed Dr Matt Younger (Poitier) who runs a clinic in a ghettoised area of Washington, DC, in the USA. As a doctor, he is a man of means, and he travels to England for a holiday with his daughter, Stephanie (Yvette Curtis). Here he falls in love with the mysterious African princess, Catherine (played by Jamaican actress Esther Anderson). This film – produced by First Artists and filmed at Pinewood Studios – is something of a rarity, showing, as it does, transnational, middle-class black characters in Britain in a positive light as successful professional people.

Other films of the period also develop nuanced takes on racial politics. *Man Friday* (Jack Gold, 1975), for example, is an adaptation of the 1973 play by Adrian Mitchell, which itself is based on Daniel Defoe's novel *Robinson Crusoe* (1719). This film effectively reverses the roles of Crusoe and Friday. Here, Crusoe (Peter O'Toole) is a blunt Englishman, while Man Friday (Richard Roundtree) is an altogether more intelligent figure. As such, *Man Friday* operates as a critique of colonisation and Western imperialism, but also, at the same time, as an examination of contemporary race relations. This film was a UK/US co-production, backed by Lew Grade's ITC and ABC Motion Pictures. Another film that demonstrates the problematical relationship between Britain and its disintegrating empire is *Game for Vultures* (James Fargo, 1979), a Columbia Pictures thriller starring Richard Harris and Richard Roundtree. Set in the late 1970s, during the last years of the Rhodesian Bush War, this film tells the story of attempts by David Swansey (Harris) to import a number of helicopters which might be used in the fight against insurgents led by Gideon Marunga (Roundtree). *Game for Vultures* can be read in a postcolonial context – Rhodesia declared unilateral independence from Britain in 1965, but remained unrecognised as a state until 1979. It became the Republic of Zimbabwe in 1980.

But while racial stereotypes proliferated across British cinema and television, the 1970s was also a key period of artistic innovation among immigrant communities. For example, *A Private*

Enterprise (Peter K. Smith, 1974), backed by the British Film Institute Production Board, was the first British film to depict the lives of a British Asian community in a realistic way. Black culture was celebrated during this period, too. Writing in a book published in 1987, Lauretta Ngcobo argues that 'A few years ago there was nothing called Black British Art and Culture. Today there is.'[13] Examples of these types of positive artistic developments include the creation of the Black Theatre of Brixton and the Black Theatre Co-operative. The Notting Hill Carnival also expanded considerably during the decade. In the field of poetry, the work of Linton Kwesi Johnson managed to richly capture aspects of the politics of race in modern Britain.[14] Meanwhile, in cinema, an important and influential film appeared, made by black people, and centred on black urban experience.

Bacon and eggs, or avocado? *Pressure*

The Western metropole must confront its postcolonial history, told by its influx of postwar migrants and refugees, as an indigeneous or native internal to its national identity.

Homi K. Bhabha[15]

Made in 1975, *Pressure* was directed by Trinidadian-born Horace Ové, scripted by Trinidadian-born writer Sam Selvon, and backed by the British Film Institute Production Board after an intense struggle to get the film financed. Alexander Walker points out that 'In spite of its urgency (and moderation), *Pressure* had to wait over two years to get a commercial showing: it is not being unduly cynical to suggest that the Notting Hill race riots on August Bank Holiday 1978 helped it "surface".'[16] This powerful and influential film is concerned with racial prejudice and injustice in 1970s London. It is notable for the anger and passion displayed by black characters and, at the same time, the hatred evidently felt for these characters by many white Britons. *Pressure* features a number of non-actors, was partly improvised, and was shot on location in the Ladbroke Grove area of west London. The film follows the travails of a likeable black teenager, Tony (Herbert Norville), who was born in London to immigrants from Trinidad. It documents Tony's efforts to secure a job on leaving school, and though we see that he is clearly capable (having passed his O-level examinations), potential employers treat him with suspicion, primarily because of the colour of his skin. As a result of continued rejections, Tony grows increasingly disillusioned and alienated from the white British culture he had previously embraced. Indeed, he gradually begins to see casual and overt racism almost everywhere.

The 'pressure' of the film's title is applied to Tony from a variety of angles. His parents, Lucas (Frank Singuineau) and Bopsie (Lucita Lijertwood), hardworking immigrants of the *Windrush* generation, have sacrificed much to raise him, and are frustrated by his apparent inability to move into a steady career in London. His older brother, Colin (Oscar James), however, was born in Trinidad, and aggressively maintains his black identity as a means of surviving in what he sees as a white-run, racist nation. Tony initially has a number of white friends, but because he does not manage to get a job, he finds he is forced to accept their charity. He then begins to mix with other disillusioned young blacks, who indulge in petty crime and smoke marijuana. Subsequent circumstances lead Tony to confront the realities of the world in which he finds himself, and he begins to move closer to sharing Colin's outlook on black politics. We see Tony angrily challenge his parents about their conformity to a way of life in a country that does no more than treat them as second-class citizens. He is further moved to drift towards radical politics when a black power event he is attending is raided by the police, and Colin is arrested and fitted up as a suspected drug dealer. After Colin's arrest, the family's flat is smashed up by the police, further forcing Tony to acknowledge the levels to which white racism has become institutionalised in modern Britain. The film ends with a rained-out demonstration by the black power group outside the Old Bailey. Overall, *Pressure* demonstrates that Tony ultimately finds himself inhabiting a liminal socio-cultural space. He has grown up with an awareness of (even an admiration of) white British culture, and still in his heart he cannot believe that all whites are prejudiced. But he is black, and he comes to the realisation that this blackness must become a source of pride if he is to make a life in a racist nation.

On its release, reviews of *Pressure* were generally positive. Writing in *Monthly Film Bulletin* in April 1978, David Wilson saw it as a 'film about options'. *Pressure*'s achievement 'is to have so persuasively incorporated within its narrative format a set of options which succinctly characterise the position of blacks in Britain'.[17] It was also a successful film for Wilson because Tony sees beyond the points of view of his parents and his brother to begin to fully understand the immense complexities of his predicament. In doing this, Wilson argued, Tony articulates the real contemporary issues confronting blacks in Britain: 'whether their position is specifically a symptom of white racism, discreet or otherwise, or generally a condition of the social and political system under which they happen to live and which equally affects the majority of whites'.[18] *Pressure* certainly speaks of the ongoing struggle of immigrants trying to make lives for themselves in Britain, but also of the ways in which the increased visibility of immigration brought about profound shifts in how the nation saw itself.

One of the key themes of *Pressure*, and an inventive way of exploring identity politics, is food. After the pencil sketches of black experience featured in the opening credits sequence, the film cuts to a close-up of a frying pan, with bacon and eggs bubbling away in hot fat. Bopsie is cooking breakfast for Tony, who walks into the kitchen putting on a tie. Much is made in this sequence of the ways in which everyday cultural choices impact upon the immigrant sense of identity. Tony's food choice here – bacon and eggs – clearly marks him as a second-generation immigrant who initially chooses to embrace mythological aspects of British culture. Tony's older brother, Colin, on the other hand, chooses a breakfast of avocado and hot pepper sauce. A conversation ensues about the merits of each particular food. This sequence is shot from a variety of angles, bringing the room to life; bringing the audience into the home space of this family, and therefore into a space of tension fuelled by fiercely-contested identity politics. For example, speaking of Tony, Bopsie tells Colin, 'Don't forget he is not like us. He was born here.'

But elsewhere in the film, food provides ways of dealing with other complicated issues concerning British identity. When Tony and a young female acquaintance wander home after a dance and stop to pick up a late night snack at a Kentucky Fried Chicken outlet, the choice of fast food establishment here can be taken as a sign of the creeping power of American consumer culture in Britain at that historical moment (the first British McDonald's restaurant opened in London in 1974). But Tony's journey towards Colin's vision of blackness is symbolised by his later food choices. Just before the end of the film – after Tony's attempts to find work in white Britain are thwarted; after he has been racially discriminated against by his young woman friend's landlady; and after he returns home from the police station – he chooses to eat rice. The camera faces him, seated at the now-familiar kitchen table. A hand reaches across and passes him a bottle of pepper sauce from outside the frame, as if to welcome him into black consciousness.

In terms of its formal and aesthetic structure, performances and iconography, *Pressure* mixes cinematic influences, and is another British generic hybrid of the period. There are moments in the film which are naturalist in style, such as the improvised sequences shot at the market in Ladbroke Grove, when Tony's young black friends indulge in petty crime, thieving fruit from market stalls. Shots of these same young men in a supermarket certainly offer documentary evidence of life in London in the mid-1970s, capturing as they do the type of consumer culture that was coming to shape the modern nation. Here the camera picks out piles of colourful cans and Green Shield stamps signs. A documentary realist style is also evident in sequences in the church, and at the black power meeting, both of which feature members of the real Ladbroke Grove community.

But elsewhere the film moves away from documentary realist aesthetics in significant and sometimes even shocking ways. The sequences featuring dialogue are reminiscent of British social realist film-making. But other sequences feel more obviously modernist in their formal qualities. This is achieved through inventive editing and multiple camera angles. In the sequence in which Tony goes to work at a hospital, cross-cutting makes it appear as if he is in two places at once. The later drugs raid is captured with hand-held cameras, lending the action energy and a sense of urgency. Another intriguing example of editing in the film occurs when Tony has a flashback – a memory from childhood of a school playground – which features modified sound.

But the most extraordinary example in *Pressure* of a move away from the aesthetics of documentary realism, social realism, and naturalism towards modernism and the avant-garde comes towards the end of the film. A cut takes us abruptly from a scene in which the young black activists are smoking and talking in a house. Tony has been handed a joint, and has apparently fallen asleep on the sofa. We are suddenly in a bedroom at night. Having seemingly just slept with her, Tony leaves Sister Louise (Sheila Scott-Wilkinson) in bed. He dresses slowly and quietly, takes a knife from a chest of drawers, and leaves. The film cuts to a shot of Louise, now awake, her head lifted up off the pillow. Slowly, the camera zooms in on her face, which has a knowing, wise look. Is the following action to be read as Tony's stoned daydream? This much remains unclear at this stage. The film cuts to a dark street. Tony wanders past the Mangrove restaurant and down another street. Suddenly we are in daylight. Tony walks close to high iron gates. The faint sound of African singers can be heard on the soundtrack. So too can birdsong. Tony subsequently climbs over the gates and walks through gardens, towards the camera. On he walks, through well-tended plants and shrubs, past looming statues; his feet crunching through scattered autumn leaves. Gradually the camera picks out an impressive Georgian mansion house – no doubt built with wealth accumulated in the British colonies. Tony walks towards this building. The film cuts to an interior. A bed is situated in the middle of a dark room. Tony, now naked, approaches this bed, and begins stabbing a body which lies hidden under pink silk sheets. Blood pours from this body. Eventually, the body rolls out of the bed. It now becomes clear that this is a pig. Blood pours from the head of the animal and on to the wooden floor. The next shot is of Tony, in close up. He appears to be drowsy; waking up.

This, then, we might read as a drug-fuelled daydream sequence. But the ontological status of these images remains ambiguous. Parts of this sequence certainly do not take place in the 'real' diegetic world in which the central narrative of the film unfolds. As such, the sequence echoes in some ways the work of surrealists Luis Buñuel and Salvador Dali (most obviously their 1929 masterpiece *Un Chien Andalou*) among others. If this is a daydream or fantasy, Stewart Home argues that Tony's killing of the pig symbolises a battle against the establishment and, specifically, the police (still widely reviled in common parlance as 'pigs'). Home points out that this pig 'simultaneously harks back to the opening scene in which Colin criticises Tony's liking for white English food, and specifically bacon. Likewise, to the many black power activists who embraced the Muslim faith, 'pork was impure and they refuse to eat it.'[19] Interestingly, Home further argues that this pig-stabbing sequence might lead hypothetical white viewers to imagine a white woman in the bed before a pig is revealed, and that this expectation would be primarily driven by racist fears surrounding instances of black men engaging in sexual relations with white women. This is a rich idea, but it comes close to conjecture. Ové does nothing to clearly suggest this.

There is another potential reading of this sequence. In terms of its formal hybridity, it echoes developments seen in the work of a number of postcolonial writers and theorists who were attempting to develop new ways of articulating aspects of black experience that might resist the rigid binaries of 'Self' and 'Other'. After all, the sequence, as it develops, does not clearly signal a shift from reality to fantasy. Instead, it draws upon the aesthetics of both representational systems in order to construct a hybrid territory.

Michael Dash notes how the West Indian writers Stephen Aléxis (Haitian) and Wilson Harris (Guyanese) turn to myths, legends and superstitions of the 'folk' in order to develop a new aesthetic, because 'colonization and slavery did not make things of men, but in their own way the enslaved peoples might have in their own imagination so recorded their reality as to reach beyond the tangible and concrete to acquire a new re-creative sensibility which could aid in the harsh battle for survival.'[20] Dash argues that these writers thus effectively circumvent the 'ironies of history' in order to avoid the 'negativity of pure protest.'[21] In other words, a new language might move outside and beyond the discourses of the oppressed and oppressor. In such a way, the formal qualities of their work 'would signify an adoption of the positive imaginative reconstruction of reality developed in the consciousness of the folk, by the contemporary writer.'[22] In the dream sequence in *Pressure*, the sound of black singers certainly evokes black consciousness, while the image track serves to subvert the ideologies of Western iconography as Tony wanders through the gardens – an archetype of the historical white Western desire to design and control territories. So the sequence does not straightforwardly operate as reality followed by fantasy, but rather speaks of another indeterminate, 'inbetween' language, which also, at the same time, is evocative of aspects of white culture and black folk culture and heritage.

In his influential book *The Location of Culture* (1994), Homi K. Bhabha reflects on the ways in which cultural difference might be articulated in terms other than the binaries of 'Otherness':

> What is at issue is the performative nature of differential identities: the regulation and negotiation of those spaces that are continually, *contingently*, 'opening out', remaking the boundaries, exposing the limits of any claim to a singular or autonomous sign of difference – be it class, gender or race. Such assignations of social differences – where difference is neither One nor the Other but *something else besides, in-between* – find their agency in a form of the 'future' where the past is not originatory, where the present is not simply transitory. [emphasis in original][23]

Bhabha writes of the liminality of the migrant experience – 'no less a transitional phenomenon than a translational one'[24] – and suggests that 'The "newness" of migrant or minority discourse has to be discovered *in media res*: a newness that is not part of the "progressivist" division between past and present, or the archaic and the modern: nor is it a "newness" that can be contained in the mimesis of "original and copy".'[25] Elsewhere in his book, Bhabha focuses on a Moroccan daydream recalled by Roland Barthes, as he remembers the effect of hearing, half-asleep, foreign voices in a bar.[26] For Bhabha, Barthes's daydream – a 'hybrid moment outside the sentence' – was 'not quite experience, not yet concept; part dream, part analysis; neither signifier nor signified'. This is evocative, then, of a possible postcolonial discourse which might become 'one of indeterminism, unexpectability, one that is neither "pure" contingency or negativity nor endless deferral'.[27] Thus we might read Tony's daydream in *Pressure* as similarly evocative of a new postcolonial discourse, which, in its temporary refusal to align itself with white discourse or an 'Othered' black voice of protest, articulates a subaltern consciousness in terms of relocation and reinscription. As Bhabha puts it in another context, 'a curious indeterminacy enters the chain of discourse. This becomes the space for a new discursive temporality, another place of enunciation that will not allow the argument to expand into an unproblematic generality'.[28] It is significant that Tony's daydream is framed by activity in the house occupied by the black power activists, as the dream temporarily pulls Tony away from their oppositional politics towards a space that is 'ex-centric, interruptive, in-between, on the borderlines, turning inside outside'.[29]

Pressure, then, is a formally inventive piece of work which draws upon realist traditions while at the same time choosing to subvert them. But Horace Ové has demonstrated a mastery of documentary aesthetics elsewhere. He has made a range of factual documentary and realist fiction films including *Reggae* (1970); *King Carnival* (1973) – a film made for the *World About Us* television series on BBC2; and *The Skateboard Kings* (1978), made for the same series. *A Hole in Babylon*, co-written by Ové and Jim Hawkins, was broadcast on BBC television as part of the *Play for Today* series in 1979.[30] This drama is based on events leading up to the Spaghetti House siege in London in September 1975, when the robbery of an Italian restaurant by three black men developed into a full blown siege. *A Hole in Babylon* develops an aesthetic that mixes drama-documentary with archive footage.[31] At the time of (and after) the release of *Pressure*, other film-makers began to tell stories of black immigrant communities in a style that very much echoes aspects of Ové's film.

Dickensian dub: *Black Joy*

Films are not necessarily good because black people make them. They are not necessarily 'right-on' by virtue of the fact that they deal with black experience.

Stuart Hall[32]

If *Pressure* offers insights into a nation fragmenting along racial lines, or the development of a new, more obviously multicultural identity for the British, other films of the period explore similar thematic territory. One example is *Black Joy* (Anthony Simmons, 1977). This film was also low-budget, costing less that £300,000 to make, with the National Film Finance Corporation (NFFC) providing approximately half of the funds.[33] Other finance was provided by West One, an independent production company run by the American, Elliott Kastner. Kastner usually looked towards action films and casting major stars to ensure profits for the films that he backed, but in this case he was prepared to make a low-budget 'quality' film with high cultural capital, which could be screened at the Cannes Film Festival.[34] Anthony Simmons was the (white) director, but *Black Joy* is 'notable for its all black cast'.[35]

Like *Pressure*, *Black Joy* is set in the mid-1970s. The film begins with a credits sequence featuring location shots of Brixton (south London) – grey, drab, and damp, with the reggae soundtrack providing the only warmth (a soundtrack LP was released by Ronco). The film tells the story of a Guyanese immigrant, Ben Jones (Trevor Thomas), who arrives at Heathrow Airport on an Air Jamaica flight with one suitcase and a wallet full of money. The white immigration officials are suspicious, immediately treating him like a criminal. The film cuts to a black cleaner, hunched over a bucket, who is mopping the floor – a clear sign that Britain might not be as welcoming as black immigrants would hope. Ben is subsequently subjected to a rectal examination by immigration officers. This strip-search sees him violated symbolically by the white man before he has even entered the country. After this humiliation, Ben travels to Brixton. Here he meets (and is robbed by) a cheeky young boy, Devon (Paul Medford) – a twentieth-century, black Artful Dodger. Indeed, this film feels Dickensian in a number of ways, not least in its grim London settings, its range of strong characters, and its development of a tale documenting financial struggle and hardship.[36]

Intriguingly, *Black Joy* appears to demonstrate a distinct lack of solidarity within the black community. We see Devon having Ben's wallet taken off him by Dave King (Norman Beaton), a charismatic petty crook and lover of Devon's mother, Miriam (Floella Benjamin). Ben also loses money to a fraudulent landlord. Moreover, this is a community characterised by casual sex and broken families, drug-taking, and foul language. The men are happy to visit prostitutes and sex shops. But there is hope in this community. Miriam (Benjamin) is a strong, independent woman, evidently not afraid to stand up to the misogynistic men in her life. During one confrontation, Dave shouts at her 'Woman been fightin' for de power, but let me tell you something, babe, we ain't equal yet, no fuckin' way.' Miriam balks at this sexist remark. The film shows Brixton to be a ghettoised space defined in terms of social, political, ideological, and racial struggles. Having said this, Anthony Simmons often gives the film a light-hearted or even comedic tone. Dylan Cave argues that the film, in its vivid depiction of strong characters, action-led narrative and vibrant soundtrack, has led to comparisons with 1970s American blaxploitation.[37] Stylistically, Cave argues, *Black Joy* 'shares some of the genre's tropes with flamboyant costume designs; an extremely episodic narrative motivated by dramatic confrontation; exaggerated protagonists with sharp dialogue and a fetishism of the urban ghetto'.[38] This appropriation of the aesthetics of blaxploitation is best exemplified by the trip that Ben, Dave, Miriam, and Saffar (Dawn Hope) take to Margate, on the Kent coast, in a large Buick. Overall, this sequence has a warm and amusing tone. We see the group dressed in funky clothes, enjoying an evening in a club. The sequence clearly provides a much-needed break for the characters (but also the audience) from the tense claustrophobia of Brixton. But Cave further points out that 'The ghettoised setting – within a mostly black populated Brixton – creates a hermetically sealed world for the (larger, non-black) audience to peer into, delighting in their petty crime, fast insults and sexual titillation.'[39] And at the time of the film's release, David Badder noticed that 'the question of integration with the white population is completely excluded'.[40] So this is a complex film which supports a range of readings in terms of its depiction of blackness in 1970s Britain.

Interestingly, Andrew Spicer and Josie Dolan notice what they see as *Black Joy*'s marginal position within existing interpretative frameworks, which tend to be split between 'white misrepresentation' and 'resistant black representations'.[41] They argue that the film 'does not lend itself to conventional critiques suggesting that white directors reproduce the imperial gaze through a reliance on stereotypical characters or generic verisimilitude'.[42] On the contrary, they advocate that *Black Joy* 'is interspersed with scenes that interrogate the white gaze and which expose institutionalised racist strategies'.[43] Spicer and Dolan offer the opening immigration hall sequence (mentioned earlier) as an example of this, which they suggest 'illuminates the extent to which the black body is constituted as a site of the colonising white gaze and white regulatory regimes'. In doing this, the film effectively produces 'a marginal gaze that is neither white and colonising nor black and resistant'.[44] This is a broadly generous response to the racial politics of the film, which lend it an air of radicalism. Others have been more critical. Akua Rugg argues that *Black Joy* does no more than pander to 'white society's prurient interest in certain aspects of black social life'.[45] This has clearly been a key problem with the film for a number of critics. Linked to this is the non-black racial profile of the director, Simmons, and the issue of how far his 'whiteness' might impact upon any 'authenticity' the film may lay claim to in its representation of black culture.

Great black hope: *Babylon*

Another film that throws up similar problems concerning whose view of the black community we are witnessing is *Babylon* (1980), directed by the Italian immigrant Franco Rosso, which captures tensions developing between the black community, local whites, and the police in south London during the late 1970s. *Babylon* was filmed entirely on location (mainly in Deptford), and was produced independently by Gavrik Losey, who had worked in British cinema since the late 1950s, with, among others, Lindsay Anderson on *If...* (1968); Tony Richardson on *Laughter in the Dark* (1969), *Hamlet* (1969), and *Ned Kelly* (1970); and, as we have seen, David Puttnam on *Melody* (aka *S.W.A.L.K.*) (1971), *That'll Be the Day* (1973), and *Stardust* (1974).[46] Although white, Franco Rosso had considerable experience in dealing with black stories. He had worked with Horace Ové – editing *Reggae* (1970) – and went to Trinidad to operate second camera and edit Ové's documentary *King Carnival* for the BBC. Ové's influence can certainly be seen in *Babylon* in terms of its formal and aesthetic qualities, but also in terms of its subject matter. Interestingly, Rosso and Ové also both directed two parts of a drama series for Peter Ansorge at BBC Birmingham, *East End at Your Feet*, based on the 1976 book of short stories by Farrukh Dhondy.

Babylon, like *Pressure* and *Black Joy*, has its roots in the social realist and documentary traditions of British film-making. Visually, the film recalls the work of Ken Loach in particular. Indeed, Rosso has admitted that the presence of the cinematographer Chris Menges (who worked with Loach on *Kes*) on the shoot was 'very, very, very important', and that the finished film owed much to his vision.[47] *Babylon* attempts to offer a realistic portrayal of young black men living in south London in the 1970s who are trying to forge a positive identity for themselves by embracing the Jamaican 'toasting' musical culture of the sound systems that was proving so popular at the time.[48] Blue (Brinsley Forde – a singer with Aswad) is a toaster with Ital Lion, a sound system preparing to enter a competition. Before this competition, Blue loses both his job and his girlfriend, is arrested by the police on a 'sus' charge, and is racially abused. The Ital Lion sound system is trashed by racists, too, and, in his rage at the injustice he has witnessed, Blue stabs with a screwdriver the man he thinks is responsible for this act, before turning up at the toasting competition and losing himself in his performance.[49] Overall, the film attempts to offer a balanced and truthful representation of black culture. In *Babylon*, these young men are not depicted as black stereotypes, but as complex and likeable individuals struggling to live in a 1970s urban Britain plagued by racism, poverty, and injustice.

At the black power meeting in *Pressure*, Sister Louise (Sheila Scott-Wilkinson) tells the assembled group, 'Music is one of the most important parts of the black man's heritage.' *Pressure* features a reggae soundtrack which provides a rich rhythm to the lives of the characters and to the film itself. But music is also absolutely central to *Babylon*. It provides young black men living in south London with a shared sense of identity forged in their West Indian heritage. And reggae also provides one of the central aesthetic pleasures of the film, featuring Jah Shaka, Mighty Observer, and Rootsman Hi Fi.[50] Like Anthony Simmons' film *Black Joy*, *Babylon* employs realist visual aesthetics alongside a pumping reggae soundtrack. Indeed, a *Babylon* soundtrack LP was released, and enjoyed considerable chart success.[51] But the pleasures of the reggae soundtracks in these films were not there purely for a black audience and black listeners. As Spicer and Dolan point out, in *Black Joy*, 'Reggae fuses the distinctive rhythms of Afro-Caribbean culture with an emergent language of political protest and it was the first indigenous form of black British music. Moreover, its popularity cuts across both white and black identities.'[52]

Babylon was screened in the Critic's Week at the Cannes Film Festival in May 1980, and at the Toronto Festival of Festivals, where it drew a favourable response. According to David Robinson, the black life depicted in the film is 'lively and resilient'. He also felt that *Babylon* offered a 'wholly believable, unsentimentalized, unglamorized feeling' of what it is like to belong to a black community in London'.[53] Derek Malcolm found *Babylon* to be a 'genuinely good film in a year when we are much in need of something that isn't put together simply and solely to make a box-office killing'. He thought it 'a good, old-fashioned, liberal film'.[54] Writing in the *New Statesman*, John Coleman thought that *Babylon* was 'a good, disturbing movie, at once raw and accomplished, about a bad, disturbed area of our national life'. Though he did not write a glowing review, he urged his readers to go and see a film which is 'vibrant, busy, painful, provocative and *there*'.[55] Alan Brien wrote that the film was 'one of the best British-made films for years', with 'shock potential'.[56] And in the *Daily Telegraph*, David Castell pointed out that while the film is not the work of black film-makers, 'It has taken an American-born producer, Gavrik Losey, and an Italian-born director – each brought up in Britain but owning national allegiance elsewhere – to shake a stick at our complacency.'[57]

Interestingly, a reporter for *The New Standard*, Guy Pierce, accompanied three black youths (all under 18) to a preview of *Babylon*. They found the film to be an authentic representation: 'It's very true to life. That's exactly the way it happens,' said Peter. They thought, moreover, that the action in the film was 'a little toned down'. Indeed, of the scene in which Blue is followed and picked up on a 'sus' charge by plain-clothes policemen, who give him a severe beating, Peter said 'He was lucky they didn't plant anything on him. If you run from a policeman you've got to make sure you're not caught.' Further points made by these youths were particularly prescient. Brian said 'It's a very fair reflection on the way things are.' Peter added 'It should go down well in Brixton and Tooting.' Overall, they thought that the film was 'wicked'.[58]

In the USA, *Variety* called the film a 'Fiery, first rate debut feature on an inflammable theme ... a British film with more heart and soul than any home-produced feature of the last 20 years. Like the reggae music that pulses through it, *Babylon* is rich, rough and real. And like the streetlife of the young black Londoners it portrays, it's threatening, touching, violent and funny.'[59] The *Variety* reviewer also argued that 'Though blacks aren't the only likely audience, cautious handling would seem advisable in markets where to depict a bunch of young rebellious immigrants as ostensible "heroes" could be read as provocative', and that 'One key to the film's success is its lack of an overt social or political message. It presents a hard-edged narrative centred on three-dimensional characters, most of whom are black – and the chain of events appears to develop its own momentum, rather than one imposed by script or direction.'[60] *Babylon* made quite an impact in Britain for a brief period of time. The principle actors, Trevor Laird and Brinsley Forde, made the front cover of the popular weekly London magazine *Time Out* (No. 551, 7–13 November 1980) under the headline 'Great Black Hope'. And the critical reputation of the film continued to build into the following year, as Franco Rosso stepped up to receive the 1981 *Evening Standard* British Film Award for Most Promising Film-Maker.[61] But after a short run in cinemas, the film effectively vanished from public view, before eventually being released on DVD in 2008. The lack of initial box-office success of the film can be put down at least in part to its being given an X certificate by the BBFC, but also the fact that the patois spoken by the principal characters proved difficult for audiences to understand – and the film was not subtitled.[62]

British realism in the 1970s

One can locate a number of connections, then, between *Pressure*, *Black Joy*, and *Babylon*. All three films are interested in contemporary black urban experience, and all three locate dub and reggae as a key cultural reference point for black youth, and celebrate the raw power of this influential music genre. The three films also incorporate the formal qualities of realism to varying but noticeable degrees. I want to now to consider the possible ramifications of this: why did these film-makers choose to tell their stories in this way stylistically, and what questions does this potentially raise about the ideological complexity of these films?

In their book, *Realism and Popular Cinema* (2000), Julia Hallam and Margaret Marshment begin with a basic definition of realism as a 'mode of representation that, at the formal level, aims at verisimilitude (or mimesis)', pointing out that 'Allied to the more formal concept of realism as verisimilitude is the notion of truth telling.'[63] André Bazin (whose ideas were published translated into English in 1967 in *What Is Cinema?*) argued that a properly realistic cinema allows spectators the freedom to choose their own interpretation of the events unfolding on-screen. This could be achieved by employing depth-of-field shooting and long takes. In Italian neo-realist films, for example, location shooting captures the lives of common people. In these films – such as *Bicycle Thieves* (aka *Ladri di biciclette*) (Vittorio De Sica, 1948) – time was spent depicting apparently trivial, quotidian events in order to develop a vision of the realities of everyday life.[64] Interestingly, in this critical work on neo-realism, the importance of shifts in technology has been noted, such as the increased employment of hand-held cameras, and the use of natural light. *Pressure*, *Black Joy*, and *Babylon* all demonstrate aspects of this film-making legacy.

In terms of British cinema, realism has historically been employed by film-makers (but also critics) to differentiate British productions from those of Hollywood. In other words, realism has been used to project aesthetics of 'Britishness' through the employment of settings and situations which are recognisably familiar.[65] It is intriguing therefore that Horace Ové, Anthony Simmons, and Franco Rosso chose to make films about black, urban experience by employing realist aesthetics. Perhaps this is no surprise, as British realist films have 'entailed creating representations that audiences would recognise as truthful accounts of their experiences'.[66] In other words, realism is a film-making language that already had a pedigree and an audience in British cinemas.

Thus we might view *Pressure*, *Black Joy*, and *Babylon* as together forming another realist moment in British cinema history, following the documentary movement of the 1930s (which often aimed to project a 'national community'), the Free Cinema movement of the 1950s, and the British 'New Wave', 'kitchen sink' dramas of the late 1950s and early 1960s, which were also characterised by social comment. These 1970s films about black culture, then, engage with questions of Britishness in a new decade, and operate as powerful social commentaries. Like the 'New Wave' films, for example, *Pressure* features, in Tony, an essentially aspirational, working-class character. Furthermore, Hallam and Marshment argue that 'Not only did the New Wave films break up the stale clichés of studio convention, creating an exciting intervention into the depiction of working-class characters at the time by placing them at the centre of the narrative, but they encouraged the vision of an independent, de-centred, regionally-based filmmaking practice rooted in local writers, actors and filmmakers.'[67] *Pressure*, *Black Joy*, and *Babylon* can thus be understood within the context of a film industry which had been changed by the path-breaking successes of British social realism.

But if the realist films of the 1970s which document black experience can be read as extensions of the type of British films of the 1950s and 1960s that brought previously under-represented British communities to the screen, they are also open to similar criticisms. Marxist critics accused the New Wave form of realism of fetishising characters in grim urban landscapes, and of creating a kind of surface realism (or even naturalism) rather than depicting 'real' working-class people and the 'real conditions of working-class life' (for such critics, '*socialist* realism' rather than social realism), 'as if there could be an unmediated referentiality of everyday life which is in some sense more truthful or more accurate than the one depicted'.[68] The debate that unfolded in the pages of the *Screen* journal in the mid-1970s saw realism as a formal system being critiqued as an inherently conservative form of representation, incapable of embodying a progressive politics.[69] Colin MacCabe, for example, argued that realism constantly reinforces dominant ideologies and values because it cannot engage with the real as contradictory.[70] Moreover, John Hill has noticed the importance of establishing shots in the New Wave films, which, he argues, create a visual spectacle of squalor and poverty set up effectively for the enjoyment of people who do not inhabit such spaces.[71] *Black Joy* and *Babylon* are open to similar criticisms. So too, perhaps, is *Pressure*. But, as we have seen, Tony's daydream sequence, among others, serves to problematise the primarily realist aesthetics of the film through its temporary negotiation of a postcolonial position outside the discourses of coloniser and colonised, which might serve to evoke what Bhabha terms 'new and hybrid agencies and articulations'.[72] In such a way, *Pressure* employs realist aesthetics elsewhere so that they can be effectively decentred in this remarkable sequence.

But we should not always think of these films in terms of the ways in which they represent blackness. After all, Horace Ové has always considered himself to be a film-maker, not a black film-maker.[73] With *Pressure*, the director wanted to make a film that was not an art film, but would be seen by as many people as possible; people who perhaps were more used to enjoying Hollywood movies.[74] Furthermore, *Pressure* is also a film about white British working-class experience. After all, as Stewart Home points out, Ové never loses sight of the fact that 'race and class are inextricably linked'.[75] When Tony says 'I just can't believe all white people are bad', an activist replies, 'White people in this country have been colonised. We can see the bars and the chains.'[76] So the film becomes more than a comment on black experience. *Pressure* documents a range of inequalities that facilitated the fragmentation of notions of Britishness during the 1970s.

A range of British film-makers worked within the formal orthodoxies of realism during the 1970s. The work of Ken Loach has become synonymous with social realism in British cinema. Loach tends to eschew generic narratives, and places much of the emphasis on the development of character, and the ways in which his characters are affected by (and deal with) events. As such, many of his narratives, such as in *Kes* (1969) and *Family Life* (1971), are left open-ended: characters cannot always determine events.[77] Loach remained busy throughout the 1970s, making films for cinema and television. According to Deborah Knight, Loach's films often situate narratives within a long tradition of naturalism, primarily because the director is interested on the effects of environments on characters.[78] Moreover, he, like Ové, Simmons, and Rosso, is interested in the ways in which social institutions often fail the very people they were designed to help.[79]

Interesting comparisons can be made between the work of Loach and a lesser-known British director, Barney Platts-Mills, who made feature films during a transitional phase for British social realist cinema.[80] The influence of Free Cinema but also the New Wave is visible in his films, but so too is naturalism. Platts-Mills mainly used non-professional actors. *Bronco Bullfrog* (1969) was followed by *Private Road* (1971) – films with a 'downbeat tone and observational style'.[81] According to James Leggott, 'Their alternation between dramatically significant and inconsequential sequences not only serves their verisimilitude – in capturing something of the texture of "real" life – but also subtly conveys the restlessness of the char-acters.'[82] But the films of Platts-Mills also have a self-reflexive air, such as when the teenagers brag about their exploits. For example, in *Private Road*, one of the composers of the musical soundtrack plays a guitarist who acknowledges the presence of the camera at the beginning of the film.[83] Locations are also used in interesting ways. Writing about *Bronco Bullfrog*, Leggott argues that 'The film's main achievement, much in the same way as Ken Loach's *Kes*, is to use a geography of exclusive or imprisoning spaces to sketch out the social and economic parameters of the characters.'[84] This type of employment of locations is certainly echoed in *Pressure*, *Black Joy*, and *Babylon*, all of which depict black areas of London as grim ghettos, but also as spaces in which, against the odds, black youth is developing a rich subculture.

Other British films made during the period which draw upon or demonstrate realist aesthetics include *Spring and Port Wine* (Peter Hammond, 1969); *Bleak Moments* (Mike Leigh, 1971); *Duffer* (Joseph Despins and William Dumaresq, 1971); *The Ragman's Daughter* (Harold Becker, 1972); *The Moon Over the Valley* (Joseph Despins and William Dumaresq, 1975); and *A Private Enterprise* (Peter K. Smith, 1974), the latter of which, as we have seen, depicts Asian British life. But British films that demonstrate elements of realism can also be found in places one might not always expect. For example, Steve Gerrard argues that 1970s 'Carry On' films have 'a more definable sense of visual realism (albeit in caricatured form)'.[85] There are certainly realist strategies at work in the formal structure of *Carry On Girls*, for example, which features wide-ranging location shooting and, as such, offers the viewer a glimpse of the living environments of working-class and lower middle-class English people at that time. One might go as far as to suggest that these spaces give the film a grounding in 'everyday believability'.[86] Indeed, Gerrard notices formal links between these films and the British realist tradition.[87] And in some ways, he has a point. After all, as Noël Carroll points out, 'realism is not a simple relation between films and the world but a relation of contrast between films that is interpreted in virtue of analogies to aspects of reality'.[88]

Julia Hallam and Margaret Marshment argue that, during the 1980s in Britain, oppositional cultural producers were encouraged to abandon avant-garde practices, because 'Only by infiltrating the mainstream and using its common language could oppositional voices hope to make themselves heard.'[89] What appeared to be at stake was the issue of how far oppositional voices needed to infiltrate dominant institutions and employ the aesthetics of the mainstream in order to critique the status quo.[90] This often saw film-makers employing realist aesthetics in films that, in many other ways, develop images and sounds that are visionary. I want to move on now to examine how far realist aesthetics were at work in depictions of historical events in British films of the 1970s.

Notes

1   Glaessner, 'The Beast Must Die', p. 120.
2   In a number of British-produced films of the 1970s, the legacy of the British Raj in India loomed large. This was certainly the case in films directed by James Ivory. Examples include *Adventures of a Brown Man in Search of Civilisation* (James Ivory, 1971), which follows Indian scholar Nirad Chaudhuri's experiences in Oxford and London, and *Autobiography of a Princess* (James Ivory, 1975), a film set in London that sees a self-exiled princess (Madhur Jaffrey) inviting her father's ex-tutor Cyril Sahib (James Mason) to tea, when they watch old films of the Raj. The television film *Hullabaloo over Georgie and Bonnie's Pictures* (James Ivory, 1978) is set in India, and tells the story of a group of people who want to

steal paintings from an Indian palace. This film stars Peggy Ashcroft, Larry Pine, Saeed Jaffrey and Victor Banerjee. But representations of the Indian subcontinent on British screens were not just the preserve of James Ivory during the 1970s. Nick Gifford's documentary films *Burra Sahib* (1975) and *General Sahib* (1976) focus on the British Raj in India.

3 Turner, *Crisis? What Crisis? Britain in the 1970s*, p. 28.
4 Turner, *Crisis? What Crisis? Britain in the 1970s*, p. 30.
5 Turner, *Crisis? What Crisis? Britain in the 1970s*, p. 31.
6 Moore-Gilbert, 'Introduction: Cultural Closure or Post-avantgardism?', p. 6.
7 Moore-Gilbert, 'Introduction: Cultural Closure or Post-avantgardism?', p. 6.
8 Turner, *Crisis? What Crisis? Britain in the 1970s*, p. 220.
9 For more on post-Empire films see Leach, *British Film*, pp. 219–34.
10 Stam and Spence, 'Colonialism, Racism and Representation', p. 243.
11 On British television, *Love Thy Neighbour* (1972–76) was a hugely successful series that featured a significant amount of racial abuse. *The Black and White Minstrel Show* (BBC, 1958–78) remained popular. This successful series featured white singers in black greasepaint. But there were also positive moves to portray an increasingly multicultural British society. The television series *Empire Road* (BBC, 1978–79), a drama set in Handsworth, Birmingham, featured a black and Asian cast and was developed by a black writer (Michael Abbensetts) and producer (Peter Ansorge). The television series *Gangsters* (BBC, 1976–78), also set in Birmingham, depicted a city of ethnic diversity.
12 Bourne, *Black in the British Frame*, p. 176.
13 Ngcobo, *Let It Be Told: Essays by Black Women on Britain*, p. viii.
14 Moore-Gilbert, 'Introduction: Cultural Closure or Post-avantgardism?', pp. 17–18.
15 Bhabha, *The Location of Culture*, p. 6.
16 A. Walker, *National Heroes*, p. 242.
17 Wilson, 'Pressure', p. 68.
18 Wilson, 'Pressure', p. 68.
19 Home, 'Pressure'; available at: www.stewarthomesociety.org/luv/pressure.htm.
20 Dash, 'Marvellous Realism', p. 200.
21 Dash, 'Marvellous Realism', p. 200.
22 Dash, 'Marvellous Realism', p. 201.
23 Bhabha, *The Location of Culture*, p. 219.
24 Bhabha, *The Location of Culture*, p. 224.
25 Bhabha, *The Location of Culture*, p. 227.
26 See Barthes, *The Pleasure of the Text*, p. 49.
27 Bhabha, *The Location of Culture*, p. 181.

28 Bhabha, *The Location of Culture*, p. 181.

29 Bhabha, *The Location of Culture*, p. 182.

30 Bourne, *Black in the British Frame: Black People in British Film and Television, 1896–1996*, p. 201.

31 Wambu; available at: www.screenonline.org.uk/tv/id/508033/index.html.

32 Hall, 'New Ethnicities', p.225.

33 A. Walker, *National Heroes*, p. 242.

34 Dolan and Spicer, 'On the Margins: Anthony Simmons, *The Optimists of Nine Elms* and *Black Joy*', p. 87.

35 Dolan and Spicer, 'On the Margins: Anthony Simmons, *The Optimists of Nine Elms* and *Black Joy*', p. 87.

36 Badder, 'Black Joy', p. 228.

37 Cave; available at: www.screenonline.org.uk/film/id/1347353/index.html.

38 Cave; available at: www.screenonline.org.uk/film/id/1347353/index.html.

39 Cave; available at: www.screenonline.org.uk/film/id/1347353/index.html.

40 Badder, 'Black Joy', p. 228.

41 Spicer and Dolan, 'On the Margins: Anthony Simmons, *The Optimists of Nine Elms* and *Black Joy*', p. 88.

42 Spicer and Dolan, 'On the Margins: Anthony Simmons, *The Optimists of Nine Elms* and *Black Joy*', p. 88.

43 Spicer and Dolan, 'On the Margins: Anthony Simmons, *The Optimists of Nine Elms* and *Black Joy*', p. 88.

44 Spicer and Dolan, 'On the Margins: Anthony Simmons, *The Optimists of Nine Elms* and *Black Joy*', p. 88.

45 Rugg, *Brickbats and Bouquets: Black Women's Critique: Literature, Theatre, Film*, 28. Quoted in Spicer and Dolan, 'On the Margins: Anthony Simmons, *The Optimists of Nine Elms* and *Black Joy*', p. 87.

46 Bakari, 'A Journey From the Cold: Rethinking Black Film-making in Britain', p. 230.

47 Franco Rosso, interviewed by the author, 18 March 2008.

48 Back, *New Ethnicities and Urban Culture: Racisms and Multiculture in Young Lives*, p. 187.

49 Stewart Home, 'Pressure'; available at: www.stewarthomesociety.org/luv/pressure.htm.

50 In *Babylon*, the Ital Lion dubs performed by Aswad are 'Warrior Charge' and 'Hey Jah Children'. The film also features performances of 'Deliver Me From My Enemies' by Yabba U; 'Babylon' by Jah Shaka; 'You Did' by Cassandra; 'Can't Give It Up' by Janey Kay; and 'Turn Me Loose' by Michael Profit.

51 Dolan and Spicer, 'On the Margins: Anthony Simmons, *The Optimists of Nine Elms* and *Black Joy*', p. 89.

52 Dolan and Spicer, 'On the Margins: Anthony Simmons, *The Optimists of Nine Elms* and *Black Joy*', p. 89.

53 Robinson, 'Babylon'.

54 Malcolm, 'Babylon'.

55 Coleman, 'Babylon'.

56 Brien, 'Babylon'.

57 Castell, 'Babylon'.

58 Pierce, 'Babylon'.

59 *Variety*, 14 May 1980.

60 *Variety*, 14 May 1980.

61 Bourne, *Black in the British Frame: Black People in British Film and Television, 1896–1996*, p. 202.

62 Shaw, 'Picking up the Tab', pp. 83–4.

63 Hallam with Marshment, *Realism and Popular Cinema*, p. xiii.

64 Hallam with Marshment, *Realism and Popular Cinema*, p. 16.

65 Hallam with Marshment, *Realism and Popular Cinema*, p. 33.

66 Hallam with Marshment, *Realism and Popular Cinema*, p. 34.

67 Hallam with Marshment, *Realism and Popular Cinema*, p. 51.

68 Hallam with Marshment, *Realism and Popular Cinema*, p. 51.

69 Hallam with Marshment, *Realism and Popular Cinema*, p. xii.

70 MacCabe, 'Realism and the Cinema: Notes on Some Brechtian Theses'.

71 Hill, *Sex, Class and Realism: British Cinema 1956–1963*, pp. 135–6.

72 Bhabha, *The Location of Culture*, p. 192.

73 Derek Malcolm, 'Horace Ové and Pressure', BFI DVD booklet.

74 Derek Malcolm, 'Horace Ové and Pressure', BFI DVD booklet.

75 Home, 'Pressure'; available at: www.stewarthomesociety.org/luv/pressure.htm.

76 Home, 'Pressure'; available at: www.stewarthomesociety.org/luv/pressure.htm.

77 Hallam and Marshment, *Realism and Popular Cinema*, p. 210.

78 Knight, 'Naturalism, Narration and Critical Perspective: Ken Loach and the Experimental Method', pp. 60–81.

79 Hallam and Marshment, *Realism and Popular Cinema*, p. 213.

80 Leggott, 'Dead Ends and Private Roads: The 1970s Films of Barney Platts-Mills', p. 231.

81 Leggott, 'Dead Ends and Private Roads: The 1970s Films of Barney Platts-Mills', p. 235.

82 Leggott, 'Dead Ends and Private Roads: The 1970s Films of Barney Platts-Mills', p. 234.

83 Leggott, 'Dead Ends and Private Roads: The 1970s Films of Barney Platts-Mills', p. 234.

84 Leggott, 'Dead Ends and Private Roads: The 1970s Films of Barney Platts-Mills', p. 236.
85 Gerrard, 'What a Carry On! The Decline and Fall of a Great British Institution', p. 39.
86 Gerrard, 'What a Carry On! The Decline and Fall of a Great British Institution', p. 39.
87 Gerrard, 'What a Carry On! The Decline and Fall of a Great British Institution', p. 41.
88 Carroll, *Theorising the Moving Image*, p. 244.
89 Hallam and Marshment, *Realism and Popular Cinema*, p. ix.
90 Hallam and Marshment, *Realism and Popular Cinema*, p. ix.

5

In memoriam:
the past in the present/
the present in the past

The year is 1872. In London's Hyde Park, Van Helsing (Peter Cushing) battles violently with Count Dracula (Christopher Lee) on a speeding horse-drawn carriage. The carriage crashes, and Dracula is impaled on a wooden spoke from one of the smashed wheels. The film then suddenly shifts to the contemporary London of 1972 by means of a 100-year jump cut. We see a jet plane leaving a vapour trail high in the sky over the modern city. Traffic jams are polluting the grey city air. Seedy sex shops line the drab streets. *Dracula A.D. 1972* (Alan Gibson, 1972) offers us a vision of London in the 1970s characterised by moral decline and socio-cultural fragmentation. Count Dracula is resurrected in the contemporary city in a groovy, far-out ceremony held by a young counter-cultural group led by Johnny Alucard (Christopher Neame), featuring a black American woman, Gaynor (Marsha Hunt); a raven-haired white temptress, Laura (Caroline Munro); a good-natured working-class Londoner, Bob (Philip Murray); and the middle-class Jessica Van Helsing (Stephanie Beacham). But while the Count has an eye for Jessica, he effectively remains on the periphery of events throughout the film.[1] The London of 1972 is clearly no place for him. Indeed, the film is intriguing in terms of the ways in which it locates this famous figure from the past within a vision of contemporary British culture, and how he struggles to function within the vicissitudes of a new moral climate.[2] It is perhaps not surprising that *Dracula A.D. 1972* has received very little critical attention. It was once even dismissed as being 'beneath discussion',[3] and has long been considered one of the lesser films of the Christopher Lee *Dracula* cycle. Indeed, James Craig Holte calls it 'a complete failure'.[4] But it has developed a cult following.

Other horror films of the 1970s exploit the legacy of the late-1960s hippy phenomenon while at the same time colliding old and new British cultures. Most noticeable is *The Wicker Man* (Robin Hardy, 1973), which sees Sergeant Neil Howie (Edward Woodward) coming into conflict with Lord Summerisle (Christopher Lee), the titular leader of a remote pagan community on a Scottish island.[5] The island community's cultural practices appear to be unacceptably hedonistic to the Christian Howie, as they are seemingly rooted in ancient pagan folk traditions. But the culture of the islanders also resonates with late-1960s hippy notions of free love.

Rather than exploring the ways in which historical socio-cultural mores operate in contemporary communities, other British films of the period transplant the activities of contemporary groups to previous historical moments. For example, Tigon's *Blood on Satan's Claw* (Piers Haggard, 1971), which is set in a seventeenth-century English village, features Linda Hayden as Angel Blake, a sexualised adolescent girl holding power over a group of youngsters who behave like late-1960s 'flower children'.[6] This narrative resembles the real-life story of Mary Bell, the 11-year-old who was convicted of strangling a smaller child, Martin Brown, in England on 25 May 1968. Moreover, while set in an English past, *Blood on Satan's Claw* also clearly echoes the notorious activities of Charles Manson and the so-called Manson Family in the USA, which climaxed in 1969 with the murder of Sharon Tate, and several other people. But *Blood on Satan's Claw*, like *The Wicker Man* and *Dracula A.D. 1972*, also exploits (in an imagined past) concerns brought about by the countercultural embrace of free sexuality and hedonism.[7] In this chapter I shall discuss the ways in which contemporary British social-cultural tensions are worked through in historical settings, and how far 1970s British historical films mediate ideas pertaining to a shifting British present and an uncertain British future.

A common treasury: *Winstanley*

In the late 1950s, two young men began working together on a film about England under an imagined Nazi occupation. *It Happened Here* was eventually released through United Artists in 1966.[8] Kevin

Brownlow and Andrew Mollo subsequently became two highly respected film-makers and historians.[9] Brownlow would later work as an editor on *The Charge of the Light Brigade* (Tony Richardson, 1968), and Mollo, a military and costume specialist, worked as a consultant on *Dr Zhivago* (David Lean, 1965). But they came together again in the late 1960s to begin work on *Winstanley*, a film about the historical figure Gerrard Winstanley, which would be based on David Caute's 1961 English Civil War novel, *Comrade Jacob*. Brownlow and Mollo worked closely with the script adviser, Marina Lewycka, and cast Miles Halliwell in the title role. But none of the cast apart from Halliwell and Jerome Willis (who played Lord Thomas Fairfax) were professional actors.

The film was shot by cinematographer Ernest Vincze, who, in agreement with Brownlow and Mollo, sought to depict the events in as realistic a way as possible; to capture scenes of life as it would have been in early-modern rural England. Mollo used his expert knowledge to make sure that all the costumes, weapons, agricultural equipment, and breeds of animal that were used were authentic. He also enlisted the help of the Roundhead Association battle recreation group to facilitate the realistic depiction of the battle scenes. The British Film Institute Production Board gave the producers £17,000. But while *Winstanley* had the support of Mamoun Hassan, it took eight years for the collaborators to see the film to fruition. When it was eventually screened, *Winstanley* was well received at film festivals, and on non-commercial circuits.[10]

Winstanley is a black and white film, shot on location in natural light. It tells the story of the attempt made by Gerrard Winstanley to set up a communal farm on common land at St George's Hill, near Weybridge in Surrey, England, in 1649. The film employs dialogue drawn almost exclusively from Winstanley's writings. Parson Platt (David Bramley), a Nonconformist Presbyterian (in whose parish St George's Hill lies), encourages the villagers to move against the Diggers (or the 'True Levellers' – a group of Protestant agrarian proto-communists), and enlists Cromwell's army (through Thomas Fairfax) to remove them from the land. For many Diggers this is evidently very hard to stomach, as they fought alongside Fairfax in the Civil War, and now feel that they should be able to live as free men.

The film begins with a prologue, set to stirring music from Prokofiev's opera *Alexander Nevsky*, which covers events leading up to April 1649. In this sequence the audience is taken through the final battles of the Civil War. Brownlow and Mollo employ close-ups of faces, hands, and weaponry, and a rapid, aggressive rhythm is set up by the montage. Some shots remain out of focus, and images of horses' hooves careering across the ground serve to increase the tension dramatically. After this prologue, the central narrative of the film deals with events following the debates in Putney Church in late 1647, the mutiny by Leveller soldiers at Corkbush Field near Ware in Hertfordshire, and the execution of the ringleaders by the army commanders, Fairfax and Cromwell.[11] The film shows the construction of the Diggers' modest dwellings in the woods, and the escalating assaults on this settlement by Platt's henchmen. *Winstanley* depicts other key events, such as the arrest for trespass of the Diggers, and their subsequent appearance before Kingston magistrates, where they are refused the right to conduct their own defence in the absence of a lawyer, and fined beyond their means.[12] The last sequence in the film shows the Digger settlement lit by flames as it is destroyed at night, and the return of Parson Platt to his village to the cheers of his parishioners.

Winstanley is, in many ways, a bleak, austere film that shows the harsh existence of early-modern rural English communities. The difficulty of their lives, and the sheer struggle to survive from day to day, is further evoked by the windswept landscapes and the almost constant bad weather. Indeed, the narrative develops under brooding skies. The film is replete with rainfall. Gerrard Winstanley is depicted as a man of peace who counsels against violent retaliation. We have direct access to his thoughts and beliefs through the formal device of a voiceover, as Halliwell reads from Winstanley's writings about his vision of all men being equal 'in the creation'. So the audience is encouraged to share Winstanley's perspective on the injustices meted out to him and his followers. Halliwell (as Winstanley) stalks through film with a permanently furrowed brow, and sometimes in his struggle he is reminiscent of a Christ-like figure. Indeed, many of the images have the weight of a biblical epic: Parson Platt's wife (Alison Halliwell) wandering in a hood to the Diggers' camp; men in silhouette on the brow of a hill. But while telling a very English story, the film clearly also has the look of a European art film. David Caute suggests that in some ways the film specifically resembles the work of Swedish director Ingmar Bergman, with its 'silhouetted figures trudging in pursuit of destiny across distant horizons'.[13] Certainly, in formal terms, the film also evidences a close affinity to the legacy of the silent period of cinema. As Christopher Durston point outs, while the early Soviet film-makers were clear influences on Brownlow and Mollo, others appear to have been Carl Dreyer – specifically, his 'play of faces and space' in films such as *The Parson's Widow* (1920) – and Arthur von Gerlach's *Zur Chronik von Grieshuus* (aka *Chronicles of the Grey House*) (1925).[14]

At the time of the release of *Winstanley*, Alexander Walker wrote that this was a 'beautiful film that shows the passion of its makers'.[15] Verina Glaessner picked up on the power of the political message of *Winstanley*, arguing that 'The film's deliberately oblique treatment of the narrative calculatedly diverts attention from the simple dramatic sequence of events and on to their underpinnings – the dynamics of the challenge Winstanley's idealism offers the status quo and of its suppression.'[16] As such, while Glaessner acknowledged its power as a political statement, *Winstanley* was arguably of limited appeal in terms of how it tells the story in formal terms. The narrative, then, was not developed in such a way that would guarantee the film a wider audience as 'entertainment'. But this did not appear to concern the film-makers. Interestingly, in a 1980 interview, Brownlow noted that 'There is no point whatever in making a historical film, unless you are going to show what happened. Fiction interests me less and less.'[17]

But having said that, *Winstanley* is not as difficult as a number of avant-garde films or other British art films. So it does not sit easily within orthodox categories of cinema. Geoff Brown notes that, on its release, *Winstanley* 'demonstrated Brownlow and Mollo's estrangement from both Britain's mainstream and independent cinemas. The film did not fit the costume drama pigeonhole, nor did it pursue the Greenaway path towards elaborate games with form and content'.[18] So *Winstanley* functions as a hybrid film in formal terms. It is an art film, but it tells a story in a linear fashion. It is also effectively a drama-documentary. And it is not beyond the realms of possibility to read the film as an English western, influenced by European silent cinema. Gerrard Winstanley and his band of Diggers, after all, are pioneer settlers trying to create a kind of new frontier, making the best out of a hostile, barren landscape. They find themselves under attack from foes who claim ownership of the land. Shots of horsemen traversing the wilderness appear uncannily familiar.

While the film is widely regarded as an authentic recreation of the past, *Winstanley* also evokes aspects of the contemporary moment, and, as such, is open to 'presentist' readings, as James Chapman notices. The intense quotidian struggle captured in the film is certainly evocative of life in a nation mired by socio-cultural conflict, as Britain clearly was in the early 1970s. The intensity of the political struggle on display in the film effectively echoed the contemporary moment at which the film was released. Many in Britain in the mid-to-late 1970s felt there was a significant amount of unfinished business; that a revolutionary moment might be just around the corner.

As James Chapman points out, the gestation period of the production of *Winstanley* coincided with the emergence of an earlier revolutionary moment, when counter-cultural movements developed, 'whose values of communal living, pacifism and free love were similar to the outlook of the Diggers'.[19] Indeed, the events of May 1968 in France 'had seemed to promise the possibility of both a political and social revolution in which the catalyst was direct action by students and workers'.[20] Towards the end of the film, for example, Fairfax argues that the Diggers are 'men of peace'. 'Peace', we should remember, is a word forever bound up with 'love' within the late 1960s hippy lexicon. In terms of the ways in which the past infiltrates the present (and aspects of the present are projected into the past), then, *Winstanley* is a very rich, complex film.

One aspect of the production of the film which clearly facilitates a 'presentist' reading is the fact that Sid Rawle was cast as a Ranter.[21] The so-called 'King of the Hippies', Rawle (who died in 2010) moved to London from the South West in the 1960s, where he set up an 'ultra-hippy cult' known as the Hyde Park Diggers, which had more than 200 members, and he played a key role in the squatting movement in North London.[22] In September 1969, the group participated in the six-day occupation (by the London Street Commune) of 144 Piccadilly, a neglected 100-room mansion. Subsequently, Rawle was approached by the Beatle, John Lennon, who offered him custodianship of a tiny island, Dornish, in Clew Bay, off the coast of County Mayo, which he had purchased in 1967. In 1971, Rawle recruited a group of 30 people to live on Dornish communally for two years. He and the Diggers also gave away free food at the 1971 Glastonbury Fayre, and he helped to establish a free festival in Windsor Great Park in 1972. But in 1974 police cleared the site, arresting 200 people. Police tactics were criticised, and Rawle helped to persuade the government to provide a site on an abandoned airbase at Watchfield, Oxfordshire, where he staged a nine-day people's free festival in 1975.[23]

In light of the casting of Rawle in *Winstanley*, one of the most interesting sections of the film shows the arrival of the Ranters at the settlement. Their hedonistic behaviour – smoking, loafing, and making bawdy sexual advances to female members of the Digger community – clearly evokes aspects of late-1960s countercultural lifestyles. But while the potential reading of the Ranters as hippies is rich here, we might also be tempted to read these characters retrospectively as proto-punks; as young people who refuse to play by the rules (and the ethics) of an older generation, and instead choose a 'do-it-yourself' approach to everyday life built upon notions of simplicity and self-sufficiency.

Arguing the case for Winstanley's enduring relevance as a historical and political figure in the film, Christopher Durston puts it that 'Gerrard Winstanley is shown as the upholder of the mid-twentieth-century values of egalitarianism, personal liberty and religious autonomy, and as an individual engaged in a heroic but uneven struggle with the forces of political, economic and religious dogmatism and oppression.'[24] As such, Winstanley might feel like a heroic figure again in the 1970s. Indeed, the film speaks to coeval British concerns such as the booming housing market and homelessness, and, as such, as Verina Glaessner points out, powerfully evokes a country 'where conservatism seems often a matter of actual physical space, of bricks and mortar'.[25]

In a nod to contemporary concerns, Brownlow himself acknowledged the fact that 'The left was divided as desperately in those days as now.'[26] What the film certainly does do is bring to life a tradition of radical politics of the left in Britain that can be traced back many generations. Further evidence that the film was in some ways designed to refer to contemporary socio-cultural concerns comes in an interview with Kevin Brownlow at the time the film was released:

> The period recreation is important but the connections with the present are there and obvious, although we didn't stress them. There was raging inflation. The army were off to beat up people in Ireland. There was terrific unemployment. There was a desperation, a sense of being at the edge of a void. It was also a time of incredibly sophisticated political thinking – which, I suppose, ours is not – nevertheless there are so many similarities.[27]

So *Winstanley* is a film about the English Interregnum. But it is also arguably a film that reflects aspects of life in Britain (or, specifically, England) in the 1970s. As Alexander Walker puts it, '*Winstanley*'s vision of England in disarray was historically apposite.'[28]

Oliver's army: *Cromwell*

Winstanley was not the only film made in Britain during the late 1960s and 1970s that looked back to events surrounding the English Interregnum. *Cromwell* (Ken Hughes, 1970) – produced by Irving Allen for Columbia – stars Richard Harris as Oliver Cromwell, and Alec Guinness as King Charles I. The film was shot primarily on location in Spain, but interiors were filmed at Shepperton Studios. *Cromwell* is an epic, big budget production, and features two battle sequences that unfold on a large scale. John Morrill argues that the film 'is both deeply committed to visual accuracy and very relaxed about combining certain characters and events, or even fictionalizing them for dramatic purposes'.[29] *Cromwell* begins with shots of an impressive English landscape; all sweeping vistas and enormous skies. We see Oliver Cromwell and his men riding through the vast expanse of a wetland location. These images are accompanied by

Frank Cordell's rousing orchestral music. The formal strategies employed here emphasise the scale of the land and, as such, speak of the scale of Cromwell's task, but also the potential reach of his power. But this, in terms of the film language employed (linear narrative, spectacular battle scenes) remains a mainstream historical film.[30]

The critical reception of *Cromwell* was muted.[31] David Robinson, writing in the *Financial Times*, argued that the film 'conforms loyally to the old traditions of the historical epic genre', while Ian Christie, in the *Daily Express*, put it that the film 'excites the imagination and stirs the emotions without insulting the intelligence'.[32] Unlike *Winstanley*, which has a *mise-en-scène* crowded with historically accurate detail, critics of *Cromwell* took issue with the ways in which the film distorts historical facts, and places the figure of Cromwell central to the action.[33] Indeed, Cromwell himself is represented as a force for democracy.[34] In *Films and Filming*, N. F. Ollenshaw called the film a 'compound of falsehoods and half-truths'.[35] In the film, after all, Oliver Cromwell becomes the commander-in-chief of the New Model Army (a position in reality held by Sir Thomas Fairfax), and meets King Charles I on at least three occasions (there is no historical evidence that this actually happened).[36] Moreover, Richard Harris's Cromwell is given a number of opportunities to give impromptu speeches, and on these occasions other characters in the frame tend to remain static as he wanders through them, glowering and blinking, forcefully stating his point of view and outlining his plans. Brenda Davies was also critical of the film in *Monthly Film Bulletin*, commenting on what she saw as its 'oversimplified approach to complex situations' and its 'kindergarten view of history'.[37] Furthermore, Davies recognised that Cromwell's brutalities in Ireland remain absent from the narrative, and that the film 'tries to combine serious intentions with the widest kind of popular appeal and falls unhappily between the two'.[38] Indeed, the film certainly does not refer to Cromwell's suppression of Irish rebels in 1649–50. Perhaps this was no coincidence, as the film-makers would, of course, have been fully aware of the fact that British troops had been sent to Northern Ireland in April 1969, and the Irish Republican Army (IRA) was engaging in its campaign of violence.[39]

Having said this, *Cromwell* certainly brings issues of corruption in government and political oppression to the fore. And just as *Winstanley* is open to 'presentist' readings, some of the speeches made by Harris as Cromwell, as well as other dialogue in the film, arguably resonate with the socio-cultural concerns of late 1960s and early 1970s Britain. The first example of this occurs towards the beginning of the film, when Cromwell makes it clear that he once had a vision for England: 'A Great nation. Prosperous. God fearing. Good laws. Strong. Respected throughout the world. That was an England I dreamed of.' Later, at the end of the film, some years after the execution of Charles I, Cromwell makes a more profound speech along similar lines, telling Parliament: 'Instead of unifying the good people of this nation with righteousness and peace, which would have been a glorious, Christian thing to have done, what do I find? Anarchy, corruption, division and dissatisfaction.' To 1970s British audiences, living in a nation that seemed to be falling apart, these words would no doubt have resonated. Minutes later, in an empty House, to the extra-diegetic swelling of strings on the soundtrack, Cromwell carries on:

> I will give this nation back its self respect. We will walk in this world with our heads held high. I will liberate men's souls from the darkness of ignorance. I will build schools, universities for all. This will become the golden age of learning. I will bring the law within the reach of every common man. There will be work and bread for all. This nation will prosper because it is a Godly nation and because we walk hand-in-hand with the Lord.

Here, then, is a man who sees a nation in crisis and decline. He is offering ways to weather a socio-cultural and political storm. One wonders whether, in 1970, the incoming Conservative Prime Minister Edward Heath could ever have dreamed of such rhetoric.

The director of *Cromwell*, Ken Hughes, had previously worked on films such as *Chitty Chitty Bang Bang* (1968), *Casino Royale* (1967), and *The Trials of Oscar Wilde* (1960) – another 'serious historical drama'.[40] He would go on to direct the 1970s films *The Internecine Project* (1974), *Alfie Darling* (1975), and *Sextette* (1978). Richard Harris's career is also demonstrative of the highly complex nature of British and transnational film production during the period. His career during the 1970s saw him feature in both US and UK films and on television. For example, he plays the central protagonist in the US film *A Man Called Horse* (Elliot Silverstein, 1970). Major roles in 1970s British films include the bomb disposal expert Lt. Cmdr Anthony Fallon in Richard Lester's *Juggernaut* (1974), and Richard the Lionheart in Lester's US film, *Robin and Marion* (1976) (shot in Spain), which also features other major British actors such as Sean Connery, Robert Shaw, Nicol Williamson, and the Belgian-born Audrey Hepburn. Harris also stars in the international co-production *The Cassandra Crossing* (George P. Cosmatos, 1976) alongside Sophia Loren and Martin Sheen, and in the British/Belgian co-produced part live action/part animated *Gulliver's Travels* (Peter R. Hunt, 1977). He stars alongside Richard Burton and Roger Moore in *The Wild Geese* (Andrew V. McLaglen, 1978) (shot in South Africa). And he stars in *Game for Vultures* (James Fargo, 1979) as David Swansey, a South African businessman delivering helicopters illegally to Rhodesia. Here, then, is another film actor who worked throughout the 1970s, in British, US, and European films, and across the globe.

Alec Guinness, who plays King Charles I in *Cromwell*, also worked throughout the 1970s, mostly in Britain. He plays Jacob Marley's ghost in the musical *Scrooge* (Ronald Neame, 1970). He appears in the Franco Zeffirelli-directed British/Italian co-production *Brother Sun, Sister Moon* (1972). And he plays Adolf Hitler in another British/Italian co-production, *Hitler: The Last Ten Days* (Ennio De Concini, 1973). He was cast as Ben Obi-Wan Kenobi in the US science fiction films *Star Wars* (George Lucas, 1977) and *The Empire Strikes Back* (Irvin Kershner, 1980), which were largely filmed on sets built at Elstree Studios. Guinness played George Smiley in seven episodes of the successful late-1970s British television series *Tinker Tailor Soldier Spy* (BBC), and appears in *Raise the Titanic* (Jerry Jameson, 1980), Lew Grade's disastrous attempt – under the aegis of Incorporated Television Company (ITC) Entertainment – to make an American-style blockbuster. Again, then, here is an actor whose variegated career clearly speaks of the vicissitudes of film-making in the 1970s in Britain and elsewhere.

A number of other historical costume dramas were made in Britain during the 1970s. These include *Royal Flash* (Richard Lester,

1975), which, according to Sue Harper, 'seeks out ludicrous images from the past which are clearly intended to provoke', and *The Man Who Would Be King* (John Huston, 1975), which 'is an admirably complex examination of Empire: its absurdities, magnificence, self-delusions and betrayals'.[41] Stanley Kubrick's *Barry Lyndon* (1975) is also a celebrated, painterly historical film of the period that carefully reconstructs a vision of the past.

Americans production companies retained something of a foothold in big British historical films in the early 1970s.[42] While Columbia backed *Cromwell* and *Young Winston* (Richard Attenborough, 1972), Hal B. Wallis produced *Anne of a Thousand Days* (Charles Jarrott, 1970) and *Mary, Queen of Scots* (Charles Jarrott, 1971) for Universal. These films were expensively produced but in most cases did not make profits, thus impacting on the subsequent withdrawal of US investment from the British film industry.[43]

A number of historical 'Carry On' films were also made during the decade, such as *Carry On Henry* (Gerald Thomas, 1971) and *Carry On Dick* (Gerald Thomas, 1974). But these films only ever 'play' at being historical; this 'play' being primarily filtered through the knowing performances of the regular ensemble. As Nicholas Cull puts it, 'Merely casting the familiar *Carry On* stars in historical roles undermined the pretence of historical filmmaking to re-create the past.'[44] Moreover, these films also 'play' at history by poking fun at the stylistic devices employed in mainstream historical films.[45] As such, we should remember that the historical 'Carry On' films essentially refer to cinematic (rather than social) history; they make a number of intertextual references to other historical films.[46] In other words, historical 'Carry On' films always operate within (and serve to evoke) the moment in time during which they were produced, as well the past they purport to depict.[47] As such, any apparent anachronisms these films display effectively allow the humour to function in the contemporary moment.[48] So, in *Carry On Henry*, for example, the past is a territory in which present sexual fantasies can be explored.[49]

Other films made in Britain during the 1970s display a strong historical focus. These include *Conduct Unbecoming* (Michael Anderson, 1975), starring Michael York, Richard Attenborough, and Trevor Howard – a film engaged in an examination of the lives of British regimental offers serving in India. *The Last Valley* (James Clavell, 1970), starring Michael Caine and Omar Sharif, is set during the Thirty Years' War in Germany. *Bequest to the Nation* (aka *The Nelson Affair*) (James Cellan Jones, 1973) tells the story of a relationship between Lord Nelson (Peter Finch) and Lady Hamilton (Glenda Jackson) during the Napoleonic Wars. In terms of representations of Welsh history (and films made in Wales), *Above Us the Earth* (Karl Francis, 1977) is a drama-documentary about Welsh miners; *Danny Jones* (Jules Bricken, 1971) tells the story of a Welsh carpenter, and was shot on location in Wales; and *In the Forest* (Phil Mulloy, 1978) is an ambitious film that seeks to offer 400 years of British history in order to evoke the origins of the British working class. It does this in a formally inventive, fragmented way, focusing centrally on three peasants walking through a forest. This is what the magazine *Time Out* termed an alternative history of 'political and cultural fragments'.[50] Films like this offer highly inventive and idiosyncratic views of aspects of British history and explore pressing issues concerning questions of British national identity.[51] But other films of the period focus primarily on threats to rural Englishness. I now want to move on to consider filmic representations of specific parts of the English countryside.

Notes

1   I develop these points in the article 'The Grateful Un-Dead: Count Dracula and the Transnational Counter Culture in *Dracula A.D. 1972*', pp. 135–51.

2   In addition to *Dracula A.D. 1972*, the wide range of films produced at this time that drew upon established British gothic figures include *Frankenstein Must be Destroyed* (Terence Fisher, 1969); *The Horror of Frankenstein* (Jimmy Sangster, 1970); *The Satanic Rites of Dracula* (Alan Gibson, 1973); *Frankenstein and the Monster from Hell* (Terence Fisher, 1973); and the television films *Dracula* (Dan Curtis, 1973) and the US-produced, but shot in Britain, *Frankenstein – the True Story* (Jack Smight, 1973). *Vampira* (Clive Donner, 1974) is a comedy/horror spoof of Dracula films starring David Niven and featuring Playboy Playmates. Critical coverage of 1970s British horror films has been provided more than adequately by Peter Hutchings, Andrew Tudor, Kim Newman and David Pirie, among others.

3   Hunt, *British Low Culture: From Safari Suits to Sexploitation*, p. 143.

4   Holte, *Dracula in the Dark: The Dracula Film Adaptations*, p. 63.

5   I develop readings of the employment of folk music in *The Wicker Man* in the article 'Folksploitation: Charting the Horrors of the British Folk Music Tradition in *The Wicker Man* (Robin Hardy, 1973)'.

6   Hunt, 'Necromancy in the UK: Witchcraft and the Occult in British Horror', p. 93.

7   Other horror films set in a British past include *Cry of the Banshee* (Gordon Hessler, 1970), an American International film, featuring titles by Terry Gilliam of Monty Python fame; Tigon's *The Creeping Flesh* (Freddie Francis, 1973); Tyburn's *The Ghoul* (Freddie Francis, 1975); and the Amicus produced *I, Monster* (Stephen Weeks, 1971).

8   Brown, 'Kevin Brownlow'; available at: www.screenonline.org.uk/people/id/547695.

9   Durston, '*Winstanley*', p. 232.

10 Harper, 'History and Representation: The Case of 1970s British Cinema', p. 37.

11 Durston, '*Winstanley*', p. 237.

12 Durston, '*Winstanley*', pp. 237–8; Caute, 'Looking Back in Regret at Winstanley'.

13 Caute, 'Looking Back in Regret at Winstanley'.

14 Durston, '*Winstanley*', p. 241.

15 *Evening News*, 14 October 1976. Quoted in Chapman, 'The World Turned Upside Down: *Cromwell* (1970), *Winstanley* (1975), *To Kill a King* (2003) and the British Historical Film', p. 123.

16 Glaessner, '*Winstanley*: An Interview with Kevin Brownlow and Andrew Mollo', p. 19.

17 Rubenstein, 'Winstanley and the Historical Film: An Interview with Kevin Brownlow', p. 25.

18 Brown, 'Kevin Brownlow'; available at: www.screenonline.org.uk/people/id/547695/index.html.

19 Chapman, 'The World Turned Upside Down: *Cromwell* (1970), *Winstanley* (1975), *To Kill a King* (2003) and the British Historical Film', p. 125.

20 Chapman, 'The World Turned Upside Down: *Cromwell* (1970), *Winstanley* (1975), *To Kill a King* (2003) and the British Historical Film', p. 126.

21 Durston, '*Winstanley*', p. 240.

22 Tibbetts, 'Kevin Brownlow's Historical Films: *It Happened Here* (1965) and *Winstanley* (1975)', p. 244.

23 May, 'Sid Rawle – Obituary'.

24 Durston, '*Winstanley*', p. 243.

25 Glaessner, '*Winstanley*: An Interview with Kevin Brownlow and Andrew Mollo', p. 19.

26 Glaessner, '*Winstanley*: An Interview with Kevin Brownlow and Andrew Mollo', p. 22.

27 Glaessner, '*Winstanley*: An Interview with Kevin Brownlow and Andrew Mollo', p. 22.

28 A. Walker, *National Heroes*, p. 224.

29 Morrill, 'Oliver Cromwell and the Civil Wars', p. 210.

30 Chapman, 'The World Turned Upside Down: *Cromwell* (1970), *Winstanley* (1975), *To Kill a King* (2003) and the British Historical Film', p. 118.

31 Chapman, 'The World Turned Upside Down: *Cromwell* (1970), *Winstanley* (1975), *To Kill a King* (2003) and the British Historical Film', p. 117.

32 Chapman, 'The World Turned Upside Down: *Cromwell* (1970), *Winstanley* (1975), *To Kill a King* (2003) and the British Historical Film', p. 117.

33 Chapman, 'The World Turned Upside Down: *Cromwell* (1970), *Winstanley* (1975), *To Kill a King* (2003) and the British Historical Film', p. 123.

34 Chapman, 'The World Turned Upside Down: *Cromwell* (1970), *Winstanley* (1975), *To Kill a King* (2003) and the British Historical Film', p. 118.

35 Ollenshaw, 'Fact and Fiction', p. 4.

36 Chapman, 'The World Turned Upside Down: *Cromwell* (1970), *Winstanley* (1975), *To Kill a King* (2003) and the British Historical Film', p. 118.

37 Davies, 'Cromwell', p. 180.

38 Davies, 'Cromwell', p. 180.

39 Chapman, 'The World Turned Upside Down: *Cromwell* (1970), *Winstanley* (1975), *To Kill a King* (2003) and the British Historical Film', p. 119.

40 Morrill, 'Oliver Cromwell and the Civil Wars', p. 209.

41 Harper, 'History and Representation: The Case of 1970s British Cinema', p. 32.

42 Harper, 'History and Representation: The Case of 1970s British Cinema', p. 30.

43 Chapman, 'The World Turned Upside Down: *Cromwell* (1970), *Winstanley* (1975), *To Kill a King* (2003) and the British Historical Film', p. 112.

44 Cull, 'Camping on the borders: History, identity and Britishness in the *Carry On* costume parodies, 1963–74', p. 94.

45 Cull, 'Camping on the Borders: History, Identity and Britishness in the *Carry On* Costume Parodies, 1963–74', p. 97.

46 Harper, 'History and Representation: The Case of 1970s British Cinema', p. 35.

47 Cull, 'Camping on the Borders: History, Identity and Britishness in the *Carry On* Costume Parodies, 1963–74', p. 104.

48 Cull, 'Camping on the Borders: History, Identity and Britishness in the *Carry On* Costume Parodies, 1963–74', p. 97.

49 Cull, 'Camping on the Borders: History, Identity and Britishness in the *Carry On* Costume Parodies, 1963–74', p. 98.

50 Available at: www.timeout.com/film/reviews/76091/in-the-forest.html.

51 While not British in their historical subject matter, a number of 1970s historical films were made under the auspices of the American Film

Theatre series. These films were adaptations of stage plays produced by Ely A. Landau between 1973 and 1975. They include *Luther* (Guy Green, 1973) (an adaptation of John Osborne's play, filmed at Shepperton); *The Maids* (Christopher Miles, 1974) (an adaptation of the play by Jean Genet); and *Three Sisters* (Laurence Olivier and John Sichel, 1970) (an adaptation of the play by Anton Chekhov, released by AFT in 1974). Key British films made for the American Film Theatre which were not historical films or costume dramas include *The Homecoming* (Peter Hall, 1973) (an adaptation of Harold Pinter's stage play); *Butley* (Harold Pinter, 1974) (an adaptation of the play by Simon Gray); and *In Celebration* (Lindsay Anderson, 1974) (an adaptation of a play by David Storey). Furthermore, while they do not deal explicitly with British history, we might also consider some of Ken Russell's 1970s music films as historical films, such as *The Music Lovers* (1970), *Mahler* (1974), and *Lizstomania* (1975). And Russell's controversial *The Devils* (1971) is set in seventeenth-century France.

6

Rural rides:
the countryside and modernity

The backbone of old England: *Akenfield*

Ronald Blythe's novel *Akenfield: Portrait of an English village* was published in 1969, and became a best-seller. The theatre director, Peter Hall (the artistic director of the National Theatre, on London's South Bank, between 1973 and 1988), decided to film an adaptation.[1] For Hall, this was clearly a story for film rather than theatre. As he told Alexander Walker in an interview on 18 July 1974, 'We were doing something only cinema could do, for the camera had to be there and "at the ready" to catch "life" when it was invented.'[2] London Weekend Television (LWT) put up £60,000 for the rights for two television broadcasts, and the National Film Finance Corporation (NFFC) invested a further £20,000.[3] Peter Hall and producer Rex Pyke deferred their fees.[4] Perhaps this is one of the reasons why the Suffolk-born director referred to the film as a 'home movie'.[5] *Akenfield* was filmed on location in a number of villages to the west of Wickham Market in Suffolk, and features a mixture of documentary-style camerawork and fictional set-ups. But while the narrative is fictional, the non-professional actors in the film were all local, and their dialogue was improvised.

Akenfield had a unique exhibition schedule. It was broadcast on LWT in January 1975 and premiered at London's Paris-Pullman cinema at almost the same time (where it opened the London Film Festival that year). This, in effect, was a challenge to a ban in force at the time, which prevented films appearing on television in Britain within four years of their cinematic release. When *Akenfield* was screened on television it drew over 13 million viewers nationally, and made the cover of the widely-read *TV Times* magazine on 26 January.[6] But, even before this, Anglia Television and the BBC had screened documentaries about the production of the film.[7] Interestingly, at that stage, Gareth Jones argued that '*Akenfield* is in no sense a television film, having been conceived and planned as a cinema feature; it merely has the advantage of the backing of a TV company.'[8] But it certainly worked on television, capturing the imagination of much of the nation. Later, the film was screened at festivals in Los Angeles, Moscow, and Tehran. It was distributed to cinemas by David Puttnam and Sandy Lieberson under their VPS banner.[9] But the film was not a box office success, and while it received positive reviews in the USA, no theatrical distributor could be found. So, as Alexander Walker put it, 'Within six months of its premiere, *Akenfield* had turned into a salvage operation.'[10]

The box office failure of *Akenfield* would have been particularly disappointing for those involved with the film, because reviews had generally been excellent. Writing in the *London Evening Standard*, Alexander Walker argued that *Akenfield* was 'one of the best films – and certainly the most unusual – made in and about England'.[11] For Valerie Jenkins, also writing in the *London Evening Standard*, the film was nothing less than a 'masterpiece'.[12] In the same newspaper, Celia Brayfield wrote that, in this 'magnificent film', 'The poetry and misery of life on the land are masterfully drawn.'[13] In *The Times*, John Higgins put it that 'It is the subjectivity and honesty of Akenfield, its total lack of [the] sentimental and picturesque … that allows it to capture part of England in a way that few films have done since the death of Humphrey Jennings.'[14] In *Films Illustrated*, Mark Whitman found *Akenfield* 'deeply moving'.[15] In the *Sunday Telegraph*, Tom Hutchinson poetically opined that 'some of its images cling to the mind like loam to a spade'.[16] The US trade paper *Variety* found the film 'seldom less than engrossing', and its depiction of rural landscape and life 'lyrical, often magical'.[17] But perhaps one of the most telling responses to the film came from Jan Dawson, who, writing in *Sight and Sound*, noticed that 'its central protagonist is the land, its subject the effects of time on it and those who toil upon it'.[18]

Akenfield opens with a panning shot of a distant rural cottage. The camera moves to the left, past mature trees and along a hedgerow, as if to remind us that even the English countryside is characterised by its boundaries; this is an ancient, historically contested space.[19] As Ann Bermingham reminds us, 'With enclosure, landowners acquired land once held in common or wasteland once thought unsuitable for cultivation. Old commons and wastes were divided into fields that were either fenced or hedged with a variety of quick-growing shrubs.'[20]

We soon find out that one character in the film seeks to escape this environment. A man is walking behind the hedgerow. This is our first glimpse of Tom – the youngest of three generations of men from the same family who share the same given name. We hear birdsong. We hear the extra-diegetic sound of violins. A title reads 'Made by People of Suffolk'. Other than a visible telephone wire, the first sign that this action is taking place in contemporary times is the t-shirt worn by Tom's friend, who appears from long grass in the graveyard (we later find out that he is digging Tom's grandfather's grave). We also hear the sound of this man's portable transistor radio. The camera gives us a close-up of this device, as if to emphasise the fact that this is a very old space into which modernity and technology are slowly creeping.

Akenfield is set in a small Suffolk village, and tells the story of local lives unfolding over approximately a hundred years. This village has been given a fictional place name, conflating Akenham (a small village north of Ipswich) and Charsfield (a village near Wickham Market, which itself lies approximately ten miles northeast of Akenham). On location, Peter Hall had the villagers act out the stories of their lives, and the lives of their parents and grandparents. The film crew worked with them at weekends (filming for nearly a year), and chronicled the quotidian activities of the community framed by the gradual shift of the landscape across the seasons. But the film itself is focused on the activities which take place on one spring day in 1974 – the day of the funeral of 'old' Tom. We find out that this character was born, grew up, and died in the village. He left Akenfield once, to fight in the First World War, but returned to spend the rest of his life there. We also learn that he tried to leave on one other occasion – walking the forty miles to Newmarket in search of work – but that he ultimately failed in this pursuit. Old Tom evidently experienced great hardship as a young man, and lost a number of friends during the First World War. He married a woman from the village, and the couple lived in a tied cottage on the farmer's estate. They had a son, Tom, who we find out was young Tom's father. He, like young Tom, was also born in the village, but was killed in the Second World War.

Events in *Akenfield* are effectively seen, remembered or imagined by young Tom (Garrow Shand). During the course of the film we witness him going about his everyday business on the day of old Tom's funeral. But a voiceover accompanies the images, serving to complicate them in terms of their status as depictions of real events. The narrative is also, as such, non-linear. We must surmise that, through the voice we hear, young Tom is remembering (or imagining) the spoken words of his now-dead grandfather. As the voice of the older man accompanies the images of young Tom, we notice that the young man appears to be preoccupied with thoughts of 'elsewhere' (in time and space), and, as such, he rarely appears to be fully engaged 'in the moment', to be absolutely focused on what is happening 'now'. Indeed, in some ways, the unseen old Tom – through his voice – feels as present as his grandson. This young man evidently keeps his late grandfather's memory alive. But, as photographs in the film show eerily, the deceased old man is also present in the younger man's DNA. Indeed, old Tom himself makes the point that, in the village, hands and other parts of bodies appear to survive across the centuries; inherited by children from parents, grandparents, uncles and aunts. There is a discernable influence of the modern poetry of T. S. Eliot on the thematics of the film here, specifically when one considers the ways in which the past and present appear to merge in the experience of successive generations. When viewing *Akenfield*, lines from Eliot's *Four Quartets* (1943) spring to mind, specifically these, from 'East Coker':

> Keeping time,
> Keeping the rhythm in their dancing
> As in their living in the living seasons
> The time of the seasons and the constellations
> The time of milking and the time of harvest

The time of the coupling of man and woman
And that of beasts. Feet rising and falling.
Eating and drinking. Dung and death.

Dawn points, and another day
Prepares for heat and silence. Out at sea the dawn wind
Wrinkles and slides. I am here
Or there, or elsewhere. In my beginning.[21]

So, as in Eliot's poem, while change is evident in the English rural space depicted in *Akenfield*, this does not necessarily occur in a linear fashion across time.

Young Tom lives with his long-widowed mother in a small cottage in the present-day 1970s. On the death of old Tom, the tied cottage becomes available. The local farmer and landowner seemingly notices an opportunity to get young Tom to work for him for life, and offers him tenancy of this cottage. Young Tom's girlfriend appears to understand that, if he agrees to take this cottage, he will be able to move out of his mother's cottage and offer her marriage. So, on the day of old Tom's funeral, young Tom has a life-changing decision to make. Will he accept the offer of the cottage, marry his girlfriend, and spend the rest of his life in Akenfield? Or is he willing to take the risk of leaving the village and seeking a new life elsewhere?

Interestingly, this decision is clearly influenced by old Tom, who, present to young Tom throughout the film (and to us, in the form of the voice over), tells stories of his own failed attempt to better himself by trying to leave the village. This voice is accompanied on the soundtrack by the haunting strings of Michael Tippett's *Fantasia Convertante on a Theme of Corelli*. At the end of the film, young Tom heads off toward Ipswich to catch a train to London. Driving out of the village down a narrow country lane, he looks out of the window of his friend's Morris Minor and sees a man, hunched and alone, wandering back towards Akenfield. Is this the ghost of old Tom wandering back from Newmarket? We never find out. Nor do we know if this vision proves enough to convince young Tom to continue to make the journey to the big city. The narrative of the film, as such, remains unresolved.

Old Tom's voiceover, then, is a key formal feature of *Akenfield*. It is a warm, colloquial voice, both wise and charming, and spoken in a strong Suffolk accent. This voice has the uncanny effect of suggesting a sense of deep history in one specific space. It is a voice that is evocative of more than just the experience of one man, but of a community, and also, perhaps, of the human condition at a moment of profound change. Tippett's swelling music also pulls the aesthetics of the film away from naturalism, lending the everyday events pictured an uncanny level of emotional depth and power. In its use of the voiceover and the music on the soundtrack, then, *Akenfield* displays innovative formal qualities. But while much of the camerawork by Ivan Strasburg is naturalistic, rapid editing occurs between young Tom and what appears to be his point of view. And handheld camerawork features throughout the film. *Akenfield* was shot in colour in little more than natural light - sunlight floods in through the cottage windows. And some sequences make it feel like a film in the British documentary tradition - the baptism ceremony, for example, and the shots of rural labourers going about their work. This is also the case with the wake sequence in Dulcie's cottage, during which the camera gets very close to the people present, and develops a real sense of community, but also, at the same time, a distinct feeling of claustrophobia.

Akenfield is a film primarily concerned with the nature of memory (individual memories, the shared memories of communities, and national memories) and how these memories facilitate a sense of 'home'. Interestingly, many of the shared memories of this rural community are developed and maintained through rituals, such as the instance when, during a harvest, a young boy is pulled up on top of a cart full of hay and crowned, and when the villagers sing and chant 'largesse' on their way home from the fields. Here, then, we see a community which remains in touch with natural cycles. But young Tom cuts a melancholy figure. He obviously longs to escape these cycles, rituals, and memories. He is trapped by the past, and Akenfield, for him, remains a place that contains his past. If his memories make him the man he is, can he ever leave?

Modernity intrudes in intriguing ways into the sleepy life of the fictional village. For example, not long after the beginning of the film, we hear the very loud sound of a fighter jet as it flies low over the church. Elsewhere in the film the new constantly erupts into the old. When a grocer turns up at Dulcie's cottage, young Tom takes a piece of factory-made sliced bread from a Sunblest plastic bag. So, even here in rural Suffolk, mass-produced, supermarket products are seemingly creeping in, speaking of the shift in consumer habits in Britain in the 1960s and 1970s. This is further evidenced by the blue milk lorry which, rumbling down the village street, invades the otherwise bucolic scene. So, in *Akenfield*, modernity sits rather uncomfortably alongside apparently unchanging rural iconography. Indeed, old Tom displays an awareness of the ways in which modernity is altering rural life: 'We wore our bodies to death. You only wear out a few machines,' he says, as a brightly-painted combine harvester stalks the country lanes. Another example of this occurs in the sequence that takes place in the funeral cars, when a conversation concerning progress develops, and an old woman tells of cottages being knocked down and new buildings going up. As such, *Akenfield* speaks of debates that were being engaged with in Britain during the 1970s concerning the dangers of mechanisation, and what might possibly be lost to the nation through this process. One should also remark that the presence of London is palpable in the film, as a distant force; as a nexus. Young Tom certainly feels the imaginative draw of the capital.

Both World Wars are seen to have profoundly shaped the experience of this rural community, and the people's knowledge of who they are. In another shift in time, we witness a dance taking place in the village hall during World War Two, when young Tom's soldier father meets his mother, Dulcie. We learn that subsequently he goes off to war and is killed in action. And elsewhere in the film we find out, through to the voice of old Tom, that joining the army was seen as a means of escape from the village for young men during the First World War. What is intriguing about these shifts in the film between talk of the First World War and images of events taking place during the Second World War is that they demonstrate just how far both conflicts still, in the 1970s, served to inform what was left of the collective memory of a fragmenting British nation. In this way, both wars feel present even in the contemporary moment, and thus also serve to disrupt notions of linear historical time and progress. When we see a jump cut depicting old Tom's cottage across decades, we are reminded that material changes to our environment over time are not always discernable, and that we can be haunted by genetic and imaginary legacies. As such, we can read the cottage here, like the village church and the village itself, as a deep repository of memories. On this and other occasions in the film, the past and present appear to merge into each other. These moments are often breathtaking, such as the moment when the film cuts from the interior of the church when the congregation is singing in the present day to the same space decades earlier, when soldiers take up the hymn. Time appears to shift and break down in other interesting ways. The potential for current and future warfare is evoked by the roar of the jet fighter which appears over the church again as the congregation leaves. Interestingly, in all probability this fighter jet would have been stationed at RAF Lakenheath, an air base in Suffolk also used by US Air Force units and personnel, and is thus suggestive of the developing political relationship between Britain and the USA during the Cold War.

Akenfield was shot on 35mm film in Techniscope, which provides a 'letter-box' widescreen image that Alexander Walker points out was suited to Suffolk's wide, low horizons.[22] But this part of the English countryside had long been eulogised in literature. William Cobbett wrote of the Suffolk landscape near Ipswich in his famous *Rural Rides* (1832) thus:

> From the town itself you can see nothing; but you can, in no direction, go from it a quarter of a mile without finding views that a painter might crave, and then the country round about it so well cultivated; the land in such a beautiful state, the farmhouses all white, and all so much alike; the barns, and everything about the homesteads so snug; the stocks of turnips so abundant everywhere; the sheep and cattle in such fine order; the wheat all drilled; the ploughman so expert; the furrows, if a quarter of a mile long, as straight as a line, and laid as truly as if with a level: in short, here is everything to delight the eye, and to make the people proud of their country.[23]

Akenfield is an elegiac, bucolic British film which features a number of shots of the type of rural Suffolk landscape that is seemingly little changed since Cobbett's time. But these shots are distinctly pictorial, and, in addition to echoing representations in literature, they also evoke a rich tradition of British landscape painting.

The harvest shots of the workers in the fields in *Akenfield* specifically resemble the work of a number of English landscape artists. The most obvious comparison to make here would be to John Constable's paintings of the Stour Valley in Suffolk. But other key works of art also spring to mind. George Lambert's 1733 painting *A View of Boxhill in Surrey* was arguably the first proper British landscape painting – the first painting of a British landscape for its own sake. We see farm labourers harvesting corn in a rural setting. Thomas Gainsborough painted a number of georgic landscapes in his Suffolk period (1748–59). These were often simple images of the human condition, or images of rural communities existing in 'nature', such as *Landscape with a Woodcutter Courting a Milkmaid* (1755), which depicts a young couple on uncultivated common ground, and *The Harvest Wagon* (1767). Other examples of paintings that *Akenfield* echoes in visual terms include George Morland's rustic landscapes, such as *Ferreting* (1792) and *Bargaining for Sheep* (1794), which effectively pulled the tradition of landscape painting in Britain away from the classical preferences of the upper classes. *Ferreting* depicts poaching – a form of thieving from landowners. Men could be hanged for this activity. Sequences in *Akenfield* certainly share Morland's preoccupation with the everyday activities of the rural poor; the things they have to do to survive.

Akenfield also features beautiful haymaking sequences shot in the rural Suffolk landscape. In their pictorial quality, these shots certainly echo a range of paintings from the eighteenth and nineteenth centuries. Again, these paintings are very rich ideological texts, and the works of various artists encourage very different readings concerning the political implications of how the rural poor are depicted. On the one hand, as the art historian Michael Rosenthal points out, 'hawking parties or haymaking rustics are … typical signifiers of the philosophy of country life in which the patrons of these pictures liked to believe'.[24] In paintings of the mid-1700s, 'Haymaking meant that summer had come and with it relaxation and dalliance.'[25] Examples include George Lambert's *Hilly Landscape with a Cornfield* (1733), in which the cornfield is cut by a solitary, token reaper. But, unlike the work of George Lambert,

George Stubbs' paintings display an order which evokes the composition of classical paintings. A number of his works, including
Haymakers (1785) and *Reapers* (1785), feature people toiling in rural
landscapes. These staffage paintings have divided critical opinion.
Some argue that they display the heroism of everyday rural life.
Rosenthal puts it that Stubbs' landscapes display a 'detached objec-
tivity' which portrays 'actual labourers'.[26] But other critics argue
that these images dehumanise rural labourers, or that they are too
clean and tidy to be doing this type of work.[27] It does seem as
though the labourers in Stubbs' paintings appear contented and
comfortable with their lot. They are not struggling, covered in dirt
or sweat. Perhaps, then, these are rural workers as the upper classes
would like to have imagined them.

But this is not the case with portrayals of figures in the rural
landscape in *Akenfield*. This is a film at pains to capture the realistic nature of agricultural toil, both in its hardship, but also in its
moments of celebration; the community's evident enjoyment of life
when the work is done. As such, the film is closer, in its representation of rural labourers, to John Constable's *The Wheatfield* (1816),
which depicts a scene of tranquility and rural contentment with
no clear evidence of rural unrest. As Christina Payne points out,
'A painting of a good harvest was not only an illustration of the
goodness of God; it could also be a symbol of peace, prosperity,
social harmony and good government, and thus an expression of
patriotic pride.'[28] In *Akenfield*, Peter Hall shows us rural landscapes
that speak of the community that works them. Images of the
haymakers are characterised by movement as we witness the end
of the corn harvest, the 'horkey' (harvest feast), and the 'last load'.
But there is also the palpable sense here that this way of life is in
danger of retreating into memory.

Akenfield, then, is a film about the passing of a life, but also about
the passing of a way of life. Here we see the potential death of
an old, traditional, rural community. This film might also be read
as a requiem for the old nation. After all, a letter of condolence
read out at old Tom's wake refers to him as 'the backbone of Old
England'. We might go so far as to read the village of Akenfield
itself as representative of aspects of 1970s Britain; or, at best, as a
microcosm of a threatened rural England. It is, after all, on the one

hand a space of stasis – a space in which some things appear never to change; or, if they do change, to change extremely slowly. But this is also a space into which change (and modernity) will inevitably come. It is no surprise to discover that other film-makers were engaged in exploring the emergence of a new vision of Britain in the mid-1970s.

The Lord gave and the Lord hath taken away: *Requiem for a Village*

David Gladwell's *Requiem for a Village* (1975) – a 'deeply-felt expression of the unities of time and place' according to John Pym – mines very similar thematic territory to Peter Hall's coeval *Akenfield*.[29] This film too was shot primarily on location in rural Suffolk (around the villages of Witnesham and Metfield), and is also centrally engaged with what might be lost to old ways of life as modernity forces change on rural England. This poetic, elegiac film centres on the experience, thoughts and memories of one old man (Vic Smith), who, while slowly and carefully tending the graves in a village churchyard, talks about the people he knew who now lie buried there. According to Elizabeth Sussex, writing in *Sight and Sound* at the time that the film was released, 'His words drop inconsequentially out of the present.'[30] But images of the old man suggest immensely rich and complex links between the past and the present. As Sussex puts it, 'What the mind's eye has seen, quite simply becomes visible.'[31]

David Gladwell is best known for his work as an editor on Lindsay Anderson's *If...* (1968) and *O Lucky Man!* (1973), but also on the 1972 BBC television series *Ways of Seeing*, presented by the art critic, John Berger. Gladwell also made the films *A Summer Discord* (1955), *Miss Thompson Goes Shopping* (1958), *28b Camden Street* (1963) and *An Untitled Film* (aka *The Killing*) (1964). He went on to direct the feature film *Memoirs of a Survivor* (1981), adapted from Doris Lessing's 1974 novel and starring Julie Christie, who, during the 1970s, also appeared in seminal films such as the British-made *The Go-Between* (Joseph Losey, 1970), *Don't Look Now* (Nicolas Roeg, 1973), and the US science fiction film *Demon Seed* (Donald Cammell,

1975). Gladwell has stated that his influences were drawn primarily from European art cinema: 'Eisenstein, Pudovkin, Prévert, Claire, Bunuel, Cocteau, Fellini, Resnais, Vigo.'[32] But the director has also signalled the fact that the main inspiration for *Requiem for a Village* was the English painter, Stanley Spencer: 'People emerging from graves as embodied spirits in the clothes they wore in life, waking from a long sleep, yawning and rubbing their eyes: stretching and catching sight of friends and relatives among the living.'[33] Some of the camerawork in *Requiem for a Village* is by Walter Lassally, a key figure in the Free Cinema and New Wave movements, who shot films such as *Every Day Except Christmas* (Lindsay Anderson, 1957); *We Are the Lambeth Boys* (Karel Reisz, 1959); *A Taste of Honey* (Tony Richardson, 1961); *The Loneliness of the Long Distance Runner* (Tony Richardson, 1962); and *Tom Jones* (Tony Richardson, 1963). The music in *Requiem for a Village* is by David Fanshawe, and, like Tippett's work used in *Akenfield*, plays a crucial role in conjuring up the sense of a deep past in one location. As Elisabeth Sussex put it, Fanshawe's music is 'evocative of a once immovable faith'.[34] As if to anchor the music in the earth, most of the words sung in the film are taken from tombstones in the graveyard.[35]

The opening shots of *Requiem for a Village* feature the roofs of a new housing development; images accompanied on the soundtrack by the sound of a transistor radio, overheard conversations, and babies crying. The old man (Smith) takes a bicycle from a garden shed situated to the rear of one of these new properties and makes his way up the street. We see close-ups of clean, new walls and more angled roofs. This is the architecture of a new, modern Britain. But this is a nondescript place, exemplified by clean, straight lines. The streets are fresh; the lawns are well-tended. Indeed, there is an overwhelming sense of newness here. All traces of the past in this space have seemingly been erased. The film cuts to a shot of a cultivated field and mature trees beyond. The visible differences between this space and the housing estate in the previous shots are immediate and telling. The past is still evident in this rural field; enclosed generations ago, and no doubt farmed for just as long. A cockerel crows. We see an old country lane, with deep, ancient hedgerows. The film cuts to a shot of an old cottage. Then we are in the village graveyard; lichen covering the weathered headstones.

A number of other painterly shots follow, all held with a static camera. We see old, well-trodden paths. The old man comes to a busy road on his bicycle. He is clearly an anachronistic figure at this modern roadside. The film cuts again to a shot of the new housing estate. A bright pink ice cream van squats in the centre of the frame. We cut back to old cottages, and a series of close-up images of ancient walls and rickety roof tiles. This is followed by the first of a number of shots of huge land-flattening equipment in a field; giant, yellow vehicles in the livery of the Wimpey Homes construction company.[36] So we can see that changes to this ancient rural English landscape are being brought about by faceless, gigantic mechanical leviathans.

During another sequence, the old man is seen cycling down the busy A12 dual carriageway, being passed by speeding cars and a lorry taking goods to supermarket chain stores run by the Dutch company, Spar. The old man then pedals down a country lane. We see close-up shots of a cow's tail moving in slow motion, followed by a farmer feeding chickens. Offering evidence of the influence of European art cinema, Gladwell has written that his interest in incorporating slow-motion shots came from his love of sequences such as the pillow-fight in *Zéro de Conduite* (Jean Vigo, 1933), the funeral procession in *Entr'acte* (René Clair, 1924), and the boy's nightmare in *Los Olvidados* (aka *The Young and the Damned*) (Luis Buñuel, 1950).[37] This slow-motion sequence is followed by some of the first dialogue in the film.

We are in a village hall, at a meeting. The vicar speaks to those gathered of how he has lived in the village for twenty years, but admits that others present have families that have lived there for generations. We cut again to the old man, now tending a grave, and the choral music returns. This is the beginning of one of the most remarkable sequences in the film. The old man looks up, with a face of concern; perhaps even of fear. His attention has been drawn to something. As the film cuts to a point-of-view shot, we see that he has spotted the surface of a grave moving. Hands appear out of the earth, and gradually, in slow motion, a man rises up. Elsewhere in the graveyard, other people in period clothing shake off the earth and walk again, and slowly make their way into the old church. The old man follows them, and, on entering this building, discovers he is young again; perhaps fifty years younger. Here, as in *Akenfield*, the essentially unchanged environment of the church acts as a deep repository of memories. It is as if the old walls have recorded the key moments in the lives of generations of villagers. We see that the old man's younger self has appeared at his own wedding. This is followed by images of celebrations of the past. As in *Akenfield*, we see painterly shots of people making hay in the fields as they would have done for generations; these images are intercut with the marriage ceremony.

The formal qualities of *Requiem for a Village* pose problems for straightforward genre classification, because, while the images feel like documentary footage, the use of an intercutting editing style (which operates throughout) lends the film a modernist aesthetic, problematising, as it does, linear time and the construction of space. The editing and the music draw these images into uncanny territory. We see shots of blacksmiths at work, taking pride in their craft. But in a strange sequence reminiscent in some ways of a number of period-set, location-shot British horror films of the early 1970s, we see a child capture a small frog and hang it by its leg from a tree near a stream. A sudden cut takes us on through time, eliminating weeks or even months, and we now see nothing but the frog's skeleton remaining. The bones are gently broken up by hands in close-up, and tossed into the slow-moving water. This sequence clearly evokes the passing of time and the inevitability of death. And, indeed, death stalks this film. But death is seen as merely a natural aspect of 'change'; that is, as an element of natural cycles, as something that cannot be governed by modern science or altered by technological progress. In a continuation of the editing pattern we see a shot of a horse captured in slow motion. The film then cuts to shots of paving stones in a pedestrianised shopping precinct. This is effectively a 'new' space, but the damaged lettering of a sign on the roof which reads 'The Centre' suggests that this modern place is already getting old.

But other sections of the film locate us firmly within the everyday lives if the contemporary villagers in a more naturalistic way. Indeed, the charming longer sequence that covers the events around the wedding breakfast has a documentary feel to it. The gathered villagers sing old songs such as 'Daisy, Daisy', and show themselves to be an organic community. Theirs is a life in touch with nature; a simple, rural existence which is clearly coming under threat in 1970s Britain. A newly married couple's first night together is captured as a slow-moving, fumbling, nervous affair; silent but for the sounds of rustling clothes being discarded; tentative footsteps taken on creaking wooden floorboards. But the film suddenly cuts to the scream of a woman in childbirth; the baby is seen emerging from the mother's body. Time passes rapidly again, and this child, now an adult woman, watches her father (the old man – Vic Smith) leave the modern house with his bicycle. At this moment in the film, a biker gang enters the new landscape. This gang performs a complex symbolic function in the film (as youth; as rapid movement; as immorality; as modernity), and will play a key part in the narrative later on.

The bikers here are reminiscent of a gang that features in the British horror film *Psychomania* (aka *The Death Wheelers*) (Don Sharp, 1972) (discussed in Chapter 7), and exhibit traces of the characteristics of the ultra-violent Droogs in Stanley Kubrick's notorious *A Clockwork Orange* (1971). Gladwell certainly plays on the aggressive nature of their faceless movements through space, and the brute roar of the motorbike engines. They burn off down a country lane, under modern electricity pylons. Their arrival signals a darker turn for the film. The old man enters the field in which the earth-moving machine lies idle. He circles it – a process which makes its monstrous size abundantly clear – and then attacks it (if rather half-heartedly) with a clump of earth. The film then cuts to images of a man tending a horse, and the ploughing of a field about to begin. In these shots (as in shots of men cutting wood and making a wheel) one gets the sense of the amount of effort and skill required to perform this traditional labour, and the time necessarily spent to attain respectable levels of old-fashioned craftsmanship. But one also notices a sense of danger in this work and the constant possibility of injury or death. Again, pain and death are ever-present in this film, lurking in quotidian moments. But there is also a sense of purpose in the activities of the people of the past, and we get the impression that their time is taken up with very few things. Merely surviving from day-to-day and from year-to-year is enough to concern them.

But *Requiem for a Village* is troubling on occasion. In the visions of the past and the present constructed in the film, things occur that are morally repugnant, but are also depicted as being as natural as making hay. For example, as the farm labourers break for lunch in a sun-kissed field, two young men follow a young woman away from the assembled villagers (who remain oblivious, lunching on bread, cheese and onions). The men find the young woman sitting alone by some hay. They brutally force themselves on her and rape her. This sequence is intercut with shots of the male bikers raping a young woman in the contemporary moment. One questions here whether these are the memories of the old man at the centre of the film. Whichever way we choose to read these intercut sequences, they demonstrate a horrific level of sexual violence. But perhaps they are also somehow symbolic. The film cuts to images of a wood which has been flattened by machines to make way for a new development. As such, we might read these intercut sequences as evocative of a rural landscape and way of life in the process of being aggressively violated by modern technology in the service of progress. In other words, the innocence of the English past is being violently erased.

The old man leaves his day at work in the graveyard, and takes his bicycle out through a rickety gateway. Meanwhile, we see intercut images of the young biker gang careering at speed down country lanes. The editing here indicates what is about to happen; death, after all, as the film shows, is inevitable. The old man is struck by one of the bikers, and falls, twisted, on to the grass verge. As Elizabeth Sussex pointed out in *Sight and Sound*, this is the man's 'last on earth'.[38] But we have already sensed it. Modernity, technology and change have killed him. In this film, these things are also seemingly on the verge of killing an old England and an old Britain. But this is not the end. In another extraordinary sequence, the dead – the people of the past – rise again. Up from their graves they come in their Sunday best, and the old man rises again with them. On the soundtrack, a haunting musical refrain hovers like a will-o'-the-wisp in the country air; lines sung by a lover from beyond the grave: 'God will give you to me again'. The film cuts to an empty rural wasteland; an area cleared for a new development. Now the singers join in on the lines: 'The Lord gave and the Lord

hath taken away'. The film cuts again to the new housing development. The biker gang roars towards us down the street. This, then,
is 1970s Britain; a nation poised on the cusp of modernity, but also
unable to forget past traditions; a nation in which the past is ever
present, even if it is not always visible in the new developments
springing up across the countryside. As such, Rob Young notes that
Requiem for a Village, like *Akenfield*, shares some of the concerns of
Penda's Fen (Alan Clarke, 1974), a BBC television *Play for Today* –
written by David Rudkin – which features a figure from the past in
the shape of the pagan king Penda of Mercia, 'bursting out of the
earth to bring guidance to would-be radicals of the modern age'.[39]

Like many of the 1970s British films discussed in this book,
Requiem for a Village resists generic classification. At moments
it feels like a horror film – the iconography of the sequences in
which the dead rise out of their graves is a case in point, as are
the rape sequences. In other ways, though, the film functions as
a rural drama; as a neo-modernist exploration of memory; as a
documentary; and as a poetic meditation on rural England. But,
like *Akenfield*, *Requiem for a Village* can also be considered to be a rural
film concerned with the threat of change.

The modernisation of Britain in the 1970s was keenly felt and
widely feared. One response to this fear was the development of
a heritage consciousness.[40] Indeed, throughout the 1980s and in
to the 1990s, representations of the rural in English cinema were
found most notably within the heritage film genre.[41] Writing about
British heritage films, Andrew Higson argues that 'This is more
than just a breath of fresh air, it is a long vacation from present-day
realities, a rose-tinted journey into the past, a past we are invited to
visit.'[42] This heritage vision of the past often facilitated the construction and maintenance of a coherent sense of national identity. But
Requiem for a Village and *Akenfield* resist such interpretations. Though
they offer views of old rural traditions and pictorial glimpses of life
in the countryside of the past as well as the present, these are by no
means heritage films. But they might instead be called rural films.

For Catherine Fowler and Gillian Helfield, rural cinema can
be distinguished from heritage cinema.[43] As they point out, 'the
heritage film may demonstrate a harmonious relationship between
man and nature and between peasant and fellow members of

the rural community ...Within rural cinema, however, the mood is not always nostalgic, nor are the films' representations of the rural inhabitant necessarily positive'.[44] Furthermore, rural cinema is concerned primarily with the relationship between the land and its inhabitants, and how this relationship develops in terms of a merging of physical and social landscapes.[45] As we have seen, *Akenfield* and *Requiem for a Village* certainly display one important feature that provides structure to the lives of rural inhabitants (but also to the film itself): natural cycles. These films take us through the seasons, linked cycles in agriculture, but also cycles of birth and death, and long-held cultural cycles (witness the religious events and folk rituals). But, again, these are by no means heritage films. Sarah Cardwell points out that 'Landscapes in heritage films are controlled, peaceful, unthreatening.'[46] In contrast to this, there is an unremitting state of threat in both *Requiem for a Village* and *Akenfield* – the threat of change; of modernity.[47]

Akenfield and *Requiem for a Village* appeared in a Britain that was being travelled by the poet John Betjeman, who was also making BBC films about landscapes, villages and the past: *Metro-land* (1973), *A Passion for Churches* (1974), and *Summoned by Bells* (1976).[48] But unlike Hall's and Gladwell's films, Betjeman's work evoked a widely-held, nostalgic vision of the countryside. While *Akenfield* and *Requiem for a Village* do display elements of nostalgia for a vanishing rural past, this past is never simple, uncomplicated, or untroubled, and it is not without contradictory elements. In these films, then, it is the stable sense of national identity widely depicted in heritage films that is, if anything, under threat. In *Requiem for a Village* and *Akenfield*, the past haunts the present; it holds the present in a tight and suffocating grip.

But other British films of the 1970s also resist readings as heritage texts. For example, one might argue that *The Go-Between* (Joseph Losey, 1970), which was shot almost entirely at one country house location (Melton Constable Hall in Norfolk), paints far too dark a picture of the lives of the landowners and labourers for it to be seen as a heritage film.[49] And *The Ruling Class* (Peter Medak, 1972), in which a country house also features (Harlaxton Manor in Lincolnshire and Cliveden in Buckinghamshire stand in for the fictional Gurney House), is far too strange to be read as a heritage text.[50]

In terms of the ways in which *Akenfield* and *Requiem for a Village* function as films that resist classification as heritage texts, one might also compare them to modern visions of the English landscape exemplified by the poetry of Philip Larkin. Adam Nicolson notices the importance of Larkin's seminal poetry collection *The Whitsun Weddings* (1964) in terms of how the English countryside might be viewed in modern times: 'the archetype of the modern relation to landscape, a modern version of the pastoral which understands the inaccessibility of innocence, its fragile, distant nature'.[51] *Akenfield* and *Requiem for a Village* do not locate innocence, simplicity and coherence in the past, then, but instead demonstrate that the fragmentary socio-cultural life of contemporary modern Britain can be seen to be a product of contested histories. These histories exacerbate the vicissitudes of the present.

Notes

1   A. Walker, *National Heroes*, p. 227.
2   A. Walker, *National Heroes*, p. 227.
3   See Jones, 'Akenfield', p. 193.
4   A. Walker, *National Heroes*, pp. 227–8.
5   Jones, 'Akenfield', p. 193.
6   Available at: www.akenfield.com.
7   Available at: www.akenfield.com.
8   Jones, 'Akenfield', p. 193.
9   Available at: www.akenfield.com/makingakenfield.html.
10 A. Walker, *National Heroes*, p. 228.
11 A. Walker, *London Evening Standard*, 25 July 1974.
12 Jenkins, *London Evening Standard*, 23 January 1975.
13 Brayfield, *London Evening Standard*, 24 January 1975.
14 Higgins, *The Times*, 9 October 1974.
15 Whitman, 'Akenfield'.
16 Hutchinson, *Sunday Telegraph*, 26 January 1975.
17 Anon., *Variety*, 14 January 1975.
18 Dawson, 'Akenfield', p. 58.
19 See Mabey, 'Landscape: terra firma?', pp. 65–6.
20 Bermingham, *Landscape and Ideology: The English Rustic Tradition 1740–1860*, p. 9.
21 Eliot, *Collected Poems 1909–1962*, p. 197.
22 A. Walker, *National Heroes*, p. 228.

23 Cobbett, *Rural Rides Volume 2*, p. 225.

24 Rosenthal, *British Landscape Painting*, p. 24.

25 Rosenthal, *British Landscape Painting*, p. 28.

26 Rosenthal, *British Landscape Painting*, p. 92.

27 Rosenthal, *British Landscape Painting*, p. 94.

28 Payne, *Toil and Plenty: Images of the Agricultural Landscape in England, 1780–1890*, p. 40.

29 Pym, 'Requiem for a Village', p. 197.

30 Sussex, 'Requiem for a Village', p. 60.

31 Sussex, 'Requiem for a Village', p. 60.

32 Gladwell, 'David Gladwell Discusses His Work', p. 14.

33 Gladwell, 'David Gladwell Discusses His Work', p. 15.

34 Sussex, 'Requiem for a Village', p. 60.

35 Sussex, 'Requiem for a Village', p. 60.

36 Young, 'Requiem for a Village: Cinema of the Anti-Scrape', p. 10.

37 Gladwell, 'David Gladwell Discusses His Work', pp. 14–15.

38 Sussex, 'Requiem for a Village', p. 60.

39 Young, 'Requiem for a Village: Cinema of the Anti-Scrape', p. 11.

40 Mandler, 'New Towns for Old: The Fate of the Town Centre', p. 226.

41 Cardwell, 'Working the Land: Representations of Rural England in Adaptations of Thomas Hardy's Novels', p. 25.

42 Higson, 'A Green and Pleasant Land: Rural Spaces and British Cinema', p. 248.

43 Fowler and Helfield, 'Introduction', p. 5.

44 Fowler and Helfield, 'Introduction', pp. 5–6.

45 Fowler and Helfield, 'Introduction', p. 6.

46 Cardwell, 'Working the Land: Representations of Rural England in Adaptations of Thomas Hardy's Novels', p. 26.

47 For more on British heritage cinema, see Monk, 'The British Heritage-Film Debate Revisited', p. 179.

48 Young, 'Requiem for a Village: Cinema of the Anti-Scrape', pp. 10–12.

49 Broughton, 'Landscape Gardens in *The Ruling Class*', p. 244.

50 Broughton, 'Landscape Gardens in *The Ruling Class*', p. 245.

51 Nicolson, 'Introduction', in *Towards a New Landscape*, p. 11.

7

Close to the edge:
peripheral Britain

> One had forgotten how truly rural rural places can be.
>
> Mrs Hargreaves, *Killer's Moon* (Alan Birkinshaw, 1978)

The opening credits sequence of the horror film *Killer's Moon* (Alan Birkinshaw, 1978)[1] features a coach driving through the present-day Lake District, an exemplar of a rugged rural English landscape. On the coach are a group of schoolgirls singing 'Greensleeves', accompanied by their two female teachers. They are clearly on a school trip. The coach breaks down, and the party is forced to seek shelter in a remote, ramshackle old hotel. But it turns out that they are in danger. Four escaped psychiatric patients are roaming the countryside. These men have been dosed with LSD as part of their treatment, and they now appear to be convinced they are in a shared dream in which they can freely rape and murder whoever they please. The film thus revels in the dark mysteries of the English rural landscape, here painted as a wilderness dotted with whitewashed cottages in which real or imagined terrors might lurk.

The countryside is set up as the location of horrific or morally suspect behaviour in a range of British films of the period. Often this space is seen to encapsulate elements of a dark past which now feel horrific in the modern present. What is seen to go on here exemplifies modern fears concerning seemingly uncanny and irrational aspects of British life. Other films of the late 1960s and early 1970s, such as *Witchfinder General* (Michael Reeves, 1968), *The Plague of the Zombies* (John Gilling, 1966), and the Amicus-produced portmanteau horror film *And Now the Screaming Starts!* (aka *Fengriffen*) (Roy Ward Baker, 1973) depict past rural British communities in which evil stirs. But *Killer's Moon* can be read alongside coeval films such as *Doomwatch* (Peter Sasdy, 1972); *Neither the Sea Nor the Sand* (Fred Burnley, 1972); *The Wicker Man* (Robin Hardy, 1973); *Straw Dogs* (Sam Peckinpah, 1973); and *Symptoms* (José Ramón Larraz, 1974) – films of the period that locate the horrific, the uncanny and the bizarre specifically in remote rural and coastal areas. Set on the physical, material edges of the British land mass, these films uncover activity which is unfolding on the edges of mainstream British experience. In this chapter I want to examine a range of films of the 1970s (including some listed above) that deal with the horrors which might exist on the peripheries of Britain and mainstream British life. But I want to concentrate my attention primarily on one British-made film, directed by a Pole, which develops a narrative that plays out on the edge of England – but also on the edge of everyday experience – *The Shout* (Jerzy Skolimowski, 1978).[2]

I have heard some sounds in my time, you know: *The Shout*

The Shout stars Alan Bates, Susannah York and John Hurt.[3] It was nominated for the *Palme d'Or* at the Cannes Film Festival in 1978, and received the Grand Prize of the Jury in a tie with *Bye Bye Monkey* (Marco Ferreri, 1978). William Johnson thought it was 'the most engrossing' film at the New York Film Festival that year.[4] Richard Combs called the film 'the intellectual *Exorcist*' – high praise indeed.[5] *The Shout* was shot on location in North Devon in South West England, primarily around Braunton Burrows and Saunton Sands. Interiors were shot at Pinewood Studios. The film was financed by the National Film Trustee Company, the Recorded Picture Company, the Rank Organisation, and the National Film Finance Corporation (NFFC). For this film, Skolimowski adapted a short story by Robert Graves originally published in 1926. It was shot by Mike Molloy, who had worked as a camera operator with Nicolas Roeg on *Performance* (1970) and *Walkabout* (1971), and with Stanley Kubrick on *A Clockwork Orange* (1971) and *Barry Lyndon* (1975).

There is an idiosyncratic vision of Britain evident in Skolimowski's *The Shout*, as there is in his earlier, equally memorable *Deep End* (1970). This vision can be put down at least in part to his status as a trans-European exile. His outsider's view of the nation is certainly evident in the look and tone of these two films. But they still manage to remain ostensibly products of a British national cinema at the level of iconography and representation. Indeed, writing about Skolimowski's work on *The Shout*, Philip Strick argued that 'As with *Deep End*, he preserves the accents and accidents of the national character with unarguable authenticity and then proceeds to undermine it at every turn.'[6] Moreover, noting the director's peculiarities of vision, Richard Combs wrote in *Monthly Film Bulletin*, just after the release of *The Shout*:

> To a greater extent than can be explained by the caprices and misfortunes of the international film market, Jerzy Skolimowski's career has been a remarkable, halting, lurching zig-zag from country to country. And more than just a simple sense of alienness, or the feeling that each new environment becomes a purely fictional reconstruction, this erratic history seems responsible for a basic peculiarity of perspective in his films: local forms of life take on some frighteningly bizarre aspects, while the most outlandish tricks of plot and character quite naturally take their place in the scheme of things.[7]

The Shout tells the story of a mysterious loner, Charles Crossley (Alan Bates), who arrives in a remote Devon village, where he gains entry into the cottage (and thus into the lives) of a young, childless married couple, Anthony and Rachel Fielding (John Hurt and Susannah York). Anthony is an avant-garde musician. In his studio he uses synthesizers, a vocoder (a kind of synthesizer used to reproduce human speech), and a range of other electronic equipment to create experimental music. We see him bowing the edge of a sardine can, recording a wasp buzzing in a jam jar, and capturing the sonic properties of marbles rolling through water dripped on to a metal tray. Crossley tells the couple (over the

Sunday lunch to which he has invited himself) that he previously lived with Aborigines in Australia for 18 years. There, he murdered his children (allegedly according to Aboriginal custom) and learned how to kill with his shout. During his stay at their cottage, Crossley seduces Rachel, and thus temporarily usurps Anthony. Through the figure of Crossley (who carries a pointed bone to facilitate his death magic), Aboriginal culture provides a magical, unknowable, horrific force in the film in such a way, it should be said, that proves problematical at the level of the evident ideological 'Otherness' of this representation. But Aboriginal magic is introduced here as a strategy which evokes the strangeness to be found in everyday British (or, more accurately, English) culture. Mysterious stones found on the dunes near the couple's remote coastal home appear to hold the souls of some of the villagers, and Anthony later renders Crossley incapacitated when he finds his 'soul stone' and proceeds to smash it into four pieces between the soles of his shoes.

Much of the story is told retrospectively. But this is not a straight-forward flashback. The narrative remains ambiguous. In *Film Quarterly*, William Johnson pointed out that 'the film, analogically, avoids subjective camerawork or voiceover narration'.[8] *The Shout* begins with grainy, blurry images of a male Aborigine zig-zagging across an impressive dune system, gradually moving towards the camera, and carrying what we eventually see to be a sharpened death bone in his hand (later it is suggested that this could be a fragment of Anthony and Rachel's shared dream).[9] This credits sequence, with its treated sounds of blustery wind, and distant-sounding rushes of piano, sets up the ambiguous, dream-like nature of the events that follow.

The film then cuts to a more realistic mode of representation, showing a car screeching to a halt outside a large house, and Rachel (Susannah York) rushing inside, where she finds dead male bodies laid out under white sheets on long tables in the wood-panelled dining room. In its use of location shooting and some non-actors, *The Shout* draws to some degree on the aesthetics of realism and, as such, the look of a range of British realist films. But the film subverts this representational system in order to examine the nature of what occurs at the edges of everyday British reality. As Philip Strick recognised, Skolimowski admits to having an interest in the 'absurd'.[10] As such, the film can also be read as another 1970s formal hybrid, this time bridging two of the most frequently travelled aesthetic avenues of British national cinema – realism and fantasy (or excess).

A number of the more disturbing images in *The Shout* are reminiscent of the graphic, raw and often grotesque work of the Irish-born British artist, Francis Bacon. One of the ongoing themes of Bacon's work was the image of an open mouth screaming, as displayed in his *Study after Velazquez's Portrait of Pope Innocent X* (aka *The Screaming Pope*) (1953). Considering the ways in which it is composed on screen, Crossley's shout (which we shall come to shortly) certainly echoes Bacon's recurring images of mouths. As Skolimowski himself points out, like his own films, Bacon's work has the 'feeling of absurdity'.[11] It is therefore significant that the director placed printed reproductions of Bacon's paintings around Anthony's studio (including *The Screaming Pope*), because this is highly suggestive of links between the figures of the painter and the composer (here represented by Anthony). As Skolimowski puts it, 'It's that movement of (Francis) Bacon which links him with the masochism of the composer, who has to go through very painful experiences in his work.'[12] But the allusions to Bacon in the film do not stop there. The curious, dreamlike ambiguity of the film is never more apparent than during the brief sequence in which Rachel (York) walks naked on all fours – an image which directly echoes the Francis Bacon image hanging on one of Anthony's loudspeakers in his studio, *Paralytic Child Walking on All Fours (from Muybridge)* (1961). Here, the painter's work is used to hint at the absurdity not only of the human condition but also of the nature of sexual performance and, indeed, of physical human interaction. But it is as if these images are uncannily bleeding out of the reproductions hanging in Anthony's studio and into the images we see of the key characters in the film; or into the everyday lives of the characters (as might happen in a disturbing dream or nightmare).

Charles Crossley is being treated at a rural asylum. He is seemingly lucid and highly intelligent; a well-educated man who is nevertheless under the delusion of being a multiple murderer.[13] At the beginning of the film, before the shots of the cricket match that frame the narrative, a conversation develops between Crossley's doctor (Robert Stephens) and Robert Graves (Tim Curry), during which they discuss the patient:

ROBERT: Why is he here?
DOCTOR: He's not entirely normal.
ROBERT: What's normal?
DOCTOR: See that tree over there? That's normal. That one over there? That's mad.

Questions of madness are thus foregrounded in the film. We are reminded of contemporary debates concerning how far insanity, rather than being a natural phenomenon, might actually have evolved as a concept during the Age of Reason; an argument evidenced in the publication in 1964 (and subsequent reception) of Michel Foucault's *Madness and Civilization*, and the Scottish psychiatrist R.D. Laing's ideas as set out in *The Divided Self* (1960). Certainly, *The Shout* could be said to evidence a nuanced understanding of the complexities of insanity that chimes with contemporary theoretical developments.

Bearing in mind the doctor's comments about Crossley, it is clear that we as spectators and listeners (as well as Robert) need to remain suspicious of what we see and hear in this film. In the wooden scoring hut, Crossley begins to tell Robert his story of Anthony (a man who 'lost a wife who loved him'), and offers the strange caveat (which echoes Skolimowski's own authorial decisions concerning the non-linear construction of the narrative of the film): 'Every word of what I am going to tell you is true. I'm telling it in a different way. It's always the same story but I change the sequence of events.' Crossley, then, is not a reliable narrator. He admits that he makes up dreams for his doctor. And, as the film moves to the flashback (Crossley's narrative), it is clear that the sequence of events that immediately follows this (including Crossley's extraordinary shout) are effectively being viewed from Crossley's perspective. As with the employment of the Francis Bacon images, Skolimowski here appears to be commenting on the 'madness' associated with creating works of art. We might even read the storytelling Crossley as an artist who has the power/madness necessary to shape narratives – not unlike Skolimowski himself. If we read the film as an elaborate, dream-like fantasy, rather than as a tale with any real basis in reality, we might then read the cricket match as a metaphor for the elaborate game that Crossley is playing with Robert (Tim Curry), but also, of course, for the game he also plays with Anthony and Rachel. But the film depicts events which feel 'real', and, as such, it operates like a kind of game or puzzle, with Skolimowski playing with his audience; toying with issues of what is (and is not) real, but also issues of identity, madness, the uncanny, and the bizarre, all the while exploiting the recognisable iconography of Englishness in the 1970s. In the sequence at the film's climax – during which a violent storm develops, and lightning hits the wooden scoring hut – a patient delivers lines from Shakespeare's *Macbeth*, forcing home the themes of authorship and mental instability.

Before Crossley's remembered/imagined narrative begins (and at very brief moments during it), we continue to see the cricket match unfolding, with staff, patients and local villagers involved. But all is not right here. In *Monthly Film Bulletin*, Richard Combs noted the camera's insistence 'on dwelling on such blankly foreboding spaces as an expanse of grass seen through a doorway, the side of a scoring hut as it is wheeled out to the pitch'.[14] This familiar vision of the iconography of a rural cricket match serves here to anchor the dream-like and supernatural aspects of the film (and, specifically, Crossley's narrative) in a 'real-type' English world. This, then, is a disturbed representation of a distinctly English ritual in a distinctly English landscape exemplified by tall oak trees, lush green grass, grazing cows, and a distant church steeple.

The potential realism of the events unfolding here is further problematised by a non-linear editing style which, by offering us very short glimpses of things we shall see happening later in the film, affords us premonitions. An example of this occurs with the very brief shot we see of Rachel lying naked on a bed some time before Crossley's narrative subsequently brings us to that moment. This shot occurs immediately after one featuring Crossley furtively exploring her bedroom and burying his face in her nylon stockings, which he finds hanging invitingly on a line suspended across the room. At this moment, it is as if he wills – through magic – their future sexual encounter to take place. Moreover, Crossley's narrative (or his recollection of events concerning his time with Anthony and Rachel) is further disrupted by more non-linear editing which returns us to the cricket match, where it is noticeable that he does not actually appear to be recalling these past events to Graves at all.

While the location shooting and the presence of non-actors lends the images of the cricket match a realist tone, then, strange sounds puncture this territory – the seemingly incongruous call of a peacock; the loud 'thwack' of the leather cricket ball on the willow bat; sudden, seemingly extra-diegetic electronic sounds – suggesting that all is not well with this world, and, importantly, reminding us that what we are experiencing here is a representation of events. In one early sequence, Anthony cycles quickly to church because he is late for the service. We can hear the choir singing as he approaches, and a loud bicycle bell, which becomes almost shocking in its timbre and volume. When Anthony eventually arrives in the church, the singers carry a hymn without accompaniment until he sits down at the organ and takes up the tune. But the immediate, thick, rich sound of the church organ is played in a different key, thus setting up a distinct feeling of discord. So there is a kind of 'edgeness' evoked by the everyday sounds heard in *The Shout*. These sounds serve to signal the fact that much of these lives are being played out on the borders of what we might think of as rational experience. But at other moments in the film, very loud sounds play an absolutely crucial role in the narrative, and serve to further evoke the disturbing terror of the 'sonic' as well as the mysterious territory that lies between concepts of reality and fantasy.[15]

The centrepiece of the film is the extraordinary 'shout' sequence. The cobbler in the village speaks of 'that noise like a terrible music'. Anthony tells Crossley – from a position of some authority as a practitioner in sound – 'I have heard some sounds in my time, you know.' But he has clearly heard nothing like this. As Anthony and Crossley walk on the dunes, two birds are shot circling each other, one hunting the other – a visual metaphor for the developing relationship between the two men. Just before the 'death shout' we hear keyboard music (played by Tony Banks of the British progressive rock group Genesis) alongside birdsong, and the atmospheric sound of a chill wind.[16] Crossley carefully prepares for his shout by going through what appears to be a series of ritual-ised movements. The unfolding event is filmed in slow motion; first with a low-placed camera looking up at him (arms stretched out in a quasi-crucifixion pose); then in close up; then in extreme close up (with his open mouth filling the frame). The slow motion footage of this event serves to amplify its strangeness, but also to suggest that it somehow creates a rupture in time. We then hear what Richard Combs, reviewing the film in the *Monthly Film Bulletin* in 1978, called Crossley's 'death-dealing terror shout';[17] a phenomenon the critic noticed makes use of 'shattering, Dolby-boosted effects'.[18] This moment marks the apotheosis of *The Shout's* employment of the then-new Dolby Optical Stereo system. Robert Strick, interviewing Skolimowski in 1978 for *Sight and Sound*, asked the director if he had carefully planned the shout sequence. Skolimowski replied:

> Yes, this is where I used the Dolby system; it had to be applied at just the right moment so that we would be hearing something special. The shock of the sound is not a question of loudness or richness – it is sudden and it is complex, because the human voice is helped on forty or more tracks by all the things that came into my mind that might be helpful, the Niagara Falls, the launching of the moon rocket, everything. But over the top is the real human voice of a man shouting like hell.[19]

Strick commented to Skolimowski, 'What makes the shouting sequence so effective is that there are so many surprising camera angles around Bates as he shouts, and the posture he presents is really just as horrifying as the sound itself.'[20] This indeed rings true, especially when consideration is paid to the ways in which Bates is shot like an existential Francis Bacon figure. But the real horror in the film resides in the sonic. In its use of Dolby Optical Stereo technology, *The Shout* marks the sonic as a spatialised site of horror. In this film, then, horror resides in sound; in its extreme incarna-tions, but also in its quotidian incarnations.

In his book *Audio-Vision: Sound on Screen* (1994), Michel Chion talks of the 'added value' of film sound, which he describes as the 'expressive and informative value with which a sound enriches a given image', which might produce 'an immediate and necessary relationship between something one sees and something one hears'.[21] According to Paul Grainge, Dolby sound technology has 'an especially significant place at the intersection of these commercial and technological definitions of "added value"; the tangible and intangible value of Dolby as a technology and corporate name has become central to the patterning of cinematic expectation and pleasure'.[22] Interestingly, as Grainge further points out, 'Dolby Laboratories sought to move beyond the science fiction and rock music genres to which its sound technology had become coupled in the late 1970s, instead investing audio quality with envisioned meanings of cinematic policy and prestige'.[23] In a report published in *Variety* in 1978 (the year *The Shout* was released), Dolby Laboratories made it clear that they sought to bring about 'the life-like reproduction of sound'.[24] In this report, Dolby aimed to set out precisely what multichannel-sound technology could do.[25] Chion argues that the Dolby system could reconstruct sonic 'environments' rather than merely events: 'Dolby Stereo has the unique ability to construct acoustic layers on a soundtrack, and to render the sonic and spatial details of each layer with extreme accuracy.'[26]

While *Star Wars* (George Lucas, 1977) is credited with initiating the large-scale conversion to four-channel Dolby Stereo in cinemas, this did not happen as a matter of course, as exhibitors were initially reluctant to commit themselves to undergoing multichannel-sound conversion in their facilities.[27] Indeed, it is true to say that many cinemas in Britain in the late 1970s still had poor sound facilities. But it is significant that major technological advances were under way during the decade, and that they were being exploited rapidly by film-makers, many of whom were working in Britain. So, this was an important period of innovation in film sound. For example, in 1970, Dolby experimented with its A-type noise reduction on the British film *Jane Eyre* (Delbert Mann, 1970).[28] Furthermore, Dolby was used to promote the musical films of Ken Russell (*Lizstomania* being the first film to use Dolby Stereo in 1975).[29] This technology facilitated broadened frequency ranges, improved dynamics, and allowed for more extreme intensity of contrasts of sound with reduced background noise.[30] As Jay Beck argues, 'Dolby Stereo has the unique ability to construct acoustic layers on a soundtrack, and to render the sonic and spatial details of each layer with extreme accuracy.'[31] So, this new technology effectively brought about new sound aesthetics in the 1970s.

In his 1981 essay 'A Dolby Stereo Aesthetic', Michel Chion notices the ability of the Dolby soundtrack to produce a 'hyper-realism of the sounds as more precise, sharper and richer', and that these sounds were more 'present' and used 'progressively'.[32] But what is particularly interesting about the sonic properties of *The Shout* is that Skolimowski sought to problematise, at a very early stage, the realistic 'lifelike-ness' made possible by this developing technology. Chion's notion of 'hyper-realism' in Dolby sound thus becomes a means for Skolimowski to explore the ambiguous edges of reality and everyday British life in the 1970s. By exploiting ongoing advances in Dolby sound, Skolimowski makes Crossley's shout an extra-linguistic, non-cognitive, primal scream which manages to evoke something of the brute nature in all human beings. Indeed, Crossley's Dolby-enhanced shout appears to encompass or channel aspects of existence that run counter to the modern, bourgeois sensibilities largely displayed by the married couple, Anthony and Rachel. As it also seemingly has its roots in Aboriginal culture, Crossley's shout appears to channel ancient, non-Western forces. But these forces are refracted through modern experience – through the sound of a moon rocket; through the cinematic apparatus; and, specifically, through Dolby Optical Stereo technology. So Crossley's shout is a primal sound, but also a modern sound. This lends the sound a certain level of poetic tension above and beyond its undeniable aural force, as it is sugges-tive of the tensions between the ancient and the modern that were tearing at the fragmentary British culture of the time.

Writing about the ontology of film sound, Rick Altman argues that what he calls the 'sound hermeneutic' functions in cinema as follows: 'The sound asks the question *where?* And the image (or the source of the sound) responds *here!*'[33] But the 'shout' sequence in *The Shout* effectively subverts the type of sound/image synchro-nisation conventions of cinema that usually work to facilitate this hermeneutic. While, as Altman shows us, sounds in cinema usually correspond to the visual representation of the sound's source (unless the sound originates from an off-screen location), the sound of this

181

extraordinary shout does not in any real way appear to come from a clearly visible source. Skolimowski's film instead asks questions of our ability to interpret sound and visual images in cinema, and furthermore, leads us to consider how far our senses of hearing and vision always essentially fail us, or at best trick us. Issues arise here concerning the believability of the sound of the shout in the sequence, primarily because we know we are watching (and indeed listening to) a fictional film.

But in the case of Crossley's shout, we also know that we are witnessing a representation of an event, and that this representation is being channelled through the mind of a fictional (and potentially insane) character. Moreover, at a more profound level, *The Shout* encourages us to ask phenomenological questions concerning how far the sounds we hear in everyday life are always representative of their source, but, because of the way in which sound necessarily has to travel through space at a particular speed (as energy transmitted through molecules), cannot be said to be linked, in any concrete way, to their source. In other words, *The Shout* evidently shows us that a schism exists between the origin of a sound and the point of its reception. This raises profound questions about the nature of our existence. This is especially true when we consider that sound is a primary medium through which we communicate with one another. So Skolimowski's film shows us that sound in film can facilitate the questioning of our concepts of who we are and our relationship with the world around us. Perhaps the real terror of this film, then, lies in the fact that it toys with the idea that, while we experience a world full of sound, all sound might be 'nothing' or 'empty' – merely representative of its source. This notion problematises concepts of expression and communication (another theme of the narrative of the film). Interestingly, Fredric Jameson argues that

> The very concept of expression presupposes indeed some separation within the subject, and along with that a whole metaphysics of the inside and the outside, of the wordless pain within the monad and the moment in which, often cathartically, that 'emotion' is then projected out and externalized, as gesture or cry, as desperate communication and the outward dramatization of inward feeling.[34]

Crossley's shout might thus be read as a rage against the silence of nothingness; a momentary attempt to articulate some kind of presence through sonic expression.

Crossley's shout is performed high on an impressive dune system beside the Atlantic Ocean in South West England. This is a peripheral space; framed by a vast expanse of sand forming a largely unpopulated Devon beach, far away from the urban centres of 1970s Britain. This is significant, too. Other films of the period also used peripheral locations.

The wild West Country: *Straw Dogs* and other animals

One of the most controversial British-made films of the early 1970s set in a remote rural area – and all the more powerful because it is set in the contemporary moment – is Sam Peckinpah's *Straw Dogs* (1971), starring Dustin Hoffman as David Sumner, an American mathematician, and Susan George as his wife, Amy.[35] This film is set in a Cornish village (the fictional Wakeley). Sumner evidently agreed to move with Amy to an isolated farmhouse, Trencher's Farm (owned by her father) to escape the violence and brutality of contemporary America. On arrival, they get much, much more than they bargained for.

On its release, a number of critics recognised the disturbing power of the film. Writing in *Monthly Film Bulletin* in December 1971, Nigel Andrews argued that 'At once harrowingly realistic and richly suggestive, *Straw Dogs* promises to emerge as a classic of the horror film and an indispensible Peckinpah masterpiece.'[36] Furthermore, *Straw Dogs* 'assembles familiar horror-in-rural England motifs (arrival of stranger in remote village, mistrustful locals, dark hints about the past)'.[37] In *Sight and Sound*, Tom Milne wrote that 'the pale horse of the Apocalypse hovers grimly over a quiet Cornish farmhouse'.[38]

At the level of issues of representation, it is certainly significant that the action in *Straw Dogs* is set in the rural English West Country. The stereotypically backward local men who attack the Trencher's Farm retreat are depicted as brutal and animalistic in nature, most obviously in the notorious double rape scene.[39] Elsewhere they are shown to be lazy and feckless. As such, the English West Country is depicted here as a wild, uncivilised territory. Only the old Major (T. P. McKenna) and the local Vicar (Colin Welland), along with the troubled Henry Niles (David Warner – uncredited), potentially break with this representational pattern in terms of their performances of rural masculinity. Instead, the urbane, intellectual American (outsider), David (Hoffman), is marked as sensitive and pacifistic, even if this characterisation is of course challenged by his violent actions in the savage, bloodthirsty denouement of the film. It remains the case, then, that remote, seemingly backward rural England is again depicted in this film as a territory in which modern anxieties concerning the future of civilisation can be worked through. Interestingly, in a *Variety* review of *Straw Dogs*, 'Jock' argued that 'The whole might be more acceptable to British audiences if the setting had been in the past or in a still primitive territory, rather than the possibly backwards but not uncivilised West of England.'[40] It seems that a range of enduring mythologies of rural England allow the narrative of *Straw Dogs* to function, in all its bloody barbarism.

Another example of a 1970s British film set in the remote English West Country is *Endless Night* (Sidney Gilliat, 1972), produced by the director with his brother Leslie Gilliat and distributed by United Artists. The film is an adaptation of an Agatha Christie novel. Michael Rogers (Hywel Bennett) is a young man employed as a chauffeur.[41] He dreams of building a house on the remote Devon coast, on a piece of land known as 'Gypsy's Acre'. He meets Ellie (Hayley Mills), a rich young heiress who, because of her developing feelings for Mike, decides to purchase the land for him. They eventually marry, and, with the help of Ellie's friend Greta (Britt Ekland) they build a property designed by renowned modern architect, Santonix (Per Oscarsson). But Ellie's family disapproves of both the marriage and the project. A local eccentric, Miss Townsend (Patience Collier), hangs around the house.[42] And a number of mysterious accidents occur. It becomes clear that the ghost of a gypsy might haunt the grounds. Throughout the film, the ghostly goings-on in this remote setting suggest a potent, disturbing, atmospheric space which speaks of the ancient, unknowable forces haunting a nation going through the processes of modernisation.

Though not, strictly speaking, part of what is generally termed the West Country, the Isle of Wight – off the south coast of England – features prominently in *Something to Hide* (aka *Shattered*) (Alastair Reid, 1972). This film stars Peter Finch as Harry Field, a middle-aged, vegetarian, alcoholic council clerk working in the Town Hall on the island. He has an abusive, failing marriage to Gabriella (Shelley Winters), which is played out in a drunken sequence of mutual loathing in their rambling beachside house at Christmas. Later, returning home from the airport, Harry picks up a young female hitchhiker, Lorelei (Linda Hayden), who turns out to be heavily pregnant. This pick-up occurs on a recently-built dual carriageway, after he runs his car into the lorry in which she is travelling. In some ways, *Something to Hide* feels like a curious US-type road movie transported to a slowly-modernising Britain. After all, Lorelei tells Harry that she is 'on the road', and asks him where he is headed. Harry drives a Morris Traveller, which, with its external ash frame, looks like a miniature American station wagon. Harry tells Lorelei that the journey to Portsmouth is thirty miles (there can be no thousand-mile drives on the road in 1970s Britain). But when Harry explains that he lives on the Isle of Wight, he tells her 'It's an island. There's nowhere to go.'

Harry's house is situated in a strange, peripheral location on the island, overlooking a dusty white beach on which peculiar things are going on – a man filling a burning oil drum; large mechanical diggers working on the sand – alongside holiday-makers building sand castles and braving the chilly coastal breeze. It is in this house that the central narrative of the film unfolds, which sees Lorelei staying and subsequently giving birth to the baby with Harry's assistance, before leaving mysteriously. This birth is followed by an increasingly disturbing series of events, which lead up to a brutal, violent confrontation on the beach. It is fitting that a narrative that deals with characters living on the edge of rational experience, and that challenges traditions and acknowledged moral and legal frameworks, should be situated in what is made to appear to be a remote threshold of modern, 1970s Britain. Again, the spatial periphery here allows the film to mediate contemporary socio-cultural tensions.

One possible reason why rural areas in Britain were depicted so widely in challenging and horrific films of the period is the fact that the late 1960s and early 1970s saw the rapid development of Britain's motorway system. This meant that, to those who could afford a car, the nation began to feel decidedly smaller. Its peripheral rural and coastal areas – previously far from its urban centres (involving a long drive on meandering old A roads) – suddenly became much easier to access. This was certainly true of the West Country. The M4 motorway in England was constructed between 1965 and 1971, at that time running between London and Bristol (the Welsh section was completed in 1993). Construction of the M3 motorway from London to Southampton began in 1968. And the M5 motorway was extended between 1967 and 1977 in order to link Bristol with Exeter in Devon. The appearance of these modern roads facilitated the emergence of the West Country as an unusual, backward, old-fashioned territory in British cultural texts of the late 1960s and 1970s. But just as this part of England was suddenly becoming easier to access, its cultural difference and comparative lack of modernity (when compared to more developed urban areas) was becoming all the more apparent.

Further evidence of this spatial difference can be found in *Crucible of Terror* (Ted Hooker, 1971), in which Jack Davies (James Bolam), an art dealer in London, does a deal with a friend, Michael Clare (Ronald Lacey), the son of a gifted sculptor, Victor Clare (Mike Raven). Michael steals some of his father's works, and Davies places them on sale at his London gallery. They split the profits between them. But seeing a chance to make more money, they plan to drive down to Cornwall to see if they can purloin any more items. It turns out that Victor lives as a recluse in a cottage built above an abandoned tin mine, which, because of a past accident, is haunted. When Jack and Michael arrive in Cornwall with their wives, they find it to be a truly horrific place. Victor turns living young women into sculptures, and his wife has clearly regressed into a second childhood, behaving erratically, and playing with dolls. A series of grisly attacks and murders ensue in this lonely Cornish location, which again signify the potential perils of living 'on the edge' in 1970s Britain, spatially or psychologically. Other films of the period offer similar representations of the West Country.

Deadly Strangers (Sidney Hayers, 1974), for example, features action set around Bristol and Somerset. In this film, Simon Ward plays Stephen Slade, who offers a lift in his Austin Maxi to Belle Adams (Hayley Mills) after she is attacked by the lorry driver she has been riding with (Ken Hutchinson). But it turns out that Slade might actually be an escaped patient on the loose from a psychiatric hospital. *Out of Season* (Alan Bridges, 1975) was shot in Dorset, and tells the story of a mother, Ann (Vanessa Redgrave), and daughter, Joanna (Susan George), who live in a deserted seaside hotel, where, one winter, they engage in a jealous sexual battle when a figure from Ann's past, Joe (Cliff Robertson), arrives. Again, peripheral British locations operate as spaces here in which modern anxieties can be worked through.

Another example of a film which locates strange goings on within a 1970s West Country community is *Doomwatch* (Peter Sasdy, 1972), produced by Tigon. The Hungarian-born Sasdy made a number of British horror films during the period, including *Hands of the Ripper* (1971), *Countess Dracula* (1971), and *I Don't Want to Be Born* (aka *The Devil Within Her*) (1975).[43] *Doomwatch* is an adaptation of the successful television series of the same name (BBC, 1970–72), which follows the activities of a government scientific agency. The film (like the television series) places contemporary fears concerning environmental destruction at the heart of the work of this agency. Indeed, the credits sequence of the film features documentary footage of individuals cleaning up after an oil spill. The first sequence of the film proper places the emphasis firmly on modernity and the type of technology employed by Doomwatch scientists in London (large computers and scientific equipment) to monitor environmental activity. Dr Del Shaw (Ian Bannen) is tasked with travelling to a fictional island, Balfe, to uncover the principle causes of the strange bodily mutations and random violence being displayed by some members of the remote community. Balfe's status as a West Country location is marked by the old lead mines visible in some aerial shots. But, as if to make this location absolutely clear, an admiral in a London office pinpoints its position on a map: near the western edge of Cornwall.

As Shaw travels across to the island, the boatman tells him 'You'll find them a strange, close lot on Balfe.' On arrival at the dock, the boatman introduces Shaw to an islander, indicating to this man that the scientist is 'all the way from London'. The capital city is thus set up in the film as a dangerous, distant centre of the type of progressive modernity of which the islanders are clearly suspicious. By way of comparison, Balfe is a place which has hardly changed over generations. The island is therefore characterised by its 'oldness'. It is an ancient settlement of medieval cottages, and thus becomes a microcosm of 'old' Britain. Shaw's arrival in the village is accompanied on the soundtrack by a flute and harp, connoting the old, 'folk'-type nature of this community. But the villagers are depicted as unwelcoming and suspicious of new arrivals. Interestingly, reviewing the film in *Monthly Film Bulletin*, Paul Madden noticed an echo of Sasdy's Hammer films here: 'Sasdy relies on Hammer clichés (Del's early encounter with the hostile villagers in the pub might have been transplanted direct from Transylvania and Elstree)'.[44] Shaw lodges in a village house, where he meets Victoria (Judy Geeson), a schoolteacher on the island. Discussing the villagers, Shaw says to her: 'They seem an odd lot.' Shaw initially puts their physical abnormalities – protruding eyebrows and thick lips – down to 'centuries of inbreeding', and no doubt believes that their rages are no more than one would expect from such uncivilised types. As such, Shaw's initial response is to locate monstrousness as a core element of backward West Country life. But he gradually discovers that the disease from which they are suffering has in fact been caused by exposure to a hormone ingested by locals who have eaten fish chemically altered by radiation. The precise cause of these abnormalities turns out to be the illegal dumping of chemical waste by the Royal Navy at Castle Rock. So the British establishment on the mainland is seen to be responsible for this threat to the lives of these remote rural dwellers. Throughout the film, while Shaw displays a palpable anger towards anybody he thinks has been acting in environmentally unsound ways (including establishment figures), he also casts himself as the urbane, intellectual saviour of the little people in a seemingly backward part of the country. In this film, then, the centre of modern Britain and the periphery – both real and imagined; physical and psychological – are seen to have a symbiotic relationship in which each is increasingly defined in relation to the other.

Neither the Sea Nor the Sand (aka *The Exorcism of Hugh*) (Fred Burnley, 1972) is another 1970s British film that develops a narrative which takes place primarily in a peripheral island location. This Tigon-produced film is based on a story by the ITN newsreader Gordon Honeycombe. It stars Susan Hampshire as Anna Robinson, a woman who has travelled to Jersey in the Channel Islands from mainland England. She wants to spend some time away from her husband in order to consider whether she wants to work on their marriage or walk away from it. In the opening sequence of the film, captured in a long shot, Anna walks alone along a causeway, towards the camera, as if being born into a new life. Here she meets a brooding young man standing below a phallic light-house. There is no dialogue during the first three minutes of this opening sequence, lending it a dark, dream-like quality. Deciding to speak, Anna remarks: 'It's very lonely here.' 'Like the edge of the world,' replies Hugh Dabernon (Michael Petrovich). Hugh is a seemingly sensitive, deep-thinking but emotionally numb young man. He lives with his older, bachelor brother, George (Frank Finlay). Spending some enjoyable time with Hugh, Anna gradually falls in love with him, and thus begins to reassess her needs (and whether or not her distant husband can fulfil them). She is clearly frustrated by the role in which she has been cast by her husband. As she tells Hugh, 'David would rather keep me at home.' David (who remains invisible to us throughout the film) is thus marked as a traditional, old-fashioned husband in terms of how he views the roles of men and women within the institution of marriage. In a move that resonates with issues of contemporary 1970s feminism (as discussed in Chapter 2), Anna clearly feels that she wants to shake off the shackles imposed by this man. Hugh seemingly offers her something different. During the sequence when Anna and Hugh fly to Scotland together, impressive shots of the young man larking in a cave with the sea crashing around him convey his sexual potency in a manner reminiscent of the work of D. H. Lawrence, by suggesting that libidinal urges are in fact forces of nature, and that, as such, Anna might be drawn to this man uncontrollably.

The lovers chase each other playfully along a beach. Anna turns to see that Hugh has suddenly collapsed. She runs to him in terror, but he dies in her arms. A doctor records the cause of death as heart failure. This is nothing more than the 'Lord's Judgment', according to Anna's moralistic landlady, who has discovered that Hugh was not her husband after all, but her lover. After Hugh's death, a distraught Anna wanders the beach where they spent time together, as if willing him to return. Subsequently, he does reappear, mysteriously knocking on the cottage door at night, as if nothing has happened. Anna invites him to stay with her, but he remains strangely mute. It turns out that he is now 'undead'. Despite this, Anna inconceivably takes this strange, silent figure back with her on a plane to Jersey (their 'home'), and eventually Hugh manages to communicate with her via telepathy. But, at the same time, steadily and bizarrely, his body begins to disintegrate. So, this final section of the film sees a very 1970s romance (often shot in soft focus) effectively become a gothic horror. And during these sequences, Anna ironically takes on precisely the role of the doting bourgeois housewife that she has been trying to relinquish with her distant husband.

During the first section of the film, Hugh shows Anna around tombstones and a burial mound on Jersey, and remarks that the sea surrounding the lighthouse used to be a graveyard for ships. Responding to this dialogue, and the performances of Hampshire and Petrovich, it is tempting to read both of these characters as exemplars of the living dead. Indeed, in *Neither the Sea Nor the Sand*, Jersey is presented as a kind of liminal zone. It is neither France nor England, of course. But here the island is also constructed as a kind of oneiric, imaginary space on the edge of 'normal' British experience. We might also read Jersey here as being representative of a form of purgatory, to be compared with Venice and its lagoon as depicted in *Don't Look Now* (Nicolas Roeg, 1973). Death is the primary concern of *Neither the Sea Nor the Sand*, then, but also the question of what lies between life and death.

Critics were often unkind to the film. John Raisbeck pointed out in *Monthly Film Bulletin* that 'to depict the macabre in the midst of the everyday requires a greater degree of artifice than is displayed here'.[45] And, in the end, this feels like a distinctly conservative film. Anna – in her madness, in this strange, liminal, windswept place – is effectively being punished for her infidelity to her husband. Jersey becomes Anna's dream-like purgatory; a space in which the soul of a wayward 1970s British housewife might be punished. Once again, then, a peripheral space is employed here as a territory in which behaviour situated on the boundaries of traditional British socio-cultural life (in this case, extra-marital desire) can be worked through.[46]

Notes

1   *Killer's Moon* was made in 1978 but not released until 1982.
2   For more details of Skolimowski's work, see Mazierska, *Jerzy Skolimowski: The Cinema of a Nonconformist.*
3   Alan Bates remained busy in Britain throughout the 1970s, starring in (among other films) *The Go-Between* (Joseph Losey, 1970); *A Day in the Death of Joe Egg* (Peter Medak, 1972); *Butley* (Harold Pinter, 1974); *In Celebration* (Lindsay Anderson, 1974); and *Royal Flash* (Richard Lester, 1975). He also starred in the Italian/French co-production *Story of a Love Story* (John Frankenheimer, 1973), as well as the US-made films *An Unmarried Woman* (Paul Mazursky, 1978) and *The Rose* (Mark Rydell, 1979). John Hurt also remained busy in Britain during the 1970s, working across both film and television. His career during this period is another that speaks of a highly complex film-making climate in which films, performers and other industry professionals were rarely classifiable in simple terms. Key roles include Timothy John Evans in *10 Rillington Place* (Richard Fleischer, 1971); Malcolm Scrawdyke in *Little Malcolm and His Struggle Against the Eunuchs* (Stuart Cooper, 1974); Nash in *East of Elephant Rock* (Don Boyd, 1977); the voice of Hazel in the animated film *Watership Down* (Martin Rosen, 1978); Max in *Midnight Express* (Alan Parker, 1978); Kane in *Alien* (Ridley Scott, 1979); and John Merrick in a US film shot in Britain, *The Elephant Man* (David Lynch, 1980). Hurt also starred as Quentin Crisp in the successful Thames Television film *The Naked Civil Servant* (1975), for which he won a BAFTA Award for Best Actor in 1976. And he played Caligula in the highly regarded television mini-series *I, Claudius* (BBC, 1976).
4   Johnson, 'The Shout', p. 54.
5   Combs, 'The Shout', p. 143.
6   Strick, 'Skolimowski's Cricket Match', p. 146.
7   Combs, 'The Shout', p. 142.
8   Johnson, 'The Shout', p. 54.
9   Johnson, 'The Shout', p. 56.

10   Strick, 'Skolimowski's Cricket Match', p. 146.

11   Skolimowski in Strick, 'Skolimowski's Cricket Match', p. 147.

12   Skolimowski in Strick, 'Skolimowski's Cricket Match', p. 147.

13   Johnson, 'The Shout', p. 54.

14   Combs, 'The Shout', p. 142.

15   The impressive mixing of the soundtrack on *The Shout* was performed by Tony Jackson at Pinewood Studios. Sound maintenance was by Mike Bassett; Gordon K. McCullum was the dubbing mixer; and Alan Bell was the sound editor.

16   The electronics on the soundtrack were developed by Rupert Hine, a prolific English musician who had been in the band Quantum Jump, and had released two 1970s albums in his own name, *Pick Up a Bone* (1971) and *Unfinished Picture* (1973). The work of Tony Banks and Mike Rutherford (of Genesis) on the music for the soundtrack of the film is also prevalent, and can be read within the context of the trend for rock groups to provide scores for films from the late 1960s onwards – for example, Pink Floyd on *More* (Barbet Schroeder, 1969) and *Zabriskie Point* (Michelangelo Antonioni, 1970); Jerry Garcia (of The Grateful Dead) on *La Vallée* (Barbet Schroeder, 1972); and Tangerine Dream on *The Wages of Fear* (aka *Sorcerer*) (Henri-Georges Clouzot, 1977).

17   Combs, 'The Shout', p. 142.

18   Combs, 'The Shout', p. 143.

19   Skolimowski, in Strick, 'Skolimowski's Cricket Match', p. 147.

20   Strick, 'Skolimowski's Cricket Match', p. 147.

21   Chion, *Audio-Vision: Sound on Screen*, p. 5.

22   Grainge, 'Selling Spectacular Sound: Dolby and the Unheard History of Technical Trademarks', p. 254.

23   Grainge, 'Selling Spectacular Sound: Dolby and the Unheard History of Technical Trademarks', pp. 254–5.

24   Dolby Laboratories, 'Dolby Stereo: A Progress Report', p. 7.

25   Grainge, 'Selling Spectacular Sound: Dolby and the Unheard History of Technical Trademarks', p. 255.

26   Beck, 'The Sounds of "Silence": Dolby Stereo, Sound Design, and The Silence of the Lambs', p. 72.

27   Grainge, 'Selling Spectacular Sound: Dolby and the Unheard History of Technical Trademarks', p. 256.

28   Beck, 'The Sounds of "Silence": Dolby Stereo, Sound Design, and The Silence of the Lambs', p. 69.

29   Flanagan, *Ken Russell: Re-viewing England's Last Mannerist*, p. 239.

30   Chion, 'The Silence of the Loudspeakers, or Why With Dolby Sound It Is the Film That Listens to Us', p. 150.

31   Beck, 'The Sounds of "Silence": Dolby Stereo, Sound Design, and The Silence of the Lambs', p. 72.

32   Chion, 'Une esthetique Dolby stéréo', p. xii. See also Beck, 'The Sounds of "Silence": Dolby Stereo, Sound Design, and The Silence of the Lambs', p. 72.

33   Altman, 'Moving Lips: Cinema as Ventriloquism', p. 74.

34   Jameson, *Postmodernism, or, The Cultural Logic of Late Capitalism*, pp. 11–12.

35   For more on the censorship crisis surrounding *Straw Dogs* (and *A Clockwork Orange*), see Barr, '*Straw Dogs, A Clockwork Orange* and the Critics'.

36   Andrews, 'Straw Dogs', p. 250.

37   Andrews, 'Straw Dogs', p. 250.

38   Milne, 'Straw Dogs', p. 50.

39   Hall, 'Under Siege: The Double Rape of Straw Dogs'.

40   'Jock', 'Straw Dogs'.

41   For more on *Endless Night*, see Street, 'Heritage Crime: The Case of Agatha Christie', pp. 106–7.

42   McGillivray, 'Endless Night', p. 209.

43   Peter Sasdy's film *Nothing But the Night* (1972), shot in South Devon, tells the story of a retired policeman, Bingham (Christopher Lee), who tries to uncover an explanation for the deaths of some of the trustees of the Van Traylen fund, a mysterious orphanage on a remote Scottish island. Sasdy also directed the extraordinary television ghost story film, *The Stone Tape* (BBC, 1972), written by Nigel Kneale.

44   Madden, 'Doomwatch', p. 70.

45   Raisbeck, 'Neither the Sea Nor the Sand', p. 255.

46   Other films of the period locate horror within the British countryside. For example, in *Voices* (Kevin Billington, 1973), Claire (Gayle Hunnicutt) has a mental breakdown after her young son accidentally drowns (a result in part of parental neglect). On her release from a psychiatric hospital, her husband (David Hemmings) takes her for a weekend at her mother's secluded country house to relax. But on arrival they begin to feel a profound unease in the out-of-the-way house. There is a strange presence in this remote place, and Claire starts to see things. The US/British horror film *The Legacy* (Richard Marquand, 1978) features a rambling country estate owned by Jason Mountolive (John Standing). And in *Satan's Slave* (aka *Evil Heritage*) (Norman J. Warren, 1976), Catherine Yorke (Candace Gledenning) experiences horrific goings on at her strange uncle's (Michael Gough) house in the country and nearby woods. *Scream and Die* (José Ramòn Larraz, 1973) also features a house in the woods, in which characters from London experience rural terror. The Spanish director's subsequent British film, *Vampyres* (aka *Daughters of Dracula*) (1974), is also set in English countryside around a mansion. In the Tigon film *Virgin Witch* (Ray Austin, 1971), Betty (Vicki Michelle) and her sister Christine (Ann Michelle) are hitchhiking when they are lured to a remote country house for a weekend of modelling work by the lesbian head of

an agency (Patricia Haines). They discover that the house is a hotbed of sex and has a witches' coven in residence. And the action in *The Legend of Hell House* (John Hough, 1973) also takes place in a mysterious haunted country house. Remote schools are also the sites of horrific goings on in the British countryside, as in *Absolution* (Anthony Page, 1978), and *Fear in the Night* (Jimmy Sangster, 1972).

8

Old cities, new towns:
criminality and cruelty

> We find ourselves living in disturbing times. The foundations of our
> society are not firm. We're like a rudderless ship. No direction. No-one
> has any conviction anymore. You see, we don't believe ... anything.
> We are in a period of moral starvation.
>
> The Vicar, *The Shout* (Jerzy Skolimowski, 1978)

Frenzy (Alfred Hitchcock, 1972) begins with an impressive aerial
shot of early 1970s London. Mounted on a helicopter, the camera
travels westwards up the River Thames and underneath Tower
Bridge, as if through a mysterious gateway and into the criminal
city itself. This is the spot where, a few years later, Bob Hoskins,
as the East End gangster, Harold Shand, will give an impromptu
speech about 'profitable progress' in the film *The Long Good Friday*
(John Mackenzie, 1979), celebrating British links with the American
mafia. At the beginning of *Frenzy*, the camera moves on along
the Thames and eventually focuses on a crowd standing outside
County Hall on the South Bank by Westminster Bridge. Here, a
politician, Sir George (John Boxer), is speaking to an assembled
audience of onlookers. He talks of clearing the Thames of 'waste
products of society', and proclaims 'Let us rejoice that pollution
will soon be banished from the waters of this river.'

This oratory offers evidence of a shift that was occurring in
Britain during the early 1970s towards a more pressing engagement with environmental issues. But Hitchcock toys with this idea,
by thematically linking the issue of the pollution of the natural
environment with the type of criminal and sexual activity so often

seen to pollute British society. As Sir George speaks, a woman's naked body is spotted floating in the river, with a man's tie wrapped around her neck – a piece of 'all too solid pollution', according to critic Penelope Houston.[1]

A narrative subsequently develops in the film concerning the activity and identity of the mysterious necktie strangler, and the police begin to search for a man, David Blaney (Jon Finch), whom they believe to be the criminal. But Blaney is mistakenly accused of murdering his wife, Brenda (Barbara Leigh-Hunt). Indeed, the audience knows this from an early stage, and, furthermore, gains the knowledge that the rapist and murderer is actually Blaney's friend, the Covent Garden fruit merchant, Robert Rusk (Barry Foster). The policeman charged with the task of solving the mystery is Chief Inspector Oxford (Alec McCowen), but he receives a considerable amount of help from his wife (Vivien Merchant), who makes subtly insightful suggestions while dishing up poorly cooked, pretentious suppers for her husband at their bourgeois home.

Chief Inspector Oxford operates out of the new international-style police headquarters at New Scotland Yard, which appears to have been catapulted into the fabric of the dingy, drab old city from a bright, clean, ambitious future (the Metropolitan Police moved here in 1967). But the size of this building also speaks of the size of the task that the police expect to have to clean up the streets of the 1970s city. *Frenzy* was the penultimate film in Hitchcock's career. It was distributed by Universal and made at Pinewood. This film, like a number of crime and gangster films of the period, speaks in interesting ways of some of the tensions that were developing within notions of Britishness concerning sex and sexless marriages; criminality, childhood innocence and adult experience; and modernity and traditional ways of life. In this chapter I shall examine a range of these films.

Darkness on the edge of town: *The Offence*

Sergeant Johnson (Sean Connery) walks slowly up a suburban street past a little school. We are in southern England – close to London. Johnson is wearing a thick sheepskin coat and a deerstalker hat.

The tarmac on the street is damp; the skies are grey. This is clearly a stakeout. Johnson signals to other policemen sitting in a car to move back. On the soundtrack we hear drills, a bulldozer, and other building machinery – evidence that this is an unfinished housing development. Children leave the little school under the watchful gaze of worried-looking teaching staff. Mothers bundle their offspring into cars and quickly leave the area. All is not right here. A young girl in a white coat (Maxine Gordon) is left alone by her friends and their parents and walks down the cul-de-sac ('Cross Fell'). Then she walks along another road, away from the school and the housing development, on to a well-trodden, grassy path and off across scrubby wasteland. Later the camera picks out her white coat stopping in the distance; a dot of light by a dark culvert under a dual carriageway. Here she is intercepted by a mysterious male figure in a black coat. Throughout this sequence we see several shots of the new housing estate. The tarmac on the street appears to be new. The trees around the school are newly planted; mere saplings, held on to wooden supports by string. The lawns are apparently weed-free, and other plants are juvenile. This, then, is a young space. As such, it is also seemingly an innocent space. But as *The Offence* (1972) shows us, this innocence masks a darkness that lurks; socio-cultural shadows cast by the clean lines of this new British architecture.

The Offence was directed by the American Sidney Lumet, shot by Gerry Fisher, and distributed by United Artists.[2] Sean Connery had recently agreed to return as James Bond in the United Artists film *Diamonds Are Forever* (Guy Hamilton, 1971), and was allowed to pursue two of his own lower-budget projects as part of the deal. One of these was *The Offence*, which had a budget of $1 million and was based on the 1968 play *This Story of Yours* by John Hopkins, who was best known at the time as a writer on the successful BBC television series *Z Cars* (1962–78).

The narrative in *The Offence* initially appears to be concerned with the police search for a man who has been abducting school-girls and raping them. We learn that three have already been abducted before the young girl, Janie (Maxine Gordon), whom we see being intercepted in the sequence described above. But there is a strange sense of inevitability about this abduction. The police are present at the school just before it takes place, but leave too soon. Teachers stand looking concerned outside the school building but do not make the effort to ensure that all of the children are safely accounted for. A middle-aged woman witnesses Janie being approached in the distance by the man, but does not report this to the police until much later. All of these people appear resigned to the fact that another criminal event is about to take place here in 1970s Britain. Crime is seemingly to be expected. The fourth abduction does trigger a manhunt. Police officers gather around a mobile snack van in order to hear their orders (a catering facility which speaks of prior planning for many such major police operations), nursing steaming cups of tea before moving off to search the scrubland.

However, it becomes clear that the manhunt will not be the primary drive of the narrative. Instead, *The Offence* becomes what *New York Times* reviewer Vincent Canby termed a 'psychological striptease'.[3] It is a film primarily concerned with the breakdown of Johnson, a tough, hard-drinking, foul-mouthed, old-fashioned detective. Johnson, we begin to see, is haunted by the awful things he has witnessed during his two decades on the force. Lumet allows us to share Johnson's blurred visions: memories of suicides; a murdered child's arm dangling through the slats of a crib; the lifeless body of a woman who has been tied to a bed and murdered; a body in an advanced state of decomposition found hanging from the branch of a tree. But Johnson is also a loose cannon. He treats his colleagues with contempt, and believes himself to be 'one hundred per cent right' about aspects of the investigation, but also about aspects of human psychology. At the crime scene, he displays a lack of patience and little respect for police procedure. The arrest of Baxter (Ian Bannen) as the only suspect gives Johnson an opportunity to work through his anger and frustration. He does this by brutally beating Baxter to death while he is in police custody. But we, like Johnson, never find out, beyond reasonable doubt, whether Baxter is the guilty man.

The Offence features figures that either bear the brunt of Johnson's misanthropic anger or hear his confession: his wife (Vivien Merchant); the suspected rapist, Baxter; and Detective Superintendent Cartwright (Trevor Howard), the superior officer assigned to interrogate the detective after his violent killing of Baxter. Johnson lives in a flat in a brutalist tower block, which, in its interior decoration and furnishings, is a strange mixture of the modern and the antique (not unlike a wider 1970s Britain).[4] His marriage to Maureen is tired and miserable, and characterised by verbal cruelty. A single bed has been set up in the living room. This says a great deal about the state of their relationship.

Kenneth Baxter is also a married man, with two teenage children. Johnson discovers this during questioning. But when he suggests that Baxter is sexually unfulfilled in his marriage, it becomes evident that the detective might also suffer from a poor sex life. Moreover, there is more than a hint of the suggestion that Johnson has also had to deal with (or repress) the same type of sexual desires that he thinks Baxter has acted upon. Indeed, there are moments in the film which are particularly shocking because they offer evidence that Johnson might actually have paedophilic tendencies himself; desires he has tried to bury. For example, when Johnson discovers Janie in the bushes, his gestures and looks speak of his own potential proclivity towards sexual perversion. The camera captures him in the pose of a man molesting a child. When the other policemen arrive – their torches lighting his face in the dark bushes – Johnson has the look of a criminal; of a man caught in the middle of a despicable act. And Baxter seems to register Johnson's dark thoughts and desires. Shortly before he is beaten to the ground by the larger man and dies, he tells Johnson, 'There's nothing I can say you haven't imagined.' This strikes to the heart of the main theme of the film – moral ambiguity.

Writing in *The New York Times* in 1973, Vincent Canby pointed out that the abduction of Janie takes place 'where lawns fade into scrubby fields that don't give one a feeling of space as much as emptiness'.[5] The *mise-en-scène* provided by this place is certainly very rich in terms of the ways in which it frames the issues of criminality and morality explored in the film. This location clearly invites consideration of the fact that the authorities that govern the nation, and that plan, fund and build its modern living spaces, are essentially powerless to control every aspect of life therein. Ungoverned territory lies alongside designed and managed territory. The planted trees and kept lawns bleed into wasteland. The wildness of nature is waiting to reclaim this place from the planners. These visible tensions in this location, then, effectively facilitate the exploration of the key themes of the narrative, as uncontrollable aspects of behaviour gradually take hold of those that are seemingly controlled.

The geographer, John Rennie Short, argues that 'As a symbol of the wild, the untamed, the wilderness became a symbolic representation of the id ...Wilderness becomes an environmental metaphor for the dark side of the psyche.'[6] Short further advocates that 'The creation of livable places and usable spaces is a mark of civilization. Human use confers meaning on space. Outside of society, wilderness is something to be feared, an area of waste and desolation.'[7] But, in *The Offence*, uncontrollable wildness is not relegated to the wilderness or the woods. Instead, wildness erupts in modern, seemingly controlled spaces. The modern locations employed in this film thus speak, in rich, poetic ways, of tensions at the heart of a 1970s Britain undergoing profound socio-cultural changes, struggling through the processes of modernisation. These spaces can be read as exemplars of a new vision of Britain, then, encapsulating as they do the developing nation's uncertainty about the future. *The Offence* suggests that all is not right in this new, modern nation.

During the night search for the child molester (after Janie is discovered and taken to hospital), Johnson and other police officers are depicted searching the dark, alienating, modern town centre. Footsteps echo off concrete paving stones and stairwells. Figures lurk in corners unlit by streetlights or shop fronts. We hear the sound of dogs barking, and the hum of distant cars. A solitary Baxter (Bannen) is noticed by two policemen, who watch him staggering drunkenly around a pedestrianised shopping precinct. He wobbles, disorientated, down a circular walkway. One of the most interesting things about the film in this sequence (and elsewhere) is the way in which it features characters acting in often irrational ways in spaces that were clearly designed rationally with the intent to best serve a healthy community and thus improve socio-cultural behaviour.

The Offence was shot on location in and around Bracknell, Berkshire (but this is not made clear in the film). Bracknell is situated approximately 35 miles from central London. It became a New Town in 1949, three years after the passing of the New Towns Act 1946. A new development was planned here for approximately 25,000 inhabitants. As we can see in this film, Bracknell town centre is of broadly modern, 1960s design, and very little of the original old town remains. As also evidenced by the film, at the heart of most of Bracknell's outlying, newly built neighbourhoods can be found a church, a small parade of shops, a primary school, a community centre and a pub. So here, then, is an archetypal, manufactured socio-cultural space. Government-sponsored New Towns first appeared in Patrick Abercrombie's plans for London, commissioned in 1943. The idea was to relegate industry to areas away from new neighbourhoods, and civic and shopping centres.[8] Some New Towns were grafted on to sizeable, settled communities. But in most cases, existing hamlets and villages were overwhelmed.[9] Anthony Alexander points out that 'The New Towns were intended to produce healthier places to live'[10] and that 'Environmental determinism – the notion that crime and immorality were created or amplified by the urban environment – led to a tacit view that a better environment would therefore produce a better society.'[11] So, the growth of the New Towns was pushed by planners along balanced and healthy lines. They essentially sprang from a moral imperative.[12] After the Second World War, the population of old industrial urban areas and bombed inner-city zones were to be re-housed in order to be brought back to health.

Interestingly, as Alexander further points out, most of the first generation relocating to New Towns were in their mid-twenties, and had (or were expecting) babies. This gained the towns the nick-name 'pram towns'.[13] These, then, were fresh places in which new life might develop; life which might produce positive outcomes for the nation as opposed to draining its resources. This idea is certainly evoked in the sequence detailed above in *The Offence*, in which Janie walks away from school before being abducted. Here, we see young mothers and their children going about their everyday business in clean, new surroundings. But, as I have demonstrated, most of the sequences shot in Bracknell in the film serve to problematise the new, modern, planned nature of these 'urban locations in the country' through the depiction of the dark and traumatic events that unfold here.

The spatial and socio-cultural tensions between newness and immaturity on the one hand, and oldness and maturity on the other, are explored by other films of the period which utilise the *mise-en-scène* of similar, New Town-type locations. For example, *Psychomania* (aka *The Death Wheelers*) (Don Sharp, 1972) tells the story of a biker gang that hangs out at a pagan stone circle situated in the English countryside. They commit suicide so they can return as the 'undead', and then take trips into town in order to wreak havoc on the living. The bikers, led by Tom (Nicky Henson), call themselves 'The Living Dead'. A key sequence in this film features the gang terrorising shoppers in a provincial 1960s-built shopping precinct (shot in Walton-on-Thames, near Shepperton Studios, approximately fifteen miles south-west of central London). Here we can see the fresh newness of the building development; the sleek, modern lines of the shops, and the colourful, abundant, ordered piles of mass-produced consumer goods on display in the supermarket. The bikers trash this building – a clear symbol of a new Britain (by 1974, ASDA had opened twenty-seven 'super-stores' of more than 25,000 square feet in Britain; the Co-op had opened twenty-three; Fine Fare, twenty-one; Tesco, twenty; and Morrisons, eleven).[14] Young mothers and children feature heavily in this sequence of the film, too. The undead bikers aggressively invade this immature territory, bringing dark, horrific, criminal activity into a planned and controlled, 'young' space.

Similarly, *Villain* (Michael Tuchner, 1971), which stars Richard Burton as East End gangster Vic Dakin, features a key sequence depicting a wages snatch, which was filmed in Ellesfield Avenue, on the Southern Industrial Estate, Bracknell, about half a mile to the other side of the A3095 from 'Cross Fell' (the location of the little school in *The Offence*). Here we see a new, modern, out-of-town office development. The wide roads and bridges lend this space the look of suburban America. As the robbery takes place, and gangsters violently crash their cars and viciously beat security men, office workers rush out of a sleek new building, and are clearly stunned by the brutality being displayed by these men, no doubt because it appears strangely out of place in this new, modern, 'country' location. In *Villain*, then, we see pessimism, misery, and lawlessness invade a new development, and thus problematise a vision of a clean, modern Britain.

New Towns have much in common with suburbs. They are, after all, places which have become synonymous with family values and community.[15] Like suburbs, New Towns resist stable and separate spatial categories such as 'urban' and 'countryside'. Interestingly, Short points out that 'By the 1970s the suburbs had become part of the psyche and intellectual landscape and supporters of the suburbs began to emerge.'[16] But the geographer David Matless recognises that the suburb became a 'contentious English landscape', 'valued by some as essentially English in its modest scale, domestic values and humdrum life, and castigated by others for the same characteristics'.[17] Comfortable suburban life certainly became a fixture in some notable British television sitcoms of the period, in which it was celebrated or critiqued. These include *Happy Ever After* (BBC, 1974–78); *The Good Life* (BBC, 1975–78); *The Fall and Rise of Reginald Perrin* (BBC, 1976–79); *Butterflies* (BBC, 1978–83); and *Terry and June* (BBC, 1979–87). But suburbs also feature widely in sex comedy films such as *Confessions of a Window Cleaner* (Val Guest, 1974). In these texts, manufactured landscapes and socio-cultural territories stand as exemplars of modern Britishness.

Interestingly, writing in a book published in 2009, Anthony Alexander notices that, if New Towns were conceived during the post-war period as brand new places for young families to inhabit and mature in, they themselves were, now, in the new century and new millennium, 'moving from youth into adulthood, maturing as places'.[18] Developing this point, Alexander states that 'Perhaps their recent ageing has been a period of adolescence on the road to maturity.'[19] *The Offence* very much evokes the ways in which New Towns such as Bracknell might necessarily go through a phase of immaturity before entering a mature state. The film certainly raises the issue of British innocence being taken away. But this loss of innocence is problematised by the film, as the narrative seems to suggest that wildness is everywhere, even in these 'young', immature spaces. In other words, the changes to the British landscape that the film documents might demonstrate an old country moving towards modernity, but this bland and soulless modernity cannot in fact banish darker, seemingly uncivilised aspects of human nature and experience.

If there is a level of ambiguity concerning how *The Offence* chooses to deal with issues of morality, criminality and policing, this is never more evident than in the title of the film. The 'offence' might be the abduction and rape of Janie, or it might be the killing of Baxter by Johnson while in police custody. It might even be the modernisation of Britain. Like the New Town exteriors, the *mise-en-scène* of the interior of the new, brutalist police station which features centrally in the film (designed by John Clark) is also invested with a powerful dramatic charge. This building is a huge, rambling edifice; long, winding corridors make it appear like a futuristic, machine-like labyrinth. It is also clearly still under construction. We can see loose wiring and light fittings still waiting to be screwed on to walls; step ladders resting on the floor; a cement mixer; piles of hardboard. The rooms and corridors are grey and colourless, harshly lit by fluorescent tubes. The walls are fitted with modern air-conditioning vents. Plastic chairs are piled high in the interrogation room. The building features modern cigarette, coffee and confectionery vending machines. Just as this police station is in the process of being built, so too is a new Britain. But, as with the edifice of New Scotland Yard in Hitchcock's *Frenzy*, the sheer scale of this building suggests that its architects were working on the premise that the police expect criminal activity to take place here on a very large scale. Conversely, this large, unfinished building might also signify the fact that the police are not properly ready for the modern Britain in which they find themselves. A new nation is being constructed, then. But this new nation will be unpredictable and difficult to police. It will be no modern utopia.

The Offence features a tour-de-force pre-credits sequence which unfolds in this police station. Here we have fuzzy, disturbed, slow-motion footage of a commotion taking place. There is no dialogue or realistic sound to accompany these images. Instead, the soundtrack features dull, menacing, treated sounds and electronic drones. Superimposed over the footage of policemen moving around the building is a circular pattern of white light. This produces an uncanny effect, and makes us question the ontology of the images we are viewing. Is this a dream or some kind of hellish nightmare? Is this an extreme close-up of a human eye, in which images are reflected? Generically, this sequence feels more reminiscent of a horror film, or even an art film, than a mainstream crime film. It ends with a shot of Johnson (Connery). At this moment, the film moves to a more realistic mode of representation, as Johnson utters the words 'Oh, my God', as if to signal that he has just had a kind of epiphany; he has suddenly realised the potential consequences of his actions. This sequence certainly serves to set up the ambiguous nature of the film narrative in terms of how it blurs distinctions between crime and the criminal on the one hand, and institutions on the other. It is only towards the end of the film that it becomes apparent that the circles of white light that we see in the opening sequence are in fact abstracted from an image of a large fluorescent light fitted into the ceiling of the interrogation room. This, then, is the last thing Baxter sees as he lies on the floor and dies.

The Offence features another extraordinary, quasi-experimental sequence which occurs after Johnson is sent home from the police station by his superiors. To the sound of low drones, discordant music (by Harrison Birtwistle), electronic synthesized sounds (by Peter Zinovieff – developed at his EMS studios in Putney) and location sounds (such as a train rattling over points), Johnson drives home late at night in the rain. With windscreen wipers moving slowly and rhythmically from side to side, and distant streetlights fuzzy in the darkness, we share his disturbed visions of his past experiences as a police officer. This sequence, like the pre-credits sequence, is reminiscent of a psychological horror film. Andrew Spicer argues that the 'explicit oneirism' of this sequence 'expertly orchestrates a visual and aural correlative for Johnson's confusion and anguish'.[20] The film thus employs experimental formal strategies here to examine the nature of psychological trauma. During the sequence in which Johnson is being interrogated by Cartwright, he says to his superior: 'What's happening to me? All I can see is pictures in my mind.' Here is a man who feels his identity fragmenting in a fragmenting nation in which criminality has become a central aspect of everyday life.

So, *The Offence* is effectively another 1970s generic hybrid. For Kim Newman, British 'psycho-thrillers' demonstrate 'An overlap between the crime film and the horror film, the psycho-thriller is something of a pedant to both and, as such, often slips through the cracks in studies of either form.'[21] We might think of *The Offence* as a prime example of this. In some ways it also shares an interest in exploiting potential harm to schoolchildren evidenced in the horror film *The Face of Darkness* (Ian F. H. Lloyd, 1976), in which an extremist MP plans to plant a bomb in a school playground, and resurrects a long dead man to carry this out.[22]

Brutalism: *Get Carter*

Get Carter (Mike Hodges, 1971)was co-financed by MGM's British production company and EMI, and was produced by Michael Klinger, who, as we have seen, remained busy during the 1970s, producing the *Confessions* series and mainstream films such as *Gold* (Peter R. Hunt, 1974).[23] In *Get Carter*, Michael Caine portrays gangster Jack Carter as a brutal, largely emotionless, humourless man who shows no mercy to others.[24] The pre-credits sequence of the film features Carter and his gangland bosses, the Fletcher brothers, drinking and viewing pornographic slides in their penthouse. Here and elsewhere, as Steve Chibnall points out, the narrative is driven by a dammed-up sexual energy which finds its release in violence and perversion.[25] The well-known credits sequence follows Carter as he travels north from London to Newcastle on a train. We see him travelling first class, solicitously sipping soup in the restaurant car. On arrival in grey, rain-sodden Newcastle, Carter enters a busy pub and orders a pint of bitter 'in a thin glass', signifying his cultural difference as a southerner, even though it later turns out that he was born in the northern city.

Carter subsequently meets Doreen (Petra Markham), who is apparently the daughter of his dead brother. Doreen says that she works in a Woolworths store. Carter suggests that he has plans to go to South America, and invites Doreen to join him there with his girlfriend. But there can be no such happy ending. The brutal denouement of the film appears to be driven by Carter's anger and pain on discovering that Doreen has been forced to appear in pornographic films. And interestingly, later in the film, the barman, Keith (Alun Armstrong), lying beaten up on a bed, seems to suggest that Doreen might in fact be Carter's daughter. This would explain the lengths to which the man up from London goes to in his role as avenger, and the pain he registers on his face on seeing her performing in the porn film. According to Chibnall, 'the corruption of Doreen by pornographers is also a metaphor for a much more general malaise affecting urban Britain at the end of the 1960s'.[26] So, the film articulates a sickness seemingly lurking under the skin of contemporary British culture.

Get Carter constructs a vicious, brutal, and fragmentary vision of Britain, in which thugs and pornographers work in the dark socio-cultural crevasses of a northern city which remains, on the surface at least, apparently untouched by their activities. This is also a city in which so-called legitimate businessmen are clearly corrupt. But *Get Carter* also depicts a nation torn between modernity and tradition. While some things such as the working-class ritual of drinking in old pubs appears unchanged, Newcastle and Gateshead are shown to be urban spaces moving from an industrial past towards an uncertain, post-industrial future. The memorable sequence in the film which takes place in the windswept, brutalist Trinity Square multi-storey car park in Gateshead – and which ends with Cliff Brumby (Bryan Mosley) being thrown to his death by Carter – depicts a new British urban landscape on the verge of being born. As such, Newcastle and Gateshead are shown to be spaces in flux; their rotten old terraced houses falling apart while modern, brutalist architecture rises above them. Steve Chibnall notes that the cinematographer Wolfgang Suschitzky 'uses the bleak industrial landscape of Tyneside to express an oppressive sense of dereliction and a poverty of the soul, contrasting the belching chimneys and grimy terraces with the tawdry glamour of the bingo and dance hall and the uncompromising concrete slabs that pass for redevelopment'.[27] *Get Carter*, then, operates as 'an elegy for a passing world'.[28] This is evoked most clearly in the memorable closing sequence of the film, which sees Carter shot on a beach by a nameless sniper after he has deposited the body of his last victim, Eric (Ian Hendry), in a hoist. Filmed on Blackhall Beach in County Durham, this sequence sees Eric's body being dropped unceremoniously into the angry North Sea. This piece of hoisting machinery, representative of the mining industry, also operates as a symbol of a bygone era.[29] Here, then, it feels as though we are at the end of the world. How will Britain look in the future? The Britain of the 1970s, this film seems to suggest, will be a fragmented space of change.

Innocence and experience: *The Black Windmill*

As with Janie in *The Offence*, through the figure of a youthful female character, Doreen (Petra Markham), *Get Carter* develops a narrative which centres on the sexual exploitation of an inculpable young individual. Another film of the 1970s which suggests links between a loss of innocence (and, specifically, the cruel mistreatment of children) and adult criminality is *The Black Windmill* (Don Siegel, 1974), distributed by Universal. This film also stars Michael Caine, this time as Major John Tarrant, a British secret service agent. It begins with a credits sequence which displays nostalgic, bucolic images of school life accompanied by the sound of boys singing. Two schoolboys trespass on what appears to be Ministry of Defence land, but it turns out that they have stumbled upon the den of a criminal gang. One of the boys, David (Paul Moss), is kidnapped by this gang. He is John Tarrant's son. John Vernon plays the gang leader, and Delphine Seyrig plays his moll. Donald Pleasence plays Cedric Harper, Tarrant's sickly, sniffling boss – a performance that recalls his role as Inspector Calhoun in the horror film *Death Line* (aka *Raw Meat*) (Gary Sherman, 1972).

Tarrant (Caine) attends a meeting at the large country house of MI6 boss Sir Edward Julyan (Joseph O'Conor), where discussions turn to the issue of Soviet weapons allegedly being smuggled into Northern Ireland. But, learning of the kidnap of his young son, Tarrant speeds home to wait for news. The kidnappers eventually telephone, and it becomes abundantly clear that they are torturing young David (Moss). His terrible screams can be heard on the line, causing his mother, Alex (Janet Suzman) – Tarrant's estranged wife – to be physically sick. Tarrant subsequently travels to Paris in an attempt to pay the ransom with stolen diamonds. Ultimately failing in this task, he returns to England on a hovercraft. *The Black Windmill*, then, is another film of the 1970s that features a separated modern couple, and, as such, it signifies a crisis deemed to be affecting traditional British family life during the period. But when Tarrant eventually rescues his son from the kidnappers in the closing sequence in the windmill, he clearly intends to patch things up with Alex, telling the boy: 'We both love her very much, don't we, eh?' Things might not be too difficult to put right in the relationship, as Alex (Suzman) still lives in the family house; a stylish, modernist building (shot on location in Hampstead, London). It becomes clear that the Tarrants have evidently used the events around the kidnapping of their son to rediscover their feelings for each other. One might read the harrowing events of the film, and specifically the suffering of the young boy, as a form of punishment being meted out for the failure of their marriage. This, as we have seen, is a recurring theme of 1970s British films.

A bestial thriller: *The Squeeze*

The Squeeze (1977) was produced and distributed by Warner Bros. The director of the film, Michael Apted, worked throughout the 1970s, on *The Triple Echo* (1972), *Stardust* (1974), and *Agatha* (1979). In *Monthly Film Bulletin*, Richard Combs thought *The Squeeze* was a 'neat and skilful' film.[30] But, according to the *Daily Mail*'s Margaret Hinxman, it was a 'bestial thriller'.[31] The film certainly deals with a cruel threat to childhood innocence. It stars US actor Stacy Keach as the ex-Scotland Yard detective, Jim Naboth. This troubled man has a chronic alcohol problem. During the opening credits sequence we see him staggering up out of the depths of a London underground station, as if trying to escape the darkness of his own personal hell. This sequence certainly signifies the depths to which this man of the British law has sunk. Like *The Black Windmill*, *The Squeeze* features lovers who have parted, and explores the tensions at the heart of another broken family.[32] Naboth has two young sons, but his wife, Jill (Carol White), now lives with a wealthy businessman, Foreman (Edward Fox), and their young daughter, Christine (Alison Portes).[33]

Jill and Christine are kidnapped in broad daylight in a leafy London park by a gang led by Keith (David Hemmings), and subsequent events are often harrowing in their cruelty. There are a number of sequences in the film that feature Jill's daughter, the young Christine, in great distress, being manhandled by her captors. As in *The Black Windmill*, a child is seen to suffer horribly, while the parents contemplate their own failures as a couple. But the sexual politics of this film also evidence a distinct level of sickness, especially during the highly problematical sequence during which Jill (White) agrees to strip for her captors and have sex with one of them in a particularly extreme example of Stockholm Syndrome. Indeed, the representation of Jill in *The Squeeze* speaks little of the impact of the Women's Movement and the rise of feminism in Britain during the period (as discussed in Chapter 2). This sequence is just one example of the spiritual, ethical and moral 'lack' depicted in the film. Writing about *The Squeeze* and the 1970s *Sweeney* films, Steve Chibnall and Robert Murphy argue that they 'exhibit a cynical pessimism, not only about the administration of justice but also about the failure of Britain as a prosperous and honourable society'.[34] *The Squeeze* certainly depicts a troubled nation seized by moral decline.[35]

Overall, then, *The Squeeze* offers a grim portrayal of London in which, just as in the New Town of *The Offence*, cruelty is rampant, and a sense of threat is overwhelming. But in this film, the threat often operates at the level of the national as well as the individual. For example, 'IRA Rules' graffiti is visible on the side of a terraced house as Naboth plays football in the street with his young sons, signalling local support for the activities of this organisation. Furthermore, one of the central characters in the film is Vic (played by Northern Irish actor Stephen Boyd), a wealthy Irish gangster who lives in the upmarket London area of Hampstead. He is upwardly-mobile, watching his daughter compete at a gymkhana, and wishing to be around 'decent people'. The centrality of criminality to London life, and the sense of threat this induces, is further evidenced by the nature of the business of Foreman (Fox), who runs a security firm – a sign that there is money to be made in helping people protect their property from criminals in 1970s Britain.

Hands across the ocean: *The Long Good Friday*

At the beginning of the 1970s, the so-called 'Irish question' became a source of increasing concern in Britain. Some films depict the nation (and especially London) experiencing a crippling level of tension as the ramifications of the perceived cruelties of IRA actions are felt increasingly. But these 'terrorist' actions were part of an ongoing struggle. In Belfast, on Saturday, 6 February 1971, a Provisional IRA volunteer, Billy Reid, reportedly shot at a group of soldiers, killing Gunner Robert Curtis. He was the first British soldier to be killed in Northern Ireland.[36] On Wednesday, 10 March of that year, three young Royal Highland Fusiliers were shot by the IRA. The British Home Secretary, Reginald Maudling, authorised the introduction of internment without trial for suspected Irish terrorists and sympathisers in August 1971.[37] But despite this, overall, during that year, IRA gunmen killed forty-two British soldiers. In 1972 they killed sixty-four.[38] The most significant and infamous event to take place in Northern Ireland during this period was the so-called 'Bloody Sunday', when, on 30 January 1972, thirteen unarmed civilians were shot dead by members of the Parachute Regiment in Derry. This event – 'a catastrophe for Britain's image abroad'[39] – signalled an escalation of violence which led to a bomb attack at the Parachute Regiment's headquarters at Aldershot in Hampshire, which killed seven, and brought the 'terror' to the mainland. In London, over the Christmas period in 1973, bombs were going off at the rate of one a night.[40] As Dominic Sandbrook puts it, 'By the end of 1972, the bloody rampage had accounted for 2,000 bomb explosions, 2,000 armed robberies and more than 10,000 shooting incidents, while 5,000 people had been badly injured and 479 people killed – all in just twelve months'.[41] In 1973, the IRA set off car and parcel bombs across west London (in Westminster, Pentonville and Hampstead). They also bombed the Old Bailey, and planted explosives at Harrods, King's Cross, Euston and in Birmingham. On 4 February 1974, eleven people lost their lives in the IRA bombing of a coach carrying soldiers and their families along the M62 motorway.

John Hill argues that film representations of resistance in Ireland to British rule are often decontextualised; that is, the troubles are dealt with without a proper thought for (or engagement with) historical or political explanations. Moreover, Hill points out that, in cinema, the Irish are often depicted as having an irrational proclivity towards violence.[42] It is certainly the case that a range of British films of the 1970s present the Irish as a source of deadly threat at worst and a cause of ongoing unease at best. This certainly appears to be the case in *Hennessy* (Don Sharp, 1975), for example, a film in which Neil Hennessy (Rod Steiger) plans to blow up the Houses of Parliament in Westminster after his family is killed during a riot in Belfast (the film also stars Trevor Howard and Lee Remick).

One film that places the activities of the IRA at centre stage in 1970s London is *The Long Good Friday*,[43] which was scripted by Barrie Keeffe and directed by John Mackenzie.[44] Here, the cruel actions of the Provos (often unseen or undeveloped as characters) are set against the brutal behaviour of East End gangsters. *The Long Good Friday* is a film about the crime boss, Harold Shand (Bob Hoskins), who is trying to secure investment for his plan to rebuild part of the London docks in time for the fictional London Olympics of 1988.[45] Helen Mirren plays Shand's girlfriend – the seemingly middle-class, impressive Victoria.[46] Harold's plans do not succeed, primarily because it turns out that the East End is no longer his 'manor', so to speak. It has been infiltrated by the IRA. As the venal Police Inspector 'Parky' (Dave King) reminds him: 'They've taken it away from you.' Indeed, during the course of the film, Harold's wooing of his American mafia backers is constantly thwarted by a series of events which, it turns out, were caused by the IRA. A bomb destroys one of his status symbols, his Rolls-Royce; another bomb blows up his riverside pub; and various members of his 'corporation' are murdered. An unexploded bomb is also found in his West End casino. As Harold himself puts it, 'Two or three Micks have been very busy.' In this film, then, the tensions created between Harold's old-fashioned, parochial nationalism and his love of Britain on the one hand, and his recognition of the importance of doing business with the USA and Europe on the other, explode into physical violence on the streets of London. If Harold's life is falling apart, so is his idea of Britain. As Bart Moore-Gilbert points out, during the 1970s, 'The tendency towards polarization (and fragmentation) was also reflected in the rise of separatism in Scotland, Wales and Northern Ireland – movements which were in ironic contrast to the integrationist and supra-nationalist implications of Britain's entry into the European Community in 1973.'[47] Harold Shand's tragedy is that, while he knows how to control a distinct urban territory, he has hubristic ambitions to develop his corporation into a global enterprise, and he over-reaches himself in this new, complicated world. Indeed, the fragmentation of his criminal empire effectively reflects the fragmentation of Britain during this period.

As well as evoking the threat to Londoners posed by the IRA during the 1970s, *The Long Good Friday* fruitfully explores links between what would soon become Thatcherite free-market enterprise and the underground culture of gangsters.[48] Stuart Hall has argued that, while the early 1970s saw the dis-articulation of the post-war consensus, by the mid-1970s the elements of Thatcherism were establishing themselves within public discourse.[49] *The Long Good Friday* mediates these historical developments, and presciently anticipates the free-market capitalism of the 1980s. Indeed, Charlie Gere has suggested that the film is 'an allegorical anticipation of the dislocations about to be wrought by a decade or so of capitalist deregulation, unfettered development and globalization'.[50] Moreover, by blurring the distinctions between criminality and legitimate business, the film demonstrates how far criminal organisations had become increasingly global enterprises during the 1970s.[51] Indeed, although an old-fashioned gangster in the style of the infamous Kray twins, Hoskins plays Harold Shand as a capitalist.[52] In some ways we can read this figure as an archetypal working-class proto-Thatcherite. As he welcomes his American mafia partner Charlie (Eddie Constantine), Harold makes an impressive speech to assembled guests on his boat on the Thames, framed by Tower Bridge:

> Our country's not an island anymore. We're a leading European state. And I believe that this is the decade in which

London will become Europe's capital, having cleared away the
outdated. We've got mile after mile and acre after acre of land
for our future prosperity. No other city in the world has got,
right in its centre, such an opportunity for profitable progress.

Harold further talks of 'the global nature of this venture', and
seemingly welcomes the free flow of capital across traditional
boundaries of nation and class. He makes a toast to transatlantic
trade: 'Hands across the ocean.' Harold obviously takes pride in
the fact that Britain was the first truly global nation, and that the
east London docks performed a crucial role in the maintenance
of the British Empire. But we soon see that it is the idea of this
old, 'Great' Britain in which he really feels comfortable, not the
vicissitudes of a new, troubled, modern Britain. On making the
decision to renege on the deal, Charlie's lawyer, Tony, spitefully
tells Harold that Britain is worse than Cuba – a 'banana republic'.
Feeling let down by the Americans, Harold responds by telling
Tony and Charlie that he is going into partnership with a German
organisation, because Britain is now in the 'common market'. The
future is seemingly in Europe.[53] In reality, though, Harold (who has
been given the name of old kings from a distant English past) is
not equipped to change with the times. The American gangster,
Charlie (Constantine), recognises Harold's folly, telling him 'Things
change, Harold. Don't get nostalgic. Look to the future.' As we
have seen, Britain in the 1970s, like Harold, was fragmenting: a
nation torn between tradition and modernity; a nation on the edge
of change.

Notes

1   Houston, 'Frenzy', p. 166.
2   During the 1970s Lumet directed two more films in Britain – *Murder
    on the Orient Express* (1974) and *Equus* (1977). Gerry Fisher was Director
    of Photography for Joseph Losey a number of times, including on *The
    Go-Between* (1970), *A Doll's House* (1973), *The Romantic Englishwoman* (1975),
    and *Mr Klein* (1976). He also worked on *Bequest to the Nation* (James Cellan
    Jones, 1973), *Butley* (Harold Pinter, 1974), *Juggernaut* (Richard Lester,
    1974), and on the John Wayne film *Brannigan* (Douglas Hickox, 1975).

3 Canby, 'The Offence'.
4 The art director on *The Offence* was John Clark.
5 Canby, 'The Offence', *New York Times*, 12 May 1973.
6 Short, *Imagined Country: Environment, Culture and Society*, p. 9.
7 Short, *Imagined Country: Environment, Culture and Society*, p. 6.
8 Saint, 'The New Towns', p. 149.
9 Saint, 'The New Towns', p. 149.
10 Alexander, *Britain's New Towns*, p. 8.
11 Alexander, *Britain's New Towns*, p. 72.
12 Saint, 'The New Towns', p. 147.
13 Alexander, *Britain's New Towns*, p. 102.
14 Sandbrook, *State of Emergency*, p. 339.
15 Short, *Imagined Country: Environment, Culture and Society*, p. 50.
16 Short, *Imagined Country: Environment, Culture and Society*, p. 52.
17 Matless, *Landscape and Englishness*, p. 34.
18 Alexander, *Britain's New Towns*, p. 8.
19 Alexander, *Britain's New Towns*, p. 132.
20 Spicer, 'British Neo-Noir', p. 117.
21 Newman, 'Psycho-thriller, qu'est-ce que c'est?', p. 71.
22 Sarah Street (*British National Cinema*, pp. 100–1) argues that British crime/thriller films can be divided into four general categories during the 1970s – gangster films, police films, Agatha Christie adaptations, and spy thrillers (including the James Bond films). British gangster films of the period might include *Man of Violence* (Pete Walker, 1970); *Freelance* (Francis Megahy, 1970); *Get Carter* (Mike Hodges, 1971); *Villain* (Michael Tuchner, 1971); *The Marseille Contract* (aka *The Destructors*) (Robert Parrish, 1974); *Brannigan* (Douglas Hickox, 1975); and *The Long Good Friday* (John Mackenzie, 1979). Police or private-eye films include *Gumshoe* (Stephen Frears, 1971); *Callan* (Don Sharp, 1974); *Tomorrow Never Comes* (Peter Collinson, 1977); *Sweeney!* (David Wickes, 1977); and *Sweeney 2* (Tom Clegg, 1978). Agatha Christie adaptations include *Endless Night* (Sidney Gilliat, 1972); *Murder on the Orient Express* (Sidney Lumet, 1974); and *Death on the Nile* (John Guillermin, 1978). Spy thrillers include the James Bond films *Diamonds Are Forever* (Guy Hamilton, 1971); *Live and Let Die* (Guy Hamilton, 1973); and *The Spy Who Loved Me* (Lewis Gilbert, 1977); but also *Who?* (Jack Gold, 1974); *Yellow Dog* (Terence Donovan, 1973); *The Thirty-Nine Steps* (Don Sharp, 1978); and *The Eye of the Needle* (Richard Marquand, 1978). But to these sub-genres we might add adaptations of Alistair MacLean thrillers, which include *When Eight Bells Toll* (Etienne Périer, 1971); *Fear is the Key* (Michael Tuchner, 1972); *Caravan to Vaccarès* (Geoffrey Reeve, 1974); and *Bear Island* (Don Sharp, 1979); and robbery or heist films, which include *Perfect Friday* (Peter Hall, 1970); *11 Harrowhouse* (Aram Avakian, 1974); *Give Us Tomorrow* (Donovan Winter, 1978); and

The First Great Train Robbery (Michael Crichton, 1979). Furthermore, other British murder mysteries appeared during the 1970s, including *Fragment of Fear* (Richard C. Sarafian, 1970) and *Night Watch* (Brian G. Hutton, 1973).

23   Spicer, 'The Precariousness of Production: Michael Klinger and the Role of the Film Producer in the British Film Industry during the 1970s'.

24   A. Walker, *National Heroes*, p. 25.

25   Chibnall, *Get Carter*, p. 10.

26   Chibnall, *Get Carter*, p. 47.

27   Chibnall, *Get Carter*, p. 10.

28   Turner, *Crisis? What Crisis? Britain in the 1970s*, p. 60.

29   Spicer, 'British Neo-Noir', p. 119.

30   Combs, 'The Squeeze', p. 81.

31   Hinxman, 'The Squeeze'.

32   David Hetschel wrote an electronic progressive rock score for the film, which is in some ways reminiscent of Pink Floyd and the work of Goblin employed in the 1970s Italian *giallo* films of Dario Argento.

33   Carol White came to prominence working with director Ken Loach on the television drama *Cathy Come Home* (BBC, 1966) and in *Poor Cow* (1967), the director's first feature film.

34   Chibnall and Murphy, 'Parole Overdue: Releasing the British Crime Film into the Critical Community', p. 13.

35   Harper and Smith, *British Film Culture in the 1970s: The Boundaries of Pleasure*, p. 142.

36   Sandbrook, *State of Emergency*, p. 234.

37   Turner, *Crisis? What Crisis? Britain in the 1970s*, pp. 68–9.

38   Sandbrook, *State of Emergency*, p. 476.

39   Sandbrook, *State of Emergency*, p. 483.

40   Turner, *Crisis? What Crisis? Britain in the 1970s*, p. 21.

41   Sandbrook, *State of Emergency*, p. 498.

42   Hill, 'Images of Violence'.

43   *The Long Good Friday* was initially made for television in 1979 but was picked up for cinema distribution by Handmade Films in 1980.

44   During the decade, John Mackenzie had directed *One Brief Summer* (1970), *Unman, Wittering and Zigo* (1971), and *Made* (1972), the latter starring singer/songwriter Roy Harper and Carol White.

45   See Newland, *The Cultural Construction of London's East End*, pp. 193–9.

46   Helen Mirren also remained busy in the 1970s, appearing in *Savage Messiah* (Ken Russell, 1972), *O Lucky Man!* (Lindsay Anderson, 1973), and *Hussy* (Matthew Chapman, 1980).

47   Moore-Gilbert, 'Introduction: Cultural Closure or Post-avantgardism?', p. 6.

48   Hill, 'Allegorising the Nation: British Gangster Films of the 1980s', pp. 161–2.

49   See Hall, 'The Great Moving Right Show'.
50   Gere, 'Armagideon Time', p. 117.
51   Dear, *The Postmodern Urban Condition*, p. 270.
52   A. Walker, *National Heroes*, p. 252.
53   See Newland, *The Cultural Construction of London's East End*, pp. 193–9.

Conclusion

This book set out to examine a range of British films of the 1970s, to try to obtain a clearer understanding of two things – the fragmented state of the film-making culture of the period, and the fragmented nature of the nation that these films represent. What has become clear is that this is not a period of film-making that offers itself up for easy and clear conclusions. So I will not attempt to offer a definitive conclusion here. Rather, I want to reflect briefly on some of the themes that have emerged in this book, and the ways in which I have chosen to explain them.

I have purposefully left the analysis of the films open-ended and perhaps even fragmented at times, because this, it seems to me, was a sensible thing to do when confronted with an object of scrutiny that, when viewed from a variety of different critical positions, shifts and mutates in front of one's eyes. It has become clear that, in terms of British film-making, the 1970s was a period of openings as much as it was a period of closure. Films of the period, like the contested British identity they depict, cannot and should not be packaged into tidy compartments. British films of the 1970s mediate the flux and mutability of a shifting nation. These films speak of (and to) an increasingly diverse culture, and are replete with inconsistencies. All in all, then, this is a period in British history and British film and cinema history which resists interpretative closure. There is no singular narrative to be drawn here, other than the fact that the films of the period offer evidence of a Britain (and Britishness) characterised by vicissitudes. I hope that this book, through its form and structure, then, has served to evoke and even celebrate the fragmented nature of 1970s British national identity and British film-making. I now want to reconsider briefly some of these fragments.

One way in which the fragmented nature of British film production of the 1970s is evidenced is through the existence of generic hybrids. This hybridisation, as we have seen on numerous occasions, was facilitated by actors and other professionals who worked across a wide range of films and television shows. While genre films continued to be produced (especially horrors, sex films, comedies, and thrillers), a surprising number of even these films appear to be uncertain of their potential audiences. But while genre is often problematised in 1970s British cinema, we can see some common themes developing across a wide range of films. These themes are usually related to anxieties concerning a British way of life that appeared to be shifting irrevocably, as a nation so beholden to tradition struggled to cope with modernisation and change.

For example, tensions are often evident concerning the shifting racial profile of the British and disconnected ideas of Britain and/ or the United Kingdom. Indeed, many films across genres (and indeed crossing genres) deal with the rise of racial tensions, or offer a level of engagement with the idiosyncrasies of the immigrant experience. One such film is *The Sailor's Return* (Jack Gold, 1978), which tells the story of a sailor, William Targett (Tom Bell), who returns home to his West County village with a black African wife, Princess Tulip (Shope Shodeinde), where they are met with incredulity and prejudice.

The ongoing iniquities of the British class system, and shifts in responses to this, are also evident in a range of films of the period, such as *The Hireling* (Alan Bridges, 1973), starring Robert Shaw as Steven Ledbetter, a chauffeur who falls in love with a beautiful but damaged aristocratic widow, Lady Franklin (Sarah Miles). Lady Franklin is happy to sit in the front of the car with Ledbetter (temporarily crossing a class divide of sorts), and the pair picnic together. But when she subsequently falls for the aristocratic Captain Cantrip (Peter Egan), and shuns Ledbetter's passionate advances, the chauffeur spins out of control into drunkenness and violence. The film makes much of the pernicious aspects of class in Britain; the ways in which it inhibits individual as well as national change. After all, as Ledbetter himself acknowledges, in Britain 'we all have our place in life'. Set just after the First World War, the film was adapted by Wolf Mankowitz from a novel by L. P. Hartley. It won the Palme d'Or (Grand Prix) at Cannes in a tie with the US film *Scarecrow* (Jerry Schatzberg, 1973).

As we have also seen, a plethora of anxieties about permissiveness, sexual activity and the legacies of the socio-cultural revolutions of the 1960s are worked through across a range of British films of the 1970s. These films often refer to shifts in acknowledged norms or perceived perversions in sexual behaviour. Often, sexually innocent or weak individuals are seen to be taken advantage of by more experienced figures, as is the case in *The Walking Stick* (Eric Till, 1970), a film in which the shy, controlled Deborah (Samantha Eggar) – who has recovered from childhood polio but has been left with a lame leg – meets and falls in love with the artist, Leigh Hartley (David Hemmings), but subsequently discovers that she is being used, and grows stronger in the process. Indeed, the struggle of women to gain equality with men, and a concomitant crisis in masculinity, is prevalent in many films, and twisted responses to these shifts are exemplified by the cruel debasement of young women elsewhere, such as in *Straw Dogs* (Sam Peckinpah, 1973) and *Get Carter* (Mike Hodges, 1971).

Shifting attitudes to sex play a central role in many British films of the 1970s. The theme of the commodification of sexuality is widespread, as evidenced in *Every Home Should Have One* (Jim Clark, 1970), starring Marty Feldman and Judy Cornwell, which tells the story of an advertising man, Teddy (Feldman), who comes up with a sexy television advert to help sell frozen porridge, but subsequently comes into conflict with the 'Keep Television Clean' movement. Films also often demonstrate transforming attitudes towards the traditional structure of the family. Linked to this, we have seen that anxieties are displayed across a range of films concerning the breakdown of monogamous relationships, but also the breakdown of communication between individuals, and the ultimate alienation of the individual.

Films also depict individuals living on the psychological 'edge'. Madness stalks many characters, such as City worker, Harold Pelham (Roger Moore), who has a serious accident in *The Man Who Haunted Himself* (Basil Dearden, 1970) and is subsequently unsure whether he has a doppelgänger, or if he is being haunted by his own ghost.

A number of films represent the apparent strangeness of rural lives on the spatial 'edge' or under threat of change, as in *The Moon and the Sledgehammer* (Philip Trevelyan, 1971), a documentary portrait of the Page family, who live an essentially pre-modern life in the contemporary Sussex countryside.

We have also seen that a range of films deal with corruption occurring across the strata of British life, and a prevailing sense of lawlessness, as witnessed in *Villain* (Michael Tuchner, 1971), which sees corrupt MP, Gerald Draycott (Donald Sinden), occupying the same spaces as gangsters, and Inspector Matthews (Nigel Davenport) exclaiming at one point 'You can buy yourself out of anything with money in this bloody country.'

The two world wars haunt many British films of the period, suggesting that a deep, unshakeable vision of a traumatic but also glorious past informs aspects of a troubled British present. And a number of films deal with a looming apocalypse; or, at the very least, develop fears around a sense of an ending. Examples here include *Zardoz* (John Boorman, 1974), a science-fiction fantasy starring Sean Connery, set on a post-apocalyptic earth, and *The Medusa Touch* (Jack Gold, 1978), a supernatural thriller starring Richard Burton as John Morlar, a man with telekinetic abilities who can seemingly cause disasters.

A wide range of films appear to be ideologically ambivalent – on the one hand socially conservative, while on the other offering a critique of seemingly traditional aspects of the socio-cultural climate. This, then, is evidently a Janus-faced nation on film; a nation with one eye on its past and one eye on a modern future, even as its socio-cultural body is seen to be falling apart. This is evidenced in the *mise-en-scène* of Britain on film in the 1970s, which is often characterised by an uneasy mixture of the sleek, clean and modern, and the dusty, weathered and antique. In addition, it is evident that British films of the 1970s rarely depict a coherent or stable national identity. Indeed, very few films of the 1970s set in the contemporary moment display a coherent concept of Britishness.

One intriguing aspect of British cinema of the 1970s is the increasingly transnational nature of production. For example,

Deep End (Jerzy Skolimowski, 1970) is set in London and works with recognisably British iconography (the crumbling municipal swimming pool, grey skies, and drab Victorian-built suburban architecture), picking out the minutiae of a certain type of provincial British life, and featuring recognisably British actors such as Jane Asher and Diana Dors. But this film was directed by a Pole and funded by West German and American backers.

Another example, *A Day at the Beach* (1970), is an oneiric film being made by Roman Polanski at the time that his wife, Sharon Tate, was murdered by Charles Manson and his followers, and finished by (and thus credited to) Simon Hesera as director. Backed by Paramount, this film tells the story of Bernie (Mike Burns), an intelligent, self-destructive alcoholic who takes his young niece, Winnie (Beatie Edney), to the beach for the day. As he proceeds to drink himself to death in driving rain, Winnie's bright yellow rubber mac burns off the screen, through the dark browns, beiges and greys so typical of British fashion and style (and thus films) of the period. But what is most intriguing about this film is that it transports British characters (and their attendant socio-cultural mores) to an unspecified, peripheral northern European location. The street signs and buttons for floors in an elevator are in Danish, but Bernie pays for drinks in sterling. Britishness is thus seen to be dislocated; ripped away from its traditional iconography, and severely problematised. We might note here the ubiquity of the well-stocked drinks cabinet in this and many other British films of the period, and the centrality of alcohol in the breakdown of many lives on film.

Other transnational films use foreign locations to work through shifts in British codes of behaviour. *A Candle for the Devil* (aka *Una vela para el Diablo* and *It Happened at Nightmare Inn*) (Eugenio Martin, 1973) is a Spanish/British co-production starring Judy Geeson as Laura, a young woman on holiday in Spain. Two sisters, Marta (Aurora Bautista) and Veronica (Esperanza Roy) run a hotel in a sleepy Spanish village. They are devoutly religious, and find the free sexuality of young British women in particular too much to take. Marta finds one young woman sunbathing topless on the roof, and during the ensuing argument accidentally pushes her to her death. The sisters subsequently chop up this British woman's body and cook it for their guests to consume unknowingly.

A range of transnational 1970s films further problematise the identity of Britain. *Horror Express* (Eugenio Martin, 1972) is a Spanish-produced horror film, but stars British horror stalwarts Peter Cushing and Christopher Lee alongside US star Telly Savalas. *The Devil's Men* (Costas Carayiannis, 1976) features Peter Cushing as the leader of a Greek Devil-worshipping sect. *Holocaust 2000* (Alberto de Martino, 1977) is a UK/Italian co-production starring Kirk Douglas as Robert Caine, a man who plans to build a nuclear power station near a sacred cave in the Middle East. *Lizard in a Woman's Skin* (aka *Una lucertola con la pelle di donna* and *Schizoid*) (Lucio Fulci, 1971) is an American International Pictures release, shot at Dear Studios in Rome, and in London. This might not, strictly speaking, be a British film, but it certainly depicts British culture, or at least the white, upper-middle-class culture of 1970s London and the Home Counties. It stars Stanley Baker as a policeman (Inspector Colvin) tasked with uncovering the identity of the murderer of a woman who lives in the flat next door to Carol Hammond, the daughter of an English politician (Florinda Bolkan).

Other films which clearly fragment at the level of Britishness (in terms of production but also in terms of representation) include *Hannie Caulder* (Burt Kennedy, 1971), a Tigon/Paramount-produced Western shot in Spain, featuring Raquel Welch, Robert Culp, Ernest Borgnine and Christopher Lee. *Night Hair Child* (aka *Night Child*; *Child of the Night*; *What the Peeper Saw*; and *Diabólica Malicia*) (James Kelley and Andrea Bianchi, 1972) is another international co-production which sees a perverted 12-year-old schoolboy, Marcus (Mark Lester), sexually desiring his stepmother, Elise (Britt Ekland). The British film-making culture of the 1970s was so fragmented that even *Star Wars* (George Lucas, 1977) feels British in some distinctive ways, not least in the performances of the well-known actors Alec Guinness (as Ben Obi-Wan Kenobi), Peter Cushing (as Grand Moff Tarkin), and Anthony Daniels as C-3PO – a droid which essentially behaves like an English butler.

In his influential book, *Postmodernism, or The Cultural Logic of Late Capitalism* (1991), Fredric Jameson makes the point that perhaps the 1970s were characterised by a 'peculiar aimlessness'.[1] What he appears to mean by this is that, for him, the 1960s brought about a 'strongly generational self-consciousness', while, for Jameson, the 1970s might have displayed a 'lack of just such strong self-consciousness', and perhaps even a 'constitutive lack of identity'. In other words, the 1970s had 'no specificity'.[2] This is certainly true of British film production of the period. This is a nebulous, fleeting cinema in which Britain and Britishness fall apart, for good or ill.

Notes

1 Jameson, *Postmodernism, or The Cultural Logic of Late Capitalism*, p. 296.
2 Jameson, *Postmodernism, or The Cultural Logic of Late Capitalism*, p. 296. Quoted in Lev, *American Films of the 70s*, p. 181.

Bibliography

Adams, Mark (2001) *Mike Hodges*, Harpenden: Pocket Essentials.

Alexander, Anthony (2009) *Britain's New Towns*, London: Routledge.

Alfrey, Nicholas, Paul Barker, Margaret Drabble, Norbert Lynton, Richard Mabey, David Matthews, Kathleen Raine, and William Vaughan (1993a) *Towards a New Landscape*, London: Bernard Jacobson.

Alfrey, Nicholas (1993b) 'Undiscovered Country', in Alfrey, Nicholas *et al.*, *Towards a New Landscape*, London: Bernard Jacobson, pp. 17–21.

Alibhai-Brown, Yasmin (2000) *Who Do We Think We Are? Imagining the New Britain*, London: Allen Lane/Penguin.

Allen, Dave (2012a) 'Moving Images and the Visual Arts in 1970s Britain', in Sue Harper and Justin Smith (eds), *British Film Culture in the 1970s: The Boundaries of Pleasure*, Edinburgh: Edinburgh University Press, pp. 34–49.

Allen, Dave (2012b) 'British Graffiti: Popular Music and Film in the 1970s', in Sue Harper and Justin Smith, *British Film Culture in the 1970s: The Boundaries of Pleasure*, Edinburgh: Edinburgh University Press, pp. 99–111.

Altman, Rick (1980) 'Moving Lips: Cinema as Ventriloquism', in Rick Altman (ed.), *Cinema/Sound*, special issue of *Yale French Studies*, no. 60, pp. 67–9.

Anderson, Benedict (1983) *Imagined Communities: Reflections on the Origin and Spread of Nationalism*, London: Verso.

Andrews, Nigel (1971a) 'Villain', *Monthly Film Bulletin*, vol. 38, no. 450 (July), pp. 149–50.

Andrews, Nigel (1971b) 'Straw Dogs', *Monthly Film Bulletin*, vol. 38, no. 455 (December), pp. 249–50.

Armes, Roy (1978) *A Critical History of British Cinema*, London: Secker & Warburg.

Ashby, Justine and Andrew Higson (eds) (2000) *British Cinema: Past and Present*, London: Routledge.

Ashcroft, Bill, Gareth Griffiths and Helen Tiffin (eds) (1995) *The Post-Colonial Studies Reader*, London/New York: Routledge.

Bibliography

Askwith, Robin (1978) *The Confessions of Robin Askwith*, London: Ebury Press.

Auty, Martin and Roddick, Nick (eds) (1985) *British Cinema Now*, London: British Film Institute.

Back, Les (1996) *New Ethnicities and Urban Culture: Racisms and Multiculture in Young Lives*, London: Routledge.

Badder, David (1977) 'Black Joy', *Monthly Film Bulletin*, vol. 44, no. 526 (November), pp. 227–8.

Baillieu, Bill and John Goodchild (2002) *The British Film Business*, Chichester: John Wiley.

Bakari, Imruh (2000) 'A Journey from the Cold: Rethinking Black Film-making in Britain', in Osuwu, Kwesi (ed.), *Black British Culture and Society: A Text Reader*, London: Routledge, pp. 230–8.

Barber, Sian (2011) *Censoring the 1970s: The BBFC and the Decade that Taste Forgot*, Newcastle: Cambridge Scholars Press.

Barber, Sian (2012a) 'Government Aid and Film Legislation: 'An Elastoplast to Stop a Haemorrhage', in Sue Harper and Justin Smith (eds), *British Film Culture in the 1970s: The Boundaries of Pleasure*, Edinburgh: Edinburgh University Press, pp. 10–21.

Barber, Sian (2012b) 'British Film Censorship and the BBFC in the 1970s', in Sue Harper and Justin Smith, *British Film Culture in the 1970s: The Boundaries of Pleasure*, Edinburgh: Edinburgh University Press, pp. 22–33.

Barker, Paul (1993) 'The Stones of England', in Nicholas Alfrey *et al.*, *Towards a New Landscape*, London: Bernard Jacobson, pp. 25–30.

Barr, Charles (1972) '*Straw Dogs, A Clockwork Orange* and the Critics', *Screen*, vol. 13, no. 2 (Summer), pp. 17–31.

Barr, Charles (ed.) (1986) *All Our Yesterdays: 90 Years of British Cinema*, London: British Film Institute.

Barthes, Roland (1975) *The Pleasure of the Text*, trans. R. Miller, New York: Hill.

Bartholomew, David (1977) 'The Wicker Man', *Cinefantastique*, vol. 6, no. 3 (Winter), pp. 4–19.

Barton, Ruth (2008) 'When the Chickens Came Home to Roost: British Thrillers of the 1970s', in Robert Shail (ed.), *Seventies British Cinema*, London: British Film Institute/Palgrave Macmillan, pp. 46–55.

Bassnett, Susan (ed.) (1997) *Studying British Cultures: An Introduction*, London: Routledge.

Baxter, John (1971) *An Appalling Talent: Ken Russell*, London: Michael Joseph.

Baxter, John (1997) *Stanley Kubrick: A Biography*, London: HarperCollins.

Beck, Jay (2008) 'The Sounds of "Silence": Dolby Stereo, Sound Design, and The Silence of the Lambs', in Jay Beck and Tony Grajeda (eds), *Lowering the Boom: Critical Studies in Film Sound*, Urbana/Chicago: University of Illinois Press, pp. 68–83.

Beckett, Andy (1997) *When the Lights Went Out: Britain in the 1970s*, London: Faber & Faber.

Bennett, Andy (2000) *Popular Music and Youth Culture: Music, Identity and Place*, Basingstoke: Palgrave Macmillan.

Bennett, Tony and Janet Woollacott (1987) *Bond and Beyond: The Political Career of a Popular Hero*, London: Macmillan.

Bermingham, Ann (1987) *Landscape and Ideology: The English Rustic Tradition 1740–1860*, London: Thames & Hudson.

Bhabha, Homi K. (1994) *The Location of Culture*, London and New York: Routledge.

Bhabha, Homi K. (1995) 'Cultural Diversity and Cultural Differences', in Bill Ashcroft, Gareth Griffiths and Helen Tiffin (eds), *The Post-Colonial Studies Reader*, London/New York: Routledge, pp. 206–9.

Black, Jeremy (2005) *The Politics of James Bond: From Fleming's Novels to the Big Screen*, Lincoln, NE/London: University of Nebraska Press.

Blanchard, Simon and Sylvia Harvey (1983) 'The Post-War Independent Cinema – Structure and Organisation', in James Curran and Vincent Porter (eds), *British Cinema History*, London: Weidenfeld & Nicolson, pp. 226–41.

Booker, Christopher (1980) *The Seventies: Portrait of a Decade*, London: Allen Lane.

Bordwell, David and Kristin Thompson (1994) *Film History: An Introduction*, New York: McGraw Hill.

Bourne, Stephen (1998) *Black in the British Frame: Black People in British Film and Television, 1896–1996*, London: Cassell.

Bradley, Matthew R. (1997) 'The Bloody Countess: An Interview with Ingrid Pitt', *Filmfax: The Magazine of Unusual Film and Television*, no. 62 (1 August), pp. 82–90.

Bradley, Peri (2010) 'Hideous Sexy: The Eroticized Body and Deformity in 1970s British Horror Films', in Paul Newland (ed.), *Don't Look Now: British Cinema in the 1970s*, Bristol: Intellect Books, pp. 119–29.

Brien, Alan (1980) 'Babylon', *The Sunday Times*, 9 November.

Bright, Morris and Robert Ross (2000) *Mr Carry On: The Life and Work of Peter Rogers*, London: BBC Books.

Broughton, Mark (2000) 'Landscape Gardens in *The Ruling Class*', in Paul Newland (ed.), *Don't Look Now: British Cinema in the 1970s*, Bristol: Intellect Books, pp. 243–51.

Brown, Allan (2000) *Inside the Wicker Man: The Morbid Ingenuities*, London: Sidgwick & Jackson.

Brown, Geoff (2001) 'Paradise Found and Lost: The Course of British Realism', in Robert Murphy (ed.), *The British Cinema Book* (2nd edn), London: British Film Institute, pp. 248–55.

Brown, Geoff (n.d.) 'Kevin Brownlow'. Available at: www.screenonline.org.uk/people/id/547695/; accessed 5 June 2010.

Bibliography

Brown, R. S. (1994) *Overtones and Undertones: Reading Film Music*, Berkeley: University of California Press.

Browning, John and Caroline Joan Picart (eds) (2008) *Our (Un)Invited Guest(s): Documenting Dracula and Global Identities*, Lanham, MD/Plymouth, UK: Scarecrow Press.

Brunsdon, Charlotte (2007) *London in Cinema: The Cinematic City since 1945*, London: British Film Institute.

Bryce, Allan (2000) *Amicus: The Studio that Dripped Blood*, Liskeard, Cornwall: Stray Cat Publishing.

Bryce, Allan (2007) 'Leon on Me!', *The Darkside*, no. 129 (October/November), pp. 40–3.

Burns, W. (1963) *New Towns for Old: The Technique of Urban Renewal*, London: Leonard Hill.

Caine, Michael (1992) *What's It All About?*, London: Arrow.

Canby, Vincent (1973) 'The Offence', *New York Times*, 12 May.

Cardwell, Sarah (2006) 'Working the Land: Representations of Rural England in Adaptations of Thomas Hardy's Novels', in Catherine Fowler and Gillian Helfield (eds), *Representing the Rural: Space, Place, and Identity in Films about the Land*, Detroit: Wayne State University Press, pp. 19–34.

Carney, Ray and Leonard Quart (2000) *The Films of Mike Leigh: Embracing the World*, Cambridge: Cambridge University Press.

Carroll, Noël (1990) *The Philosophy of Horror; or Paradoxes of the Heart*, New York/London: Routledge.

Carroll, Noël (1996) *Theorising the Moving Image*, Cambridge: Cambridge University Press.

Castell, David (1980) 'Babylon', *Sunday Telegraph*, 9 November.

Catterall, Ali and Simon Wells (2002) *Your Face Here: British Cult Movies since the Sixties*, London: Fourth Estate.

Caute, David (2008) 'Looking Back in Regret at Winstanley', *The Guardian*, 17 October.

Chang, Chris (2007) 'Event Horizon: Chris Petit's *Radio On* Returns from the Ether', *Film Comment*, vol. 43, no. 3 (May), p. 16.

Chapman, James (1999a) *License to Thrill: A Cultural History of the James Bond Films*, London: I.B. Tauris.

Chapman, James (1999b) '"A Bit of the Old Ultra-Violence: A Clockwork Orange', in I. Q. Hunter (ed.), *British Science Fiction Cinema*, London: Routledge, pp. 128–37.

Chapman, James (2005) *Past and Present: National Identity and the British Historical Film*, London and New York: I.B. Tauris.

Chapman, James (2007) 'The World Turned Upside Down: *Cromwell* (1970) *Winstanley* (1975), *To Kill a King* (2003) and the British Historical Film', in Leon Engelen and Roel Vande Winkel (eds), *Perspectives on European Film and History*, Gent: Academia Press, pp. 111–31.

Chapman, James (2008) 'From Amicus to Atlantis: The Lost Worlds of 1970s British Cinema', in Robert Shail (ed.), *Seventies British Cinema*, London: British Film Institute/Palgrave Macmillan, pp. 56–64.

Chibnall, Steve (1998) *Making Mischief: The Cult Films of Pete Walker*, Guildford, Surrey: FAB Press.

Chibnall, Steve (2002) 'A Heritage of Evil: Pete Walker and the Politics of Gothic Revisionism', in Steve Chibnall and Julian Petley (eds), *British Horror Cinema*, London: Routledge, pp. 156–71.

Chibnall, Steve (2003) *Get Carter*, London: I.B. Tauris.

Chibnall, Steve and Brian McFarlane (2009) *The British 'B' Film*, London: British Film Institute/Palgrave Macmillan.

Chibnall, Steve and Robert Murphy (eds) (1999a) *British Crime Cinema*, London: Routledge.

Chibnall, Steve and Robert Murphy (1999b) 'Parole Overdue: Releasing the British Crime Film into the Critical Community', in Steve Chibnall and Robert Murphy (eds) *British Crime Cinema*, London: Routledge, pp. 1–15.

Chibnall, Steve and Julian Petley (eds) (2002a) *British Horror Cinema*, London: Routledge.

Chibnall, Steve and Julian Petley (2002b) 'The Return of the Repressed? British Horror's Heritage and Future', in Steve Chibnall and Julian Petley (eds) *British Horror Cinema*, London: Routledge, pp. 1–9.

Chion, Michel (1981) 'Une esthetique Dolby stéréo', *Cahiers du Cinèma*, vol. 329, no. 18 (November), pp. xii–xiii.

Chion, Michel (1994) *Audio-Vision: Sound on Screen*, ed. and trans. Claudia Gorbman, New York: Columbia University Press.

Chion, Michel (2003) 'The Silence of the Loudspeakers, or Why with Dolby Sound It Is the Film that Listens to Us', in Larry Sider, Diane Freeman and Jerry Sider (eds), *Soundscape: The School of Sound Lectures 1998–2001*, London: Wallflower, pp. 150–4.

Ciment, Michel (1985) *Conversations with Losey*, London: Methuen.

Ciment, Michel (1986) *John Boorman*, London: Faber & Faber.

Claydon, E. Anna (2010) 'Masculinity and Deviance in British Cinema of the 1970s: Sex, Drugs and Rock 'n' Roll in *The Wicker Man*, *Tommy* and *The Rocky Horror Picture Show*', in Paul Newland (ed.), *Don't Look Now: British Cinema in the 1970s*, Bristol: Intellect Books, pp. 131–42.

Cobbett, William (2005[1832]) *Rural Rides, Vol. 2*, New York: Cosimo.

Cocks, Jay (1975) 'Stardust', *Time Magazine*, 3 March.

Coleman, John (1980) 'Babylon', *New Statesman*, 7 November.

Combs, Richard (1977) 'The Squeeze', *Monthly Film Bulletin*, vol. 44, no. 519 (April), pp. 80–1.

Combs, Richard (1978) 'The Shout', *Monthly Film Bulletin*, vol. 45, no. 534 (July), pp. 142–3.

Bibliography

Combs, Richard (1979) 'Radio On', *Sight and Sound*, vol. 49, no. 1 (December), pp. 54–5.

Combs, Richard (1985) 'Ich bin ein Englander, or Show Me the Way to Go Home', *Monthly Film Bulletin*, vol. 52, no. 616 (May), pp. 136–9.

Conekin, Becky, Frank Mort and Chris Waters (eds), *Moments of Modernity: Reconstructing Britain 1945–1964*, London/New York: Rivers Oram Press.

Connolly, Ray (1985) *Stardust Memories*, London: Pavilion.

Conrich, Ian (1998) 'Forgotten Cinema: The British Style of Sexploitation', *Journal of Popular British Cinema*, no.1, pp. 87–100.

Conrich, Ian (2001) 'Traditions of the British Horror Film', in Robert Murphy (ed.), *The British Cinema Book* (2nd edn), London: British Film Institute, pp. 226–32.

Conrich, Ian (2008) 'The Divergence and Mutation of British Horror Cinema', in Robert Shail (ed.), *Seventies British Cinema*, London: British Film Institute/Palgrave Macmillan, pp. 25–35.

Conrich, Ian and Estella Tincknell (eds) (2006) *Film's Musical Moments*, Edinburgh: Edinburgh University Press.

Cook, Pam (1996) *Fashioning the Nation: Costume and Identity in British Cinema*, London: British Film Institute.

Cooke, Les (2003) *British Television Drama: A History*, London: British Film Institute.

Corner, John and Sylvia Harvey (eds) (1991) *Enterprise and Heritage: Crosscurrents of National Culture*, London: Routledge.

Cull, Nicholas (2002) 'Camping on the Borders: History, Identity and Britishness in the *Carry On* Costume Parodies, 1963–74', in Claire Monk and Amy Sargeant (eds), *British Historical Cinema: The History, Heritage and Costume Film*, London: Routledge, pp. 92–109.

Cullingworth, J. B. (1962) *New Towns for Old: The Problem of Urban Renewal*, London: Fabian Society.

Cunningham, Frank R. (1974) 'Lindsay Anderson's *O Lucky Man!* and the Romantic Tradition', *Literature/Film Quarterly*, vol. 2, no. 3, pp. 256–62.

Curran, James and Vincent Porter (eds) (1983) *British Cinema History*, London: Weidenfeld & Nicholson.

Curtis, David (2006) *A History of Artists' Film and Video in Britain, 1897–2004*, London: British Film Institute.

Dacre, Richard (2001) 'Traditions of British Comedy', in Robert Murphy (ed.), *The British Cinema Book* (2nd edn), London: British Film Institute, pp. 233–40.

Darley, Fidelma (2002) 'Ireland, the Past and British Cinema', in Claire Monk and Amy Sargeant (eds), *British Historical Cinema: The History, Heritage and Costume Film*, London: Routledge, pp. 129–43.

Dash, Michael (1995) 'Marvellous Realism: The Way out of Négritude', in Bill Ashcroft, Gareth Griffiths and Helen Tiffin (eds), *The Post-Colonial Studies Reader*, London/New York: Routledge, pp. 199–201.

Davies, Brenda (1970) 'Cromwell', *Monthly Film Bulletin*, vol. 37, no. 440 (September), pp. 60–1.

Davies, Russell (ed.) (1994) *The Kenneth Williams Diaries*, London: HarperCollins.

Davis, Fred (1979) *Yearning for Yesterday: A Sociology of Nostalgia*, New York: Free Press.

Dawson, Jan (1971) 'Sunday Bloody Sunday', *Sight and Sound*, vol. 40, no. 3 (Summer), p. 164.

Dawson, Jan (1974/75) 'Akenfield', *Sight and Sound*, vol. 44, no.1 (Winter), pp. 58–9.

Dear, Michael J. (2000) *The Postmodern Urban Condition*, London: Blackwell.

Dickinson, Margaret (ed.) (1999) *Rogue Reels: Oppositional Film in Britain 1945–90*, London: British Film Institute.

Dickinson, Margaret and Sarah Street (1985) *Cinema and State: The Film Industry and the British Government 1927–84*, London: British Film Institute.

Dixon, Wheeler Winston (1991) *The Films of Freddie Francis*, Metuchen, NJ/London: Scarecrow Press.

Dixon, Wheeler Winston (ed.) (1994) *Re-Viewing British Cinema*, New York: State University of New York Press.

Dixon, Wheeler Winston (2008) 'The End of Hammer', in Robert Shail (ed.), *Seventies British Cinema*, London: British Film Institute/Palgrave Macmillan, pp. 14–24.

Docherty, David, David Morrison and Michael Tracey (1987) *The Last Picture Show? Britain's Changing Film Audiences*, London: British Film Institute.

Dolan, Josie and Andrew Spicer (2010) 'On the Margins: Anthony Simmons, *The Optimists of Nine Elms* and *Black Joy*', in Paul Newland (ed.), *Don't Look Now: British Cinema in the 1970s*, Bristol: Intellect Books, pp. 79–91.

Dolby Laboratories (1978) 'Dolby Stereo: A Progress Report', *Variety*, 16 August, p. 7.

Donnell, Alison (2002) *Companion to Contemporary Black British Culture*, London: Routledge.

Donnelly, Kevin J. (1998) 'British Punk Films: Rebellion into Money, Nihilism into Innovation', *Journal of Popular British Cinema*, no. 1, pp. 101–14.

Donnelly, Kevin J. (2001a) *Pop Music in British Cinema: A Chronicle*, London: British Film Institute.

Donnelly, Kevin J. (ed.) (2001b) *Film Music: Critical Approaches*, Edinburgh: Edinburgh University Press.

Donnelly, Kevin J. (2001c) 'Introduction: The Hidden Heritage of Film Music', in Kevin J. Donnelly (ed.) *Film Music: Critical Approaches*, Edinburgh: Edinburgh University Press, pp. 1–15.

Doran, Susan and Thomas S. Freeman (eds) (2009) *Tudors and Stuarts on Film*, Basingstoke: Palgrave Macmillan.

Drabble, Margaret (1993) 'The Future of Our Past', in Nicholas Alfrey *et al.*, *Towards a New Landscape*, London: Bernard Jacobson, pp. 33–8.

Bibliography

Dunleavy, P. (1981) *The Politics of Mass Housing in Britain, 1945–1975*, Oxford: Clarendon Press.

Dupin, Christophe (2008) 'The BFI and British Independent Cinema in the 1970s', in Robert Shail (ed.), *Seventies British Cinema*, London: British Film Institute/Palgrave Macmillan, pp. 159–74.

Durgnat, Raymond (1970) *A Mirror for England: British Movies from Austerity to Affluence*, London: Faber & Faber.

Durgnat, Raymond (1974) '*O Lucky Man!* Or: The Adventures of a Clockwork Cheese', *Film Comment*, vol. 10, no. 1 (January), pp. 38–40.

Durston, Christopher (2009) '*Winstanley*', in Susan Doran and Thomas S. Freeman (eds) *Tudors and Stuarts on Film*, Basingstoke: Palgrave Macmillan, pp. 232–44.

Durwood, Elissa (1976) '*O Lucky Man!*', *Crimmers: The Journal of the Narrative Arts*, (Spring), p. 14.

Ede, Laurie N. (2012) 'British Film Design in the 1970s', in Sue Harper and Justin Smith (eds), *British Film Culture in the 1970s: The Boundaries of Pleasure*, Edinburgh: Edinburgh University Press, pp. 50–61.

Edson, Barry (1980) 'Film Distribution and Exhibition in the UK', *Screen*, vol. 21, no. 3, pp. 36–44.

Edwards, Rebecca (2011) 'On 1970s Music and Nostalgia', Culture, Change and Continuity in the 1970s symposium, Aberystwyth University, 15 September.

Egan, Kate (2011) 'Exploring the Critical Reception of Ingrid Pitt: Nudity, Feminism, Nostalgia and the 1970s', Culture, Change and Continuity in the 1970s symposium, Aberystwyth University, 15 September.

Eliot, T. S. (1974) *Collected Poems 1909–1962*, London: Faber & Faber.

Ellis, John (1978) 'Art, Culture and Quality – Terms for a Cinema in the Forties and Seventies', *Screen*, vol. 19, no. 3, pp. 9–49.

Ellis, John (1982) *Visible Fictions: Cinema, Television, Video*, London: RKP.

Ellis, John (ed.) (1977) *1951–1976: British Film Institute Productions*, London: British Film Institute.

Elsaesser, Thomas (1972) 'Between Style and Ideology', *Monogram*, no. 3, pp. 2–10.

Engelen, Leon and Roel Vande Winkel (eds) (2007) *Perspectives on European Film and History*, Gent: Academia Press.

Esher, Lionel (1981) *A Broken Wave: The Rebuilding of England 1940–1980*, London: Allen Lane.

Everett, Wendy (2004) *Terence Davies*, Manchester: Manchester University Press.

Farley, Fidelma (2002) 'Ireland, the Past and British Cinema', in Claire Monk and Amy Sargeant (eds) *British Historical Cinema: The History, Heritage and Costume Film*, London: Routledge, pp. 129–43.

Flanagan, Kevin J. (ed.) (2009) *Ken Russell: Re-viewing England's Last Mannerist*, Plymouth, UK: Scarecrow Press.

Foley, D. L. (1963) *Controlling London's Growth: Planning the Great Wen, 1940–1960*, Berkeley: University of California Press.

Ford, Boris (ed.) (1988) *The Cambridge Guide to the Arts in Britain, Vol. 9: Since the Second World War*, Cambridge: Cambridge University Press.

Forster, Laurel (2012) '1970s Television: A Self-conscious Decade', in Sue Harper and Justin Smith (eds), *British Film Culture in the 1970s: The Boundaries of Pleasure*, Edinburgh: Edinburgh University Press, pp. 85–98.

Forster, Laurel and Sue Harper (eds) (2010a) *British Culture and Society in the 1970s*, Newcastle upon Tyne, Cambridge Scholars Publishing.

Forster, Laurel and Sue Harper (2010b) 'Introduction', in Laurel Forster and Sue Harper (eds) *British Culture and Society in the 1970s*, Newcastle upon Tyne, Cambridge Scholars Publishing, pp. 1–12.

Fowler, Catherine and Gillian Helfield (2006a) 'Introduction', in Catherine Fowler, and Gillian Helfield (eds), *Representing the Rural: Space, Place, and Identity in Films about the Land*, Detroit: Wayne State University Press.

Fowler, Catherine and Gillian Helfield (eds) (2006b) *Representing the Rural: Space, Place, and Identity in Films about the Land*, Detroit: Wayne State University Press.

Fowler, William (2010) 'Multiple Voices: *The Silent Cry* and Artists' Moving Image in the 1970s', in Paul Newland (ed.), *Don't Look Now: British Cinema in the 1970s*, Bristol: Intellect Books, pp. 71–7.

Fox, Julian (1972) 'Nobody Ordered Love', *Films and Filming*, vol. 18, no. 9 (June), pp. 59–60.

Fox, Julian (1973) 'That'll Be the Day', *Films and Filming*, vol. 19, no. 10 (July), pp. 53–4.

Friedman, Lester (ed.) (2006) *Fires Were Started: British Cinema and Thatcherism* (2nd edn), London: Wallflower.

Fryer, Peter (1984) *Staying Power: The History of Black People in Britain*, London: Pluto Press.

Gearing, Nigel (1974) 'Stardust', *Monthly Film Bulletin*, vol. 41, no. 489 (October), pp. 229–30.

Gere, Charlie (2003) 'Armagideon Time', in Joe Kerr and Andrew Gibson (eds), *London from Punk to Blair*, London: Reaktion Books, pp. 117–22.

Gerrard, Steve (2008) 'What a Carry On! The Decline and Fall of a Great British Institution', in Robert Shail (ed.), *Seventies British Cinema*, London: British Film Institute/Palgrave Macmillan, pp. 36–45.

Giddens, Anthony (1992) *The Transformation of Intimacy: Sexuality, Love and Eroticism in Modern Societies*, Cambridge: Polity Press.

Gladwell, David (2011) 'David Gladwell Discusses His Work, *Requiem for a Village*', British Film Institute DVD booklet, pp. 14–16.

Glaessner, Verina (1974) 'The Beast Must Die', *Monthly Film Bulletin*, vol. 41, no. 485 (June), pp. 119–20.

Bibliography

Glaessner, Verina (1976/7) '*Winstanley*: An Interview with Kevin Brownlow and Andrew Mollo', *Film Quarterly*, vol. 30, no. 2, pp. 18–23.

Gomez, Joseph A. (1976) *Ken Russell: The Adaptor as Creator*, London: Frederick Muller.

Gow, Gordon (1973) 'O Lucky Man!', *Films and Filming*, vol. 19, no. 9 (June), pp. 45–6.

Graham, Allison (1981) *Lindsay Anderson*, Boston: Twayne.

Grainge, Paul (2008) 'Selling Spectacular Sound: Dolby and the Unheard History of Technical Trademarks', in Jay Beck and Tony Grajeda (eds), *Lowering the Boom: Critical Studies in Film Sound*, Urbana, IL/Chicago: University of Illinois Press, pp. 251–68.

Hainsworth, Paul, John Hill and Martin McLoone (eds) (1994) *Border Crossing: Film in Ireland, Britain and Europe*, Belfast: US/Queen's University.

Hall, Sheldon (2001) 'The Wrong Sort of Cinema: Refashioning the Heritage Film Debate', in Robert Murphy (ed.), *The British Cinema Book* (2nd edn), pp. 191–9.

Hall, Sheldon (2008) 'Under Siege: The Double Rape of Straw Dogs', in Robert Shail, (ed.), *Seventies British Cinema*, London: British Film Institute/Palgrave Macmillan, pp. 129–38.

Hall, Stuart (1983) 'The Great Moving Right Show', in Stuart Hall and Martin Jacques (eds), *The Politics of Thatcherism*, London: Lawrence & Wishart, pp. 19–39.

Hall, Stuart (1995) 'New Ethnicities', in Bill Ashcroft, Gareth Griffiths and Helen Tiffin (eds), *The Post-Colonial Studies Reader*, London and New York: Routledge, pp. 223–7.

Hall, Stuart and Paul Du Gay (eds) (1996) *Questions of Cultural Identity*, London: Sage.

Hall, Stuart and Martin Jacques (eds) (1983) *The Politics of Thatcherism*, London: Lawrence & Wishart.

Hallam, Julia with Margaret Marshment (2000) *Realism and Popular Cinema*, Manchester: Manchester University Press.

Hamilton, John (2005) *Beasts in the Cellar: The Exploitation Film Career of Tony Tenser*, Godalming, Surrey: FAB Press.

Handzo, Stephen (1985) 'Glossary of Film Sound Technology', in Elizabeth Weis and John Belton (eds), *Film Sound: Theory and Practice*, New York: Columbia University Press, pp. 383–426.

Hannan, Michael (2009) 'Sound and Music in Hammer's Vampire Films', in Philip Hayward (ed.), *Terror Tracks: Music, Sound and Horror Cinema*, London: Equinox, pp. 60–74.

Hardy, Dennis (1991) *From New Towns to Green Politics: Campaigning for Town and Country Planning, 1946–1990*, London: E. & F. N. Spon.

Harper, Sue (1994) *Picturing the Past: The Rise and Fall of the British Costume Film*, London: British Film Institute.

Harper, Sue (2007) 'History and Representation: The Case of 1970s British Cinema', in James Chapman, Mark Glancy and Sue Harper (eds), *The New Film History*, Basingstoke: Palgrave Macmillan, pp. 27–40.

Harper, Sue (2010a) 'The British Women's Picture: Methodology, Agency And Performance in the 1970s', in Melanie Bell and Melanie Williams (eds), *British Women's Cinema*, London/New York: Routledge, pp. 124–37.

Harper, Sue (2010b) 'Keynote Lecture, Don't Look Now? British Cinema in the 1970s Conference, University of Exeter, July 2007', in Paul Newland (ed.), *Don't Look Now: British Cinema in the 1970s*, Bristol: Intellect Books, pp. 21–8.

Harper, Sue and Justin Smith (eds) (2012a) *British Film Culture in the 1970s: The Boundaries of Pleasure*, Edinburgh: Edinburgh University Press.

Harper, Sue and Justin Smith (2012b) 'Introduction', in Sue Harper and Justin Smith (eds), *British Film Culture in the 1970s: The Boundaries of Pleasure*, Edinburgh: Edinburgh University Press, pp. 1–7.

Harvey, David (1991) *The Condition of Postmodernity: An Enquiry into the Origins of Cultural Change*, Oxford: Blackwell.

Harvey, Sylvia (1986) 'The "Other Cinema" in Britain: Unfinished in Oppositional and Independent Film, 1929–1984', in Charles Barr (ed.), *All Our Yesterdays: 90 Years of British Cinema*, London: British Film Institute, pp. 225–51.

'Hawk' (1973) 'That'll Be the Day', *Variety*, 28 November, p. 14.

'Hawk' (1974) 'Stardust', *Variety*, 4 September, p. 20.

Hayward, Philip (ed.) (2004) *Off the Planet: Music, Sound and Science Fiction Cinema*, Eastleigh, Hants: John Libbey Publishing.

Hayward, Philip (ed.) (2009) *Terror Tracks: Music, Sound and Horror Cinema*, London: Equinox.

Hedling, Erik (1998) *Lindsay Anderson: Maverick Film-Maker*, London: Cassell.

Hedling, Erik (2001) 'Lindsay Anderson and the Development of British Art Cinema', in Robert Murphy (ed.) *The British Cinema Book* (2nd edn), London: British Film Institute, pp. 241–7.

Hewison, Robert, (1987) *The Heritage Industry: Britain in a Climate of Decline*, London: Methuen.

Heylin, Clinton (2004) *Can You Feel the Silence? Van Morrison – a New Biography*, London: Penguin.

Higson, Andrew (1983) 'Critical Theory and "British Cinema"', *Screen*, vol. 24, no. 4/5 (July/October), pp. 80–95.

Higson, Andrew (1984) 'Space, Place, Spectacle', *Screen*, vol. 25, no. 4/5 (July/October), pp. 2–21.

Higson, Andrew (1989) 'The Concept of National Cinema', *Screen*, vol. 30, no. 4 (Autumn), pp. 36–46.

Higson, Andrew (1993) 'Re-presenting the National Past: Nostalgia and Pastiche in the Heritage Film', in Lester Friedman (ed.), *Fires Were*

Started: British Cinema and Thatcherism, London: University College Press, pp. 109–29.

Higson, Andrew (1994) 'A Diversity of Film Practices: Renewing British Cinema in the 1970s', in Bart Moore-Gilbert (ed.), *The Arts in the 1970s: Cultural Closure?*, London: Routledge, pp. 216–39.

Higson, Andrew (1995) *Waving the Flag: Constructing a National Cinema in Britain*, Oxford: Clarendon Press.

Higson, Andrew (1996a) 'The Heritage Film and British Cinema', in Andrew Higson, (ed.), *Dissolving Views: Key Writings on British Cinema*, London: Cassell, pp. 232–48.

Higson, Andrew (ed.) (1996b) *Dissolving Views: Key Writings on British Cinema*, London: Cassell.

Higson, Andrew (1998) 'British Cinema', in John Hill and Pamela Church Gibson (eds), *The Oxford Guide to Film Studies*, Oxford: Oxford University Press, pp. 501–9.

Higson, Andrew (2003) *English Heritage, English Cinema: Costume Drama Since 1980*, Oxford: Oxford University Press.

Higson, Andrew (2006) 'A Green and Pleasant Land: Rural Spaces and British Cinema', in Catherine Fowler and Gillian Helfield (eds), *Representing the Rural: Space, Place, and Identity in Films about the Land*, Detroit: Wayne State University Press, pp. 240–55.

Higson, Andrew (2011) *Film England: Culturally English Filmmaking since the 1990s*, London and New York: I.B. Tauris.

Hill, John (1983) 'Working-class Realism and Sexual Reaction: Some Theses on the British "New Wave"', in James Curran and Vincent Porter (eds), *British Cinema History*, London: Weidenfeld & Nicolson, pp. 301–11.

Hill, John (1986) *Sex, Class and Realism: British Cinema 1956–1963*, London: British Film Institute.

Hill, John (1988) 'Images of Violence', in Kevin Rockett, Luke Gibbons and John Hill, *Cinema and Ireland*, Syracuse, NY: Syracuse University Press, pp. 147–93.

Hill, John (1996) 'Allegorising the Nation: British Gangster Films of the 1980s', in Steve Chibnall and Robert Murphy (eds), *British Crime Cinema*, London: Routledge, pp. 160–71.

Hill, John (1999) *British Cinema in the 1980s*, Oxford: Oxford University Press.

Hill, John (2004) 'A Working Class Hero Is Something to Be? Changing Representations of Class and Masculinity in British Cinema', in Phil Powrie, Ann Davies and Bruce Babington (eds), *The Trouble with Men: Masculinities in European and Hollywood Cinema*, London: Wallflower, pp. 100–9.

Hill, John (2010) 'Revisiting British Film Studies', *Journal of British Cinema and Television*, vol. 7, no. 2, pp. 299–310.

Hill, John and Pamela Church Gibson (eds) (1985) *The Oxford Guide to Film Studies*, Oxford: Oxford University Press.

Hinxman, Margaret (1977) 'The Squeeze', *Daily Mail*, 25 February.

Hjort, Mette and Scott Mackenzie (eds) (2000) *Cinema and Nation*, London: Routledge.

Holte, James Craig (1997) *Dracula in the Dark: The Dracula Film Adaptations*. Westport, CT/ London: Greenwood Press.

Home, Stewart (n.d.) 'Pressure'. Available at: www.stewarthomesociety.org/luv/pressure.htm; accessed 10 December 2010.

Houston, Penelope (1972) 'Frenzy', *Sight and Sound*, vol. 41, no. 3 (Summer), pp. 166–7.

Hoyle, Brian (2009) '*Radio On* and British Art Cinema', *Journal of British Cinema and Television*, vol. 6, no. 3, pp. 407–23.

Hunt, Leon (1998) *British Low Culture: From Safari Suits to Sexploitation*, London: Routledge.

Hunt, Leon (1999) 'Dog Eat Dog: *The Squeeze* and the *Sweeney* Films', in Steve Chibnall and Robert Murphy (eds), *British Crime Cinema*, London: Routledge, pp. 134–47.

Hunt, Leon (2002) 'Necromancy in the UK: Witchcraft and the Occult in British Horror', in Steve Chibnall and Julian Petley (eds), *British Horror Cinema*, London/New York: Routledge, pp. 82–98.

Hunter, I. Q. (2008) 'Take an Easy Ride: Sexploitation in the 1970s', in Robert Shail (ed.), *Seventies British Cinema*, London: British Film Institute/Palgrave Macmillan, pp. 3–13.

Hunter, I. Q. (ed.) (1999) *British Science Fiction Cinema*, London and New York: Routledge.

Hutchings, Peter (1993) *Hammer and Beyond: The British Horror Film*, Manchester: Manchester University Press.

Hutchings, Peter (2001) 'Beyond the New Wave: Realism in British Cinema, 1959–1963', in Robert Murphy (ed.), *The British Cinema Book* (3rd edn), London: British Film Institute, pp. 304–12.

Hutchings, Peter (2002) 'The Problem of British Horror', in Mark Jancovich (ed.), *Horror The Film Reader*, London: Routledge, pp. 115–24.

Hutchings, Peter (2004) *The Horror Film*, Harlow: Longman.

Hutchings, Peter (2009) 'The Amicus House of Horror', in Steve Chibnall and Julian Petley (eds), *British Horror Cinema*, London: Routledge, pp. 131–44.

Hutchings, Peter (2010) 'The Power to Create Catastrophe: The Idea of Apocalypse in 1970s British Cinema', in Paul Newland (ed.), *Don't Look Now: British Cinema in the 1970s*, Bristol: Intellect Books, pp. 107–17.

Inglis, Ian (2003a) 'Introduction: Popular Music and Film', in Ian Inglis (ed.), *Popular Music and Film*, London: Wallflower, pp. 1–7.

Inglis, Ian (2003b) The Act You've Known for All These Years: Telling the Tale of The Beatles', in Ian Inglis (ed.), *Popular Music and Film*, pp. 77–90.

Bibliography

Inglis, Ian (ed.) (2003c) *Popular Music and Film*, London: Wallflower.

Izod, John (1992) *The Films of Nicolas Roeg: Myth and Mind*, London: Macmillan.

Izod, John, Karl Magee, Kathryn Mackenzie and Isabelle Gourdin (2010) 'What Is There to Smile At? Lindsay Anderson's *O Lucky Man!*', in Paul Newland (ed.), *Don't Look Now: British Cinema in the 1970s*, Bristol: Intellect Books, pp. 215–27.

Jackson, L. (1988) 'Young, British and Black', *Cineaste*, vol. 16, no. 4, pp. 24–5.

Jameson, Fredric (1985) 'Postmodernism and Consumer Society', in Hal Foster (ed.), *Postmodern Culture*, London: Pluto Press, pp. 111–25.

Jameson, Fredric (1991) *Postmodernism, or The Cultural Logic of Late Capitalism*, New York: Verso.

Jeavons, Clyde (1974) 'Eskimo Nell', *Monthly Film Bulletin*, vol. 41, no. 491 (December), pp. 273–4.

Jenkins, S. (1980) 'Babylon', *Monthly Film Bulletin*, vol. 47, no. 562 (November), pp. 208–9.

'Jock' (1971) 'Straw Dogs', *Variety*, 1 December.

Johnson, Linton Kwesi (1980) *Inglan Is a Bitch*, London: Race Today.

Johnson, Tom and Deborah Del Vecchio (1995) *Hammer Films: An Exhaustive Filmography*, Jefferson, NC: McFarland.

Johnson, William (1979) 'The Shout', *Film Quarterly*, vol. 33, no. 1 (October), pp. 53–9.

Jones, Gareth (1973a) 'Carry On Girls', *Monthly Film Bulletin*, vol. 40, no. 479 (December), p. 245.

Jones, Gareth (1973b) 'Akenfield', *Sight and Sound*, vol. 42, no. 4 (Autumn), pp. 192–3.

Jordan, M. (1983) 'Carry On ... Follow That Stereotype', in James Curran and Vincent Porter (eds), *British Film History*, London: Weidenfeld & Nicolson, pp. 312–27.

Karamath, Joel (2007) 'Shooting Black Britain', *Index on Censorship*, vol. 36, no. 1 (April), pp. 142–7.

Kassabian, Anahid (2001) *Hearing Film: Tracking Identifications in Contemporary Hollywood Music*, New York/ London: Routledge.

Kermode, Mark (2002) 'The British Censors and Horror Cinema', in Steve Chibnall and Julian Petley (eds) *British Horror Cinema*, London: Routledge, pp. 10–22.

Kerr, Joe and Andrew Gibson (eds) (2003) *London From Punk to Blair*, London: Reaktion Books.

Kinsey, Wayne (2002) *Hammer Films: The Bray Studio Years*, London: Reynolds and Hearn.

Knight, Deborah (1997) 'Naturalism, Narration and Critical Perspective: Ken Loach and the Experimental Method', in George McKnight (ed.), *Agent of Challenge and Defiance: The Films of Ken Loach*, Wiltshire: Flicks Book, pp. 60–81.

Kolker, Robert Philip (1977) 'The Open Texts of Nicolas Roeg', *Sight and Sound*, vol. 46, no. 2 (Spring), pp. 82–4, 113.

Laing, Stuart (1994) 'The Politics of Culture: Institutional Change in the 1970s', in Bart Moore-Gilbert (ed.), *The Arts in the 1970s: Cultural Closure?*, London and New York: Routledge, pp. 29–56.

Landy, Marcia (1991) *British Genres: Cinema and Society, 1930–1960*, Princeton, NJ: Princeton University Press.

Landy, Marcia (ed.) (2001) *The Historical Film: History and Memory in Media*, London: The Athlone Press.

Larson, R. D. (ed.) (1996) *Music from the House of Hammer: Music in the Hammer Horror Films 1950–1980*, London: Scarecrow Press.

Lavery, David L. (1980) '*O Lucky Man!* and the Movie as Koan', *Literature/Film Quarterly*, no. 8, pp. 35–40.

Lay, Samantha (2003) *British Social Realist Drama*, London: Wallflower Press.

Leach, Jim (2004) *British Film*, Cambridge and New York: Cambridge University Press.

Leggott, James (2004) 'Like Father? Failing Parents and Angelic Children in Contemporary British Social Realist Cinema', in Phil Powrie, Ann Davies and Bruce Babington (eds), *The Trouble with Men: Masculinities in European and Hollywood Cinema*, London: Wallflower, pp. 163–75.

Leggott, James (2008) 'Nothing to Do Around Here: British Realist Cinema in the 1970s', in Robert Shail (ed.), *Seventies British Cinema*, London: British Film Institute/Palgrave Macmillan, pp. 94–104.

Leggott, James (2010) 'Dead Ends and Private Roads: The 1970s Films of Barney Platts-Mills', in Paul Newland (ed.), *Don't Look Now: British Cinema in the 1970s*, Bristol: Intellect Books, pp. 229–39.

Leigh, Jacob (2002) *Ken Loach: Art in the Service of the People*, London: Wallflower Press.

Lev, Peter (2000) *American Films of the 70s: Conflicting Visions*, Austin, TX: University of Texas Press.

Lindner, Christoph (ed.) (2003) *The James Bond Phenomenon*, Manchester: Manchester University Press.

Lippard, Chris (ed.) (1996) *By Angels Driven: The Films of Derek Jarman*, Trowbridge: Flicks Books.

Longford, Frank Pakenham (1972) *Report on Pornography*, London: Hodder & Stoughton.

Lovell, Alan (1972a) 'The Unknown Cinema of Britain', *Cinema Journal*, vol. 11, no. 2, pp. 1–8.

Lovell, Alan (1972b) 'The British Cinema: Notes on British Film Culture', *Screen*, vol. 13, no. 2, pp. 5–15.

Lovell, Alan (1975) 'Brecht in Britain – Lindsay Anderson (on *If...* and *O Lucky Man!*)', *Screen*, vol. 16, no. 4 (December), pp. 62–80.

Lovell, Alan (1976) *The Production Board*, London: British Film Institute.

Bibliography

Lovell, Alan (2001) 'The British Cinema: The Known Cinema?', in Robert Murphy (ed.) *The British Cinema Book* (2nd edn), London: British Film Institute, pp. 200–5.

Lovell, Terry (1990) 'Landscapes and Stories in 1960s British Realism', *Screen*, vol. 31, no. 4, pp. 357–76.

Lucas, Tim (2008) 'Lucky Charmer: *O Lucky Man!*', DVD Review, *Sight and Sound*, vol. 18, no. 1 (January), p. 96.

Lucie-Smith, Edward (1980) *Art in the Seventies*, London: Phaidon.

Luckett, Moya (1999) 'Image and the Nation in 1990s British Cinema', in Robert Murphy (ed.), *British Cinema of the 90s*, London: British Film Institute, pp. 88–99.

Lyons, Kevin (n.d.) 'Nobody Ordered Love'. Available at: www.bfi.org.uk/nationalarchive/news/mostwanted/nobody-ordered-love.html; accessed 13 January 2012.

McArthur, Colin (2004) 'Two Steps Forward, One Step Back: Cultural Struggle in the British Film Institute', *Journal of Popular British Cinema*, no. 4, pp. 112–27.

McArthur, Colin (ed.) (1982) *Scotch Reels: Scotland in Cinema and Television*, London: British Film Institute.

McFarlane, Brian (1997) *An Autobiography of British Cinema*, London: Methuen.

McGillivray, David (1972a) 'Endless Night', *Monthly Film Bulletin*, vol. 39, no. 465 (October), pp. 209.

McGillivray, David (1972b) 'Nobody Ordered Love', *Monthly Film Bulletin*, vol. 39, no. 460 (May), pp. 99–100.

McGillivray, David (1992) *Doing Rude Things: The History of the British Sex Film 1957–1981*, London: Sun Tavern Fields.

McKnight, George (ed.) (1997) *Agent of Challenge and Defiance: The Films of Ken Loach*, Trowbridge: Flicks Books.

MacCabe, Colin (1974) 'Realism and the Cinema: Notes on Some Brechtian Theses', *Screen*, vol. 15, no. 2 (Summer), pp. 7–27.

MacCabe, Colin (2001) *Performance*, London: British Film Institute.

Macnab, Geoffrey (ed.) (2000) *Searching for Stars: Stardom and Screen Acting in British Cinema*, London: Cassell.

Mabey, Richard (1993) 'Landscape: Terra Firma?', in Nicholas Alfrey *et al.*, *Towards a New Landscape*, London: Bernard Jacobson, pp. 63–8.

Madden, Paul (1972) 'Doomwatch', *Monthly Film Bulletin*, vol. 39, no. 459 (April), p. 70.

Malcolm, Derek (1980) 'Babylon', *The Guardian*, 6 November.

Mandler, Peter (1999) 'New Towns for Old: The Fate of the Town Centre', in Becky Conekin, Frank Mort and Chris Waters (eds), *Moments of Modernity: Reconstructing Britain 1945–1964*, London/New York: Rivers Oram Press, pp. 208–27.

Marwick, Arthur (1996) *British Society since 1945*, London: Penguin.

Matless, David (1998) *Landscape and Englishness*, London: Reaktion Books.

Maxford, Howard (1996) 'Revelations and Revolutions: Ingrid Pitt', *Shivers: The Magazine of Horror Entertainment*, 32 (1 August), pp. 44–7.

May, John (2010) 'Sid Rawle – Obituary', *The Guardian*, 15 September.

Mazierska, Ewa (2010) *Jerzy Skolimowski: The Cinema of a Nonconformist*, Oxford/ New York: Berghahn Books.

Medhurst, Andy (1986) 'Music Hall and British Cinema', in Charles Barr (ed.), *All Our Yesterdays: 90 Years of British Cinema*, London: British Film Institute, pp. 168–88.

Medhurst, Andy (1992) 'Carry On Camp', *Sight and Sound*, vol. 10, no. 3 (August), pp. 16–19.

Mercer, Korbena (ed.) (1988) *Black Film, British Cinema*, London: ICA.

Millar, Jeff (1974) 'O Lucky Man!', *Film Heritage*, vol. 9, no. 4, (July), pp. 36–7.

Milne, Tom (1971a) 'Get Carter', *Sight and Sound*, vol. 40, no. 2 (Spring), pp. 107–8.

Milne, Tom (1971b) 'Sunday Bloody Sunday', *Monthly Film Bulletin*, vol. 38, no. 450 (July), pp. 146–7.

Milne, Tom (1971c) 'Straw Dogs', *Sight and Sound*, vol. 41, no. 1 (Winter), pp. 71–2.

Milne, Tom (1972) 'Zee & Co.', *Monthly Film Bulletin*, vol. 39, no. 459 (April), pp. 82–3.

Milne, Tom (1973) 'O Lucky Man!', *Monthly Film Bulletin*, vol. 40, no. 473 (June), pp. 128–9.

Milne, Tom (1975) 'Akenfield', *Monthly Film Bulletin*, vol. 42, no. 492 (January), p. 4.

Milne, Tom (1976) 'Winstanley', *Monthly Film Bulletin*, vol. 43, no. 507 (April), p. 90.

Monaco, Paul (1987) *Ribbons in Time: Movies and Society Since 1945*, Bloomington, IN: Indiana University Press.

Monk, Claire (2002) 'The British Heritage-Film Debate Revisited', in Claire Monk and Amy Sargeant, (eds) *British Historical Cinema: The History, Heritage and Costume Film*, London: Routledge, pp. 176–98.

Monk, Claire (2008) '"Now, what are we going to call you? Scum!... Scum!... That's commercial! It's all they deserve": *Jubilee*, Punk and British Film in the Late 1970s', in Robert Shail (ed.), *Seventies British Cinema*, London: British Film Institute/Palgrave Macmillan, pp. 81–93.

Monk, Claire and Amy Sargeant (2002a) 'Introduction: The Past in British Cinema', in Claire Monk and Amy Sargeant (eds), *British Historical Cinema: The History, Heritage and Costume Film*, London: Routledge, pp. 1–14.

Monk, Claire and Amy Sargeant (eds) (2002b) *British Historical Cinema: The History, Heritage and Costume Film*, London: Routledge.

Moore-Gilbert, Bart (ed.) (1994a) *The Arts in the 1970s: Cultural Closure?* London: Routledge.

Bibliography

Moore-Gilbert, Bart (1994b) 'Introduction: Cultural Closure or Post-avantgardism?', in Bart Moore-Gilbert (ed.), *The Arts in the 1970s: Cultural Closure?* London: Routledge, pp. 1–28.

Morrill, John (2009) 'Oliver Cromwell and the Civil Wars', in Susan Doran and Thomas S. Freeman (eds) *Tudors and Stuarts on Film*, Basingstoke: Palgrave Macmillan, pp. 204–19.

Mumford, Lewis (1961) *The City in History*, London: Secker & Warburg.

Mundy, John (2007) *The British Musical Film*, Manchester: Manchester University Press.

Murphy, Robert (1989) *Realism and Tinsel*, London and New York: Routledge.

Murphy, Robert (1992) *Sixties British Cinema*, London: British Film Institute.

Murphy, Robert (1999a) 'A Revenger's Tragedy: *Get Carter*', in Steve Chibnall and Robert Murphy (eds) *British Crime Cinema*, London: Routledge, pp. 123–33.

Murphy, Robert (ed.) (1999b) *British Cinema of the 90s*, London: British Film Institute.

Murphy, Robert (ed.) (2002) *The British Cinema Book* (2nd edn), London: British Film Institute.

Murphy, Robert (ed.) (2006) *Directors in British and Irish Cinema – A Reference Guide Companion*, London: British Film Institute.

Murphy, Robert (ed.) (2009) *The British Cinema Book* (3rd edn), London: British Film Institute.

Nairn, Tom (1977) *The Break-Up of Britain: Crisis and Neo-Nationalism*, London: New Left Books.

Newland, Paul (2008a) *The Cultural Construction of London's East End: Urban Iconography, Modernity and the Spatialisation of Englishness*, Amsterdam/ New York: Rodopi.

Newland, Paul (2008b) 'Folksploitation: Charting the Horrors of the British Folk Music Tradition in *The Wicker Man*', in Robert Shail (ed.), *Seventies British Cinema*, London: British Film Institute/Palgrave Macmillan, pp. 119–128.

Newland, Paul (2008c) 'The Grateful Un-Dead: Count Dracula and the Transnational Counter Culture in *Dracula A.D. 1972*', in John Browning and Caroline Joan Picart (eds), *Our (Un)Invited Guest(s): Documenting Dracula and Global Identities*, Lanham, MD/Plymouth, UK: Scarecrow Press, pp. 135–51.

Newland, Paul (2009) 'On Location in 1970s London: Gavrik Losey', *Journal of British Cinema and Television*, vol. 6, no. 2, pp. 302–12.

Newland, Paul (2010a) 'We Know Where We're Going, We Know Where We're From: *Babylon*', in Paul Newland (ed.), *Don't Look Now: British Cinema in the 1970s*, Bristol: Intellect Books, pp. 93–104.

Newland, Paul (ed.) (2010b) *Don't Look Now: British Cinema in the 1970s*, Bristol: Intellect Books.

Newman, Kim (1988) *Nightmare Movies: A Critical History of the Horror Movie from 1968*, London: Bloomsbury.

Newman, Kim (2002) 'Psycho-thriller, qu'est-ce que c'est?', in Steve Chibnall and Julian Petley (eds), *British Horror Cinema*, London: Routledge, pp. 71–81.

Newman, Kim (2007) 'The Sound of Fear: The Influences and Production of *The Shout*', Network DVD booklet, pp. 1–7.

Ngcobo, Lauretta (ed.) (1987) *Let It Be Told: Essays by Black Women on Britain*, London: Pluto.

Nicolson, Adam (1993) 'Introduction', in Nicholas Alfrey *et al.*, *Towards a New Landscape*, Bernard Jacobson, pp. 9–14.

North, Dan (2008a) 'Don Boyd: The Accidental Producer', in Robert Shail (ed.), *Seventies British Cinema*, London: British Film Institute/Palgrave Macmillan, pp. 139–49.

North, Dan (ed.) (2008b) *Sights Unseen: Unfinished British Films*, Newcastle on Tyne: Cambridge Scholars Publishing.

Nowell-Smith, Geoffrey (1979/80) 'Radio On', *Screen*, vol. 20, no. 3/4 (Winter), pp. 29–39.

Ogidi, Ann (n.d.) 'Babylon'. Available at: www.screenonline.org.uk/film/id/475379/index.hmtl; accessed 13 January 2012.

Ogidi, Ann (n.d.) 'Black British Film'. Available at: www.screenonline.org.uk/film/id/1144245/index.hmtl; accessed 13 January 2012.

Ogundipe-Leslie, Molara (1981) 'Babylon', *The Guardian*, 7 January.

Ollenshaw, N. F. (1970) 'Fact and Fiction', *Films and Filming*, vol. 17, no. 3 (December), p. 4.

O'Pray, Michael (1996a) *Avant-Garde Film*, Luton: John Libbey.

O'Pray, Michael (1996b) *Derek Jarman: Dreams of England*, London: British Film Institute.

O'Pray, Michael (1996c) 'The British Avant-Garde and Art Cinema from the 1970s to the 1990s', in Andrew Higson (ed.), *Dissolving Views: Key Writings on British Cinema*, London and New York: Cassell, pp. 178–90.

Osuwu, Kwesi (ed.) (2000) *Black British Culture and Society: A Text Reader*, London: Routledge.

Park, James (1984) *Learning to Dream: The New British Cinema*, London: Faber & Faber.

Park, James (1990) *British Cinema: The Lights that Failed*, London: B. T. Batsford.

Patch, Andrew (2010) 'Beneath the Surface: Nicolas Roeg's *Don't Look Now*', in Paul Newland (ed.) *Don't Look Now: British Cinema in the 1970s*, Bristol: Intellect Books, pp. 253–64.

Patterson, John (2004) 'A Film Without a Cinema', *The Guardian*, 2 October.

Patterson, John (2008) 'Films We Forgot to Remember', *The Guardian Film and Music*, 19 May.

Bibliography

Payne, Christina (1993) *Toil and Plenty: Images of the Agricultural Landscape in England, 1780–1890*, New Haven, CT/ London: Yale University Press.

Perkins, Roy and Martin Stollery (2004) *British Film Editors: The Heart of the Movie*, London: British Film Institute.

Perks, Marcelle (2002) 'A Descent into the Underworld: *Death Line*', in Steve Chibnall and Julian Petley (eds) *British Horror Cinema*, London: Routledge, pp. 145–55.

Perry, George (1985) *The Great British Picture Show*, London: Pavilion.

Petit, Chris (2008) 'Road Movies: Germany–England/England–Germany', *Vertigo*, vol. 4, no. 1, pp. 40–2.

Petley, Julian (1986) 'The Lost Continent', in Charles Barr (ed.) *All Our Yesterdays: 90 Years of British Cinema*, London: British Film Institute, pp. 98–119.

Petrie, Duncan (1991) *Creativity and Constraint in the British Film Industry*, London: Macmillan.

Petrie, Duncan (ed.) (1992) *New Questions of British Cinema*, London: British Film Institute.

Petrie, Duncan (1996) *The British Cinematographer*, London: British Film Institute.

Petrie, Duncan (2000) *Screening Scotland*, London: British Film Institute.

Petrie, Duncan (2010) 'Interview with Colin Young', *Journal of British Cinema and Television*, vol. 7, no. 2, pp. 311–23.

Phelps, Guy (1975) *Film Censorship*, London: Victor Gollancz.

Phillips, Gene (1979) *Ken Russell*, Boston, MA: Twayne.

Pidduck, J. (2007) *Contemporary Costume Film: Space, Place and the Past*, London: British Film Institute.

Pierce, Guy (1980) 'Babylon', *New Standard*, 6 November.

Pines, Jim (2001) 'British Cinema and Black Representation', in Robert Murphy (ed.), *The British Cinema Book* (2nd edn), London: British Film Institute, pp. 177–83.

Pirie, David (1973) *A Heritage of Horror: The English Gothic Cinema, 1946–1972*, London: Gordon Fraser.

Pirie, David (2008) *A New Heritage of Horror: The English Gothic Horror Cinema*, London/New York: I.B. Tauris.

Porter, Vincent (2012) 'Film Education during the 1970s', in Sue Harper and Justin Smith, *British Film Culture in the 1970s: The Boundaries of Pleasure*, Edinburgh: Edinburgh University Press, pp. 62–74.

Powrie, Phil, Ann Davies and Bruce Babington (eds) (2004) *The Trouble with Men: Masculinities in European and Hollywood Cinema*, London: Wallflower.

Puttnam, David (1997) *The Undeclared War: The Struggle for Control of the World's Film Industry*, London: HarperCollins.

Pym, John (1976) 'Requiem for a Village', *Monthly Film Bulletin*, vol. 43, no. 512 (September), p. 197.

Pym, John (1977) 'Black Joy', *Sight and Sound*, vol. 46, no. 3 (Summer), p. 194.

Pym, John (1978) 'My Way Home', *Sight and Sound*, vol. 47, no. 4 (Autumn), pp. 262–3.

Pym, John (1979) 'Radio On', *Monthly Film Bulletin*, vol. 46, no. 550 (November), pp. 233–4.

Raisbeck, John (1972) 'Neither the Sea Nor the Sand', *Monthly Film Bulletin*, vol. 39, no. 467 (December), p. 255.

Ramdin, Ron (1999) *Reimagining Britain: Five Hundred Years of Black and Asian History*, London: Pluto Press.

Ravetz, A. (1980) *Remaking Cities*, London: Croom Helm.

Ravetz, A. (1986) *The Government of Space: Town Planning in Modern Society*, London: Faber & Faber.

Rayns, Tony (1973a) 'That'll Be the Day', *Monthly Film Bulletin*, vol. 40, no. 472 (May), p. 107.

Rayns, Tony (1973b) 'Claude Whatham's Day', *Sight and Sound*, vol. 42 no. 2 (April), p. 84.

Rayns, Tony (1973c) 'Dyn Amo', *Monthly Film Bulletin*, vol. 40, no. 468 (January), p. 7.

Reay, Pauline (2004) *Music in Film: Soundtracks and Synergy*, London: Wallflower Press.

Rees, A. L. (1999) *A History of Experimental Film and Video: From the Canonical Avant-Garde to Contemporary British Practice*, London: British Film Institute.

Richards, Jeffrey (1997) *Films and British National Identity: From Dickens to Dad's Army*, Manchester: Manchester University Press.

Richards, Jeffrey and Anthony Aldgate (1983) *Best of British: Cinema and Society from 1930 to the Present*, Oxford: Basil Blackwell.

Robinson, David (1973) 'Stripping the Veils Away', *The Times*, 21 April.

Robinson, David (1980) 'Babylon', *The Times*, 7 November.

Rockett, Kevin, Luke Gibbons and John Hill (1988) *Cinema and Ireland*, Syracuse, NY: Syracuse University Press.

Rolinson, Dave (2010) 'The Last Studio System: A Case for British Television Films', in Paul Newland (ed.),) *Don't Look Now: British Cinema in the 1970s*, Bristol: Intellect Books, pp. 163–76.

Rosenstone, Robert A. (2001) 'The Historical Film: Looking at the Past in a Postliterate Age', in Marcia Landy (ed.), *The Historical Film: History and Memory in Media*, London: The Athlone Press, pp. 50–66.

Rosenthal, Michael (1982) *British Landscape Painting*, Oxford: Phaidon.

Ross, Robert (1996) *The Carry On Companion*, London: B. T. Batsford.

Rubenstein, Lenny (1980) 'Winstanley and the Historical Film: An Interview with Kevin Brownlow', *Cineaste*, vol. 10, no. 4, pp. 22–5.

Bibliography

Rugg, Akua (1984) *Brickbats and Bouquets: Black Women's Critique: Literature, Theatre, Film*, London: Race Today Publications.

Saint, Andrew (1988) 'The New Towns', in Boris Ford (ed.), *The Cambridge Guide to the Arts in Britain, Vol. 9, Since the Second World War*, Cambridge: Cambridge University Press, pp. 147–59.

Salwolke, Scott (1993) *Nicolas Roeg: Film by Film*, Jefferson, NC: McFarland.

Sandbrook, Dominic (2011) *State of Emergency: The Way We Were: Britain 1970–1974*, London: Penguin.

Sandhu, Sukhdev (2008) 'Border Zones', *Radio On*, BFI DVD booklet, pp. 11–13.

Sangster, Jimmy (2001) *Inside Hammer: Behind the Scenes at the Legendary Film Studio*, London: Reynolds & Hearn.

Sargeant, Amy (2005) *British Cinema: A Critical History*, London: British Film Institute.

Sargeant, Amy (2010) 'Hovis, Ovaltine, Mackeson's and the *Days of Hope* Debate', in Paul Newland (ed.), *Don't Look Now: British Cinema in the 1970s*, Bristol: Intellect Books, pp. 199–211.

Savage, Jon (1999) '*Performance*: Interview with Donald Cammell', in Steve Chibnall and Robert Murphy (eds), *British Crime Cinema*, London: Routledge, pp. 110–16.

Shail, Robert (2008a) *Seventies British Cinema*, London: British Film Institute/Palgrave Macmillan.

Shail, Robert (2008b) 'Introduction: Cinema in the Era of 'Trouble and Strife', in Robert Shail (ed.), *Seventies British Cinema*, London: British Film Institute/Palgrave Macmillan, pp. xi–xix.

Shail, Robert (2008c) '"Much, Much More … Roger Moore": A New Bond for a New Decade', in Robert Shail (ed.), *Seventies British Cinema*, London: British Film Institute/Palgrave Macmillan, pp. 150–8.

Shaw, Sally (2012) '"Picking up the Tab" for the Whole Black Community? Industrial, Social and Institutional Challenges as Exemplified in *Babylon* (1980)', in Sue Harper and Justin Smith (eds), *British Film Culture in the 1970s: The Boundaries of Pleasure*, Edinburgh: Edinburgh University Press, pp. 75–84.

Sheridan, Simon (1999) *Come Play With Me: The Life and Times of Mary Millington*, Guildford, Surrey: FAB Books.

Sheridan, Simon (2005) *Keeping the British End Up: Four Decades of Saucy Cinema* (2nd edn), London: Reynolds & Hearn.

Sheridan, Simon (2008) *X-Rated – Adventures of an Exploitation Filmmaker*, London: Reynolds & Hearn.

Short, John Rennie (1991) *Imagined Country: Environment, Culture and Society*, London/New York: Routledge.

Sider, Larry, Diane Freeman and Jerry Sider (eds) (2003) *Soundscape: The School of Sound Lectures 1998–2001*, London: Wallflower.

Sinyard, Neil (1991) *The Films of Nicolas Roeg*, London: Letts.

Smith, Justin (2008) 'Glam, Spam and Uncle Sam: Funding Diversity in 1970s British Film Production', in Robert Shail (ed.), *Seventies British Cinema*, London: British Film Institute/Palgrave Macmillan, pp. 67–80.

Smith, Justin (2010) '"The 'Lack' and How to Get It": Reading Male Anxiety in *A Clockwork Orange, Tommy* and *The Man Who Fell to Earth*', in Paul Newland (ed.) *Don't Look Now: British Cinema in the 1970s*, Bristol: Intellect Books, pp. 143–60.

Smith, Justin (2011) 'The Boundaries of Pleasure: British Film Culture in the 1970s', *Culture, Change and Continuity* symposium, Aberystwyth University, 15 September.

Sounes, Howard (2007) *Seventies: The Sights, Sounds and Ideas of a Brilliant Decade*, London: Simon & Schuster.

Spicer, Andrew (2001) *Typical Men: The Representation of Masculinity in Popular British Cinema*, London: I.B. Tauris.

Spicer, Andrew (2007a) 'British Neo-Noir', in Andrew Spicer (ed.), *European Film Noir*, Manchester: Manchester University Press, pp. 112–37.

Spicer, Andrew (ed.) (2007b) *European Film Noir*, Manchester: Manchester University Press.

Spicer, Andrew (2010) 'The Precariousness of Production: Michael Klinger and the Role of the Film Producer in the British Film Industry during the 1970s', in Laurel Foster and Sue Harper (eds), *British Culture and Society in the 1970s: The Lost Decade*, pp. 188–200.

Spittles, Brian (1995) *Britain since 1960: An Introduction*, London: Macmillan.

Stam, Robert and Louise Spence (1998) 'Colonialism, Racism, and Representation: An Introduction', in Gerald Mast, Marshall Cohen and Leo Braudy (eds), *Film Theory: An Anthology* (5th edn), London/New York: Oxford University Press, pp. 235–50.

Storry, Mike and Peter Childs (eds) (1997) *British Cultural Identities*, London: Routledge.

Street, Sarah (1997) *British National Cinema*, London: Routledge.

Street, Sarah (2008) 'Heritage Crime: The Case of Agatha Christie', in Robert Shail (ed.) *Seventies British Cinema*, London: British Film Institute/Palgrave Macmillan, pp. 105–16.

Strick, Philip (1974) 'Zardoz and John Boorman', *Sight and Sound*, vol. 43, no. 2 (Spring), pp. 73–4.

Strick, Philip (1978) 'Skolimowski's Cricket Match', *Sight and Sound*, vol. 47, no. 3 (July), pp. 146–7.

Stuart, Alexander (1974) 'Stardust', *Films and Filming*, vol. 21, no. 3 (December), p. 39.

Sussex, Elizabeth (1975/76) 'Requiem for a Village', *Sight and Sound*, vol. 45, no. 1 (Winter), p. 60.

Sweet, Matthew (2005) *Shepperton Babylon: The Lost Worlds of British Cinema*, London: Faber & Faber.

Bibliography

Tasker, Yvonne (2011) 'Permissive British Cinema?', *Deep End* DVD Booklet, British Film Institute, pp. 8–10.

Taylor, John Russell (1974) 'Tomorrow the World: Some Reflections on the Un-Englishness of English Films', *Sight and Sound*, vol. 43, no. 2 (Spring), pp. 80–3.

Thompson, David (2011) *Deep End*, DVD Booklet, British Film Institute, pp. 1–5.

Thompson, Stacy (2004) 'Punk Cinema', *Cinema Journal*, vol. 43, no. 2 (Autumn), pp. 44–67.

Threadgall, Derek (1994) *Shepperton Studios: An Independent View*, London: British Film Institute.

Tibbetts, John C. (2000) 'Kevin Brownlow's Historical Films: *It Happened Here* (1965) and *Winstanley* (1975)', *Historical Journal of Film, Radio and Television*, vol. 20, no. 2 (June), pp. 227–51.

Tincknell, Estella (2006) 'The Soundtrack Movie, Nostalgia and Consumption', in Ian Conrich and Estella Tincknell (eds) *Film's Musical Moments*, Edinburgh: Edinburgh University Press.

Tudor, Andrew (1989) *Monsters and Mad Scientists: A Cultural History of the Horror Movie*, Oxford: Basil Blackwell.

Turner, Alwyn W. (2008) *Crisis? What Crisis? Britain in the 1970s*, London: Aurum Press.

Vitali, Valentina and Paul Willemen (eds) (2006) *Theorising National Cinema*, London: British Film Institute.

Walker, Alexander (1980) 'Babylon', *Evening Standard*, 6 November.

Walker, Alexander (1985) *National Heroes: British Cinema in the Seventies and Eighties*, London: Orion.

Walker, John (1985) *The Once and Future Film: British Cinema in the Seventies and Eighties*, London: Methuen.

Wambu, Onyekachi (n.d.) 'A Hole in Babylon'. Available at: www.screenonline. org.uk/tv/id/508033/index.html; accessed 13 January 2012.

Watson, Garry (2006) *The Cinema of Mike Leigh: A Sense of the Real*, London: Wallflower Press.

Weis, Elisabeth and John Belton (eds) (1985) *Film Sound: Theory and Practice*, New York: Columbia University Press.

Weiss, Andrea (1992) *Vampires and Violets: Lesbians in the Cinema*, London: Jonathan Cape.

Whannel, Gary (1994) 'Boxed in: Television in the 1970s', in Bart Moore-Gilbert (ed.), *The Arts in the 1970s: Cultural Closure?*, London/New York: Routledge, pp. 176–97.

Whitman, Mark (1974) 'Akenfield', *Films Illustrated*, November.

Whittaker, Tom (2009) 'Frozen Soundscapes in *Control* and *Radio On*', *Journal of British Cinema and Television*, vol. 6, no. 3, pp. 424–36.

Williams, Christopher (1980) *Realism and the Cinema: A Reader*, London: British Film Institute.

Williams, Melanie (2010) 'Staccato and Wrenchingly Modern: Reflections on the 1970s Stardom of Glenda Jackson', in Paul Newland (ed.), *Don't Look Now: British Cinema in the 1970s*, Bristol: Intellect Books, pp. 43–53.

Williams, Raymond (1973) *The Country and the City*, New York: Oxford University Press.

Williamson, Judith (1988) 'Two Kinds of Otherness: Black Film and the Avant Garde', *Screen*, vol. 29, no, 4, pp. 106–13.

Wilson, David (1973) 'O Lucky Man!', *Sight and Sound*, vol. 42, no. 3 (Summer), pp. 126–9.

Wilson, David (1974) 'Images of Britain', *Sight and Sound*, vol. 43, no. 2 (Spring), pp. 84–7.

Wilson, David (1978) 'Pressure', *Monthly Film Bulletin*, vol. 45, no. 531 (April), p. 68.

Wojcik, Pamela Robertson and Arthur Knight (2001) 'Overture', *Soundtrack Available: Essays on Film and Popular Music*, Durham, NC/London: Duke University Press, pp. 1–15.

Wood, Linda (ed.) (1983) *British Films 1971–1981*, London: British Film Institute.

Woodward, Kate (2011) 'I Was There? Rugby, National Identity and Devolution in 1970s Wales', Culture, Change and Continuity symposium, Aberystwyth University, 15 September.

Wright, Robb (2003) 'Score vs. Song: Art, Commerce and the H Factor in Film and Television Music', in Ian Inglis (ed.), *Popular Music and Film*, London: Wallflower, pp. 8–21.

Wymer, Roland (2005) *Derek Jarman*, Manchester: Manchester University Press.

Young, Lola (1996) *Fear of the Dark: 'Race', Gender and Sexuality in the Cinema*, London/New York: Routledge, 1996.

Young, Rob (2011) 'Requiem for a Village: Cinema of the Anti-Scrape', DVD booklet, British Film Institute, pp. 10–12.

Yule, Andrew (1989) *David Puttnam: The Story So Far*, London: Sphere Books.

Index

Note: 'n' preceding a page reference indicates the number of a note on that page.

Index

Index

Index

Index

Index